MW01281804

*THEY
WOULDN'T
LET US DIE*

"I don't care who you are. If I strap you up or rope you up, short of killing you, I can subject you to such pain that in a relatively short period of time your *mind* is going to overcome your *will,* and you are going to give something to get out of this pain, short of dying. Because, they will not let you die."

Colonel Thomas H. Kirk, Jr.
Prisoner of War, 1967-73

"I was hoping all during this period that they'd kill me; that I could die. But, unfortunately, that was not one of the alternatives."

Commander William R. Stark
Prisoner of War, 1967-73

THEY WOULDN'T LET US DIE

The Prisoners of War
Tell Their Story

Stephen A. Rowan

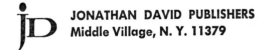

JONATHAN DAVID PUBLISHERS
Middle Village, N. Y. 11379

THEY WOULDN'T LET US DIE
The Prisoners of War Tell Their Story
Copyright © 1973

by

Stephen A. Rowan

No part of this book may be reproduced in any manner
without written permission from the publishers.

Address all inquiries to:

JONATHAN DAVID PUBLISHERS
Middle Village, New York 11379

Second Printing—1974

Library of Congress Cataloging in Publication Data

Rowan, Stephen A. 1928-
  They wouldn't let us die. The prisoners of war
  tell their story.

    1. Vietnamese Conflict, 1961-   —Prisoners and
prisons, North Vietnamese. 2. Vietnamese Conflict,
1961-   —Personal narratives, American.
I. Title.
DS557.A675R67   959.704'37   73-80414
ISBN 0-8246-0157-2

PRINTED IN THE UNITED STATES OF AMERICA

Table of Contents

Acknowledgements

In addition to the cooperation I received from the POWs themselves, and from the Project Homecoming staff of Pentagon public affairs officers, I am indebted to my secretary and trusted friend Claudia Kielich for the attitude of dedication with which she approached the preparation of this book; and to our friend Linda Arnold for pitching in to help.

I also owe much to the support and assistance I received from former CBS News colleagues including Dan Rather and Bruce Morton and to Bruce's wife, Maggie, who fed me and housed me when I was in Washington.

My children, Geoffrey and Lisa, have my thanks for undergoing long periods of fending for themselves while the book was in preparation.

Finally, the project could not have been completed without the encouragement and support of others too numerous to mention, who nevertheless have a special place in my heart.

Introduction

They are an amazing group of men.

They've become folk heroes of a sort, the only heroes most Americans are eager to honor in the wake of our longest and most unpopular war. They are not admired for their valor on the field of battle, for indeed most of them had never seen a Vietnamese face-to-face until they were captured. Their heroism derives from their ability to survive what most of us suspect we could not—years of terror at the hands of an incomprehensible enemy, and years of isolation in a medieval land.

One of the first things we all noticed about the POWs was how young they looked. Their trim bodies and their easy smiles misled some anti-war activists into believing they had been, in Tom Hayden's words: "the best treated prisoners in the history of any war." In fact they were not.

More than half of them carried worms in their intestines, worms up to a foot in length. Thirteen per cent of them had nutritional diseases, while more than eight per cent were suffering from malaria. Many had to undergo corrective surgery to repair damage done in torture sessions or when they were captured—injuries which had been untreated or illtreated. Only four of the men were diagnosed as having real psychiatric problems, but the first suicide death of a POW—in June, 1973—prompted the Pentagon to order several others back to the hospital for a careful study of mental problems.

In some ways, though, the POWs are far healthier than the vast majority of American men of similar ages. For up to eight years they slept at least eight hours a night, drank no alcoholic beverages, smoked no more than half-a-dozen cigarettes a day and existed on a diet that contained almost none of the fats and starches which add so many unwanted pounds to our bodies by the time we reach the age of 40. And most of them spent at least an hour a day doing vigorous calisthenics.

In addition to those physical "benefits" of being in prison, many of the men to whom I have talked seem to have expanded their mental capabilities and gained emotional stability.

As they did in exercising their bodies, the men followed a "use it or lose it" philosophy in keeping their minds active. Some were able to remember enough of their high school French, for example, to teach that language to others. Many found they could work out the answers to difficult problems in mathematics without pencil or paper. Some were able to recall the names of virtually every classmate from kindergarten through college.

There were pay records and shopping lists to be kept in their minds, and things to remember every day, like the names of all the other POWs. There were mental exercises to be enjoyed at the end of a day, like alphabetically listing the names of all the states or state capitals. There were homes to be built, brick by brick, and boats to be put together, and a thousand other things to be planned and constructed. Much of the actual knowledge gained in doing these mental gymnastics disappeared soon after the men returned to the United States, but at least they now know what their brains are capable of doing.

As for emotional stability, the POWs learned to look at themselves honestly, and accept everything they found—good and bad. They learned to work on those aspects of their personalities which needed changing. They discovered that their roommates could be brutally honest in assessing their behavior, and that they could provide others with similar reactions. And they seemed to achieve a sense of their own worth as human beings, and a respect for every man with whom they came in contact.

Some of us have learned about the good feelings that can be generated by intensive group interaction over periods of five days or so. The POWs emerged from North Viet Nam like men who had been in an encounter group for five *years*. Many of them straightforwardly expressed their feelings of love for each other. Two months after their release, when some of them got together in San Francisco, I heard a number exchanging invitations to "come and stay for a month or so." Obviously, they did not want to lose the good feelings they had about themselves and each other.

The catharsis they underwent in prison undoubtedly put many of these men on a somewhat different level of emotional stability than the wives they left behind, and I expect the divorce rate for the POWs will be somewhat higher than it is among the military population as a whole. I don't know what damage these divorces will do to the wives, but I believe most of the men will survive them as they survived their time in prison, stronger in their trust for their own feelings and eager to establish new relationships based on satisfying the real needs they identified while in captivity.

This was a group of POWs like no other war has produced.

The Communists released 564 American military men and 23 civilians in North Viet Nam, South Viet Nam and Laos. Only 71 of the military men were not officers, and even among the enlisted types all but a handful were career non-commissioned officers. There were no draftees among the group, and only 16 blacks.

The vast majority of the POWs were Air Force and Navy pilots and air crew members, shot down in North Viet Nam in the years 1965 through 1968 and in 1972. All of those fliers had been though survival school, and all the men had been drilled in the Code of Conduct, adopted after the Korean War, a principle feature of which is that the senior ranking man in any group of POWs is to take command and make policy decisions.

The North Vietnamese tried to keep senior officers away from the prison population as a whole, but various forms of communication were devised by the men so they could stay in touch. In any case, when one senior was removed from a particular cell block, the next highest ranking man took charge and the system remained in operation, giving the men a sense of belonging to a military organization, and unifying them in their desire to resist the Communists.

Early in 1971, that organization was formalized along the lines of an Air Force command. It was called "The Fourth Combined POW Wing," in recognition of the number of wars in this century in which Americans have been held captive.

There were many camps throughout North Viet Nam which were used from time to time, and POWs were moved from camp to camp for no apparent reason. In July of 1970, for example, all of the POWs in the Son Tay camp were moved elsewhere. No one knew why. Four months later, a daring group of U.S. Air Force and Army men staged a raid on Son Tay, hoping to rescue the POWs there. Apparently, their military intelligence was badly outdated. The camp was empty.

I set out to conduct interviews with the men on April 1st 1973, a few days after the final group had been released from prison.

The Pentagon had laid down a set of guidelines designed to protect their privacy, and it was difficult, at first, to get in touch with them. But, five years of covering the Pentagon taught me how to get around some of these roadblocks, and I received much assistance from old friends among the corps of military public affairs officers which had been dispatched to hospitals around the country to assist the men in their dealings with the press.

The major sticking point was that reporters were not allowed to talk with any POW until he had been released from his initial period in the hospital. When that day arrived, each man was given the opportunity to participate in a full-scale news conference for an hour or so, but then he was immediately free to depart for up to 90 days of convalescent leave. Quite understandably, they wanted to spend their leaves with their wives and families, and as far away from reporters as they could get.

My Navy friends were particularly helpful in putting me in touch with POWs who were continuing to undergo hospital treatment on an outpatient basis. Among the Air Force and Army public affairs officers, there also were a few who were willing to bend the rules so as to achieve the goal of providing the public with as much information as the POWs, themselves, cared to share.

Once I began contacting the men, I discovered that many were willing to spend several hours of their precious leave time so this book could be done. I found them in groups of twos and threes around some of the major military installations, Andrews Air Force base near Washington, D.C., the naval bases at Norfolk, Virginia, and San Diego, California, the Army and Air Force installations at San Antonio, Texas, and elsewhere.

It should be noted that, in many cases, the men who joined in these discussions hardly knew each other, having been in widely separated prison camps during their years in North Viet Nam. In putting men with such different backgrounds together for a discussion, it was my intention to provoke a free flow of recollections among them and from them to the reader.

My basic goal was to get more than the *facts* of their captivity. I wanted to find out about their *feelings*—how they reacted psychologically to being captured, questioned for military information, tortured, made to sign statements for political propaganda, isolated from each other and the Western world, starved and otherwise ill-treated.

To do this, I raced from coast to coast during the month of April and the first week of May talking to as many of the men as I could while they were still close enough to those feelings to be able to recapture them in our discussions.

The group technique was important because it encouraged

men who were tight-lipped or shy to open up more than they would in a one-on-one interview. In many cases, ideas and experiences spoken by one person sparked thoughts in the minds of other participants.

In some cases, the groups contained men who disagreed on such basic points as the level of resistance that was required of a POW. But men who believed it necessary to resist to the point of physical torture were never openly critical of men who did not. There seemed to be an understanding that everyone had suffered, even those few who never were "twisted."

There *was* criticism of men who openly violated the Code of Conduct by refusing to follow the orders of the senior ranking POW or by voluntarily writing statements that could be "harmful to the cause of the United States." In fact, charges were preferred by one of the seniors against eight enlisted men who collaborated with the North Vietnamese. Those charges later were dropped by Pentagon officials for lack of evidence, but not, unfortunately, until one of the eight had taken his own life—the second POW suicide.

Similar charges were preferred against two fairly high-ranking officers—a Navy captain and a Marine Corps lieutenant colonel—but they too were expected to be dropped later. The Navy captain, Walter Eugene Wilber, is the subject of Chapter Six of this book.

Most of the men were, in Commander Bob Shumaker's words, "Jack London types," who proved their loyalty and bravery over and over. Interestingly enough, their loyalty seems to have been more to each other and to the military "system" which was perpetuated by the formation of the Fourth Combined POW Wing, than to their country.

But their expressions of admiration for President Richard M. Nixon when they came home were nonetheless, honest. Commander Richard Stratton told me that many who had favorable comments on Nixon's decisions **were** "not of his party and did not appreciate his political career in any respect. But you have to understand," Stratton indicated, "that, as a group of aviators, we respect courage. For a President, in an election year, to come out with rent and price controls, to counteract the invasion of South Viet Nam by North Viet Nam in the spring, to start the bombing of the Hanoi area at an unpopular time in an unpopular war by an unpopular B-52 medium, required guts. And that guts was appreciated. We knew American public interest would save our lives, but only the 'big stick' would ever get us out of there. In no way were those pro-Nixon remarks the traditional polite things to say—suggested by a public affairs officer. And those who maintain that do us a disservice."

The POWs knew about the B-52 bombing of Hanoi in December of 1972 because they were there. But they got most of their other information about what was going on in the outside world from new prisoners. As Captain Allen Brady said: "The '72 shoot downs . . . were a real goldmine of information" about everything from X-rated movies to the economic problems of the United States.

Attempts were made by the North Vietnamese to keep the POWs from circulating information of any type, but, except for the early days—when prisoners could be physically separated by considerable distances—those efforts were largely unsuccessful. Com nets—communications networks —were established in every camp. They took many forms, but the basic means of communicating was by a simple code introduced into the system early in 1965 (described in Chapter Three). Messages were tapped from cell to cell. Sometimes they were "swept out" with the strokes of a broom, when prisoners were sent out to clean the courtyard around their cellblocks. There was also some voice communication from cell to cell. And messages sometimes were scratched out on a piece of toilet paper, with the head of a burnt match or the soft lead of a toothpaste tube, and circulated by various ingenious means.

Psychologists undoubtedly will come to the conclusion that communication was vital to maintaining the emotional stability of the POWs. And the men themselves agree. But there may have been a deeper meaning to the need for staying in touch. I believe that most military men would be totally lost without authority figures, and the "system" represented authority. Without that authority, the men might have been far more susceptible to the authority of their captors. I suspect that, in some of the cases involving men who "bought" the Communists' propaganda, it was more a matter of accepting the only available authority figure, and this could have been particularly true for the enlisted men captured in South Viet Nam and held in isolation in the jungle camps of the Viet Cong for long years.

Once they were "plugged in" to the "system," the job of the POWs was to resist. Thus, it should come as no surprise that one of their chief difficulties in re-entering society was to drop the attitude of caution and resistance that they had developed. My interview with Dick Stratton brought this point home very sharply.

Dick Stratton was a January, 1967 shoot-down. He was one of the first Prisoners of War to be seen by the American public on their TV screens. In the film that was released by the North Vietnamese, he was seen at a press conference bowing deeply and giving the impression that he had been drugged. His picture appeared on the front cover of *Life* magazine making him one of the best known of the American POWs.

Dick Stratton says he found, in his relatioship with his wife, Alice, and other members of his family, that "if a surprise is pulled on me, my instantaneous reaction is to go in the opposite direction, and at times it gets to be embarrassing." Balancing that, to some extent, is the self-discipline the men learned, because, again quoting Stratton, "You can't say the things you want to to the enemy or you'll get bashed right between the running lights."

I observed the balance of resistance and self-discipline in my discussions with the men. They spoke very slowly, choosing their words with care. And when they didn't want to talk about something, they managed to avoid it without ever simply refusing. I was reminded of the Japanese, who don't like to say "no" but who can be very difficult, nonetheless, when asked for something they don't want to provide. My reaction to this resistance, by the way, was to accept it for what it was and hope that later in our discussion the man would be willing to volunteer the information I had asked for. And that happened a number of times.

I tried to cover a broad range of subjects with each group, looking for areas where there were strong feelings. In some groups, as in Chapter One and Chapter Eleven, the strongest feelings came out during the discussion of torture. There were various forms of torture used, but the most popular with the North Vietnamese involved the use of ropes or straps, forcing the man to double up with his head between his legs. Another popular form of torture involved sitting a man on a wooden stool, and requiring him to stay there for days with no sleep (see Chapter Eight). Some of the camps had a "hot box" which usually consisted of a metal shed, completely enclosed and with no ventilation, containing a stool on which a man would be required to sit for as long as it took for him to make up his mind to answer a particular question or write a particular statement. Then, there were simple beatings, and such tricks as suspending a man upside down for periods of time. Putting a POW in leg irons, or "stocks" was a somewhat milder form of torture, but it, too, has the desired effect after several days or weeks, especially if the man was unlocked only once or twice a day to urinate and defecate. Such torture was excruciating, particularly for those suffering with dysentery as did most of the POWs who were fed a diet of soup, greens and bread.

I asked Dick Stratton to describe the food.

"The staple diet was soup, and, in season, pumpkin, kohlrabi, cabbage and some sort of green grass-type stuff that they used to cook in the soup. Sometimes, the vegetables came in a side dish; sometimes they were served all in one dish. Kohlrabi, by the way, is what we feed cows, although some health food fanatics eat it too. It has a taste between turnip and cabbage. It's rolled up like a baseball with a lot of string in it and cut into slices. Sometimes we'd get bamboo shoots. Sometimes peanuts. But the real staples were cabbage, for six months, and then pumpkin for six months—served with soup and a small loaf of bread.

"In the early days, we got about one spoonful of vegetables in a bowl of water. It was fed to you at 10:30 in the morning and 2:30 in the afternoon, and then you went from 2:30 until the next morning without anything to eat. In addition to that, we had a quart of water a day. In the winter, that was enough. But, in the summer, with the temperature up in the 90s, locked in a room with no air, it was insufficient.

"At the end, when they knew we were going home—or earlier when their balloon went up and they thought we might be going home—they'd put all three vegetables in the soup.

"Four times a year, we got holiday meals, and what they consisted of depended on what they had on the market at the time. They do have turkeys, and ducks, and roosters. For example, they might cut up two roosters for about 70 men. Or, we'd get a piece of duck, and an egg roll sort of thing, or a duck's egg. We might get half a bottle of Vietnamese beer, which is like a watered-down San Miguel [a Philippine beer known throughout the Far East] and actually not bad. We might get an ounce-and-a-half of something like an after dinner drink—a sort of apricot-tasting wine. When we finally got into larger cells, a guy would negotiate to try and get everybody's booze so he could get a full cup and get a buzz on. If he had something that he didn't like, he'd trade it. Perhaps he'd promise another guy the next orange that came up. Or, he'd auction off the traditional rice cake that he knew he'd get at the next Tet for a Christmas beer.

"About the last 12 to 18 months, we had about 12 or 14 ounces of milk every morning. It was condensed milk, powdered milk or evaporated milk, and it came from either Russia or China. It stopped when the blockade [of the harbors] started, which was one indication the blockade was going well.

"They were very conscious of the poor state of our health. We would get the vitamins from our packages from home, even though they might chop them up into a hundred pieces so that the guys who weren't getting packages would get vitamins.

"And then, as the end came, they gave us fruit: jack-fruit, oranges—some of them darn good, some of them rotten, a half a grapefruit per man, bananas, and of course, pineapple.

"We got a chance to sit outside, and we got a chance to visit between cells [in the Plantation]. Bob Craner and John McCain would come over and visit. They'd lock us all in a two-man cell in the morning, and then in the afternoon we'd get a chance to go out and wash and sit in the sun, and actually eat one of those meals outside.

"Of course as soon as the Son Tay raid hit, that was the end of that jazz and everybody was back in trouble again."

Most of the air crew members shot down in North Viet Nam eventually were moved to Hanoi, to an old French prison called Hoa Lo, which came to be known as the Hanoi Hilton. Most of the men captured in South Viet Nam and Laos eventually wound up in another prison on the northeast outskirts of Hanoi called the Citadel, which came to be known as Plantation Gardens or simply the Plantation.

Most of the POWs who were captured in the southernmost provinces of South Viet Nam were kept for long periods in the hidden jungle camps of the viet Cong, moving from place to place as the VC moved, and a few were still in the south when the peace agreements were signed.

At that point, after the Son Tay raid, the North Viet- namese shifted everyone around. They put most of the aviators, including all the seniors, into the Hanoi Hilton. Another group of fliers went to a camp on the southern edge of Hanoi called the Zoo. The Plantation, on the northeastern edge of Hanoi—which is the camp in which Stratton, McCain and others had been held—was filled thereafter with men who had been captured in South Viet Nam and in Laos, including most of the Army and Marine Corps enlisted men. That proved a benefit to the men. It gave them a chance to organize the 4th Combined POW Wing, setting up an ad- ministrative structure, dividing the men into squadrons just like they had had in the Air Force and the Navy, and es- tablishing operational procedures, communications networks and everything that could be found in a stateside military organization, up to and including chaplains.

Prior to that, a number of camps outside Hanoi had been used. In 1971 and 1972 the Vietnamese put a large number of the POWs up near the Chinese border for a time, perhaps with the thought of always having an ace up their sleeve if Hanoi was invaded. That camp was called Dogpatch by the Americans, possibly because it was way off in the boondocks.

In addition to Son Tay—which was called Camp Hope by the POWs—there were three other camps northwest of Hanoi. They were the Briar Patch, Camp Faith and Dan Hoi. Skid Row was southwest of the capital, and the Rockpile was directly south. There were also various holding areas where men were kept for brief periods, like the camp called D-1 down toward the southern panhandle, where many fliers were interrogated for a few days as they were en route to prisons in Hanoi.

Hanoi, itself, contained the Hilton, the Plantation and Alcatraz, which was just across the street from the Plantation. Then there were the Zoo and the Zoo Annex down on the southern edge of the city, and a little sector camp called Dirty Bird, near the Red River. Dirty Bird gained its fame because it was from that camp that Lieutenant Colonel George McKnight and Lieutenant Commander George Coker escaped. They just walked out, on the spur of the moment, and managed to get about 12 miles down the Red River before they were recaptured the following day.

I was unable to ascertain how all the camps got their names. But it is believed by most POWs that the Hanoi Hilton was named by Bob Shumaker, the second man there. The Vietnamese called it Hoa Lo, which translates into "fiery furnace" or "fiery crucible," and it was considered the Devil's Island of southeast Asia. It was built by the French in the 1940s, and it reminded some POWs of the Bastille they had read about in *A Tale of Two Cities*.

The Hanoi Hilton was surrounded by 20-foot high walls, topped with broken glass and four-strand electrified barbed wire. It had guard towers at the corners and bright lights all over the place.

As more men moved in, various sections of the prison were given appropriate names. One wing, described in some detail in Chapter Eleven, was called Heartbreak Hotel. It consisted of eight cells not far from the main gate. Also near the main gate was New Guy Village, right behind a room used for interrogation and torture called the Violent Room.

The entire back side of the prison was nicknamed Camp Unity, and it contained many of the larger cells, some up to about 90 feet long. At times there were 40 or 50 Americans in those cells, but the POWs learned that as many as 150 North Vietnamese prisoners had been held in cells like that before the prison was put into use as a POW camp.

Another section of the camp was called Little Vegas, named by Air Force Major Tom Storey after some other men who had served at Nellis Air Force Base outside of Las Vegas, Nevada. Various areas in that section were dubbed with the names of some of the casinos: the Desert Inn, the Thunderbird, the Riviera, and so forth.

In the Hilton and elsewhere, the men slept on bed rolls on concrete floors, or on bed boards which were sometimes put on the floor and sometimes put across saw horses, or on stanchions. In some of the larger cells they slept on huge concrete platforms. Rob Doremus recalls that in one cell in the Hilton, that had a concrete platform designed for about 30 men, there were 55 POWs. When someone got up at night to urinate, he could usually forget about trying to get back into "bed." His space would have been filled the moment he vacated it.

The second-biggest camp in the Hanoi area was formally called The Citadel, but I haven't found anyone outside of the Pentagon who knows it by that name. Most of the POWs who were there called it the Plantation, or Plantation Gardens, although it also was called the Country Club by a few. Dick Stratton says he was told that in the 1930's, it was the summer residence of the Mayor of Hanoi. In any case, it had an elegant two-story main building surrounded by many smaller outbuildings in which the POWs were kept. They

thought of the main building as the big house on a plantation, and of their rooms as the slave quarters.

One of the first photographs of a POW that was seen in the
United States showed Stratton sitting on a bunk, his hands
between his legs, his head down. Dick says: "I was hiding a
letter. They had given me my first letter from home and they
wanted me to open it while I was being photographed, and
cry for the cameras, I'm sure. So I was hiding it under the
mattress, knowing that they'd ask for it back. Then, when
they wanted it back, I claimed I had lost it outside. And I got
to read it that night.

"That room should have fooled no one. They brought
David Dellinger (the anti-war activist) in and said, 'This is
where Stratton sleeps.' There was one bunk in the far corner,
and over in the other corner was a bed board on saw horses
with nothing on it. There was one tea pot and one tooth
brush. And Dellinger said, 'Where is Stratton's roommate?'
They said, 'Oh, he's taking a shower.' He's taking a shower—
at *ten o'clock at night.*

"Actually, we called that room Movie House 4. It was a
large, airy room in which they put people for show purposes.
It was painted a sort of putrid yellow and was covered with
the ever-present cobwebs, which were a benefit because they
caught mosquitoes. The baseboards and trim were a brown-
ish, rust color. And the room smelled of urine because the
guards used to go out back by the boarded-up windows and
urinate against the wall and the sun would hit that in the
afternoon so the room had a latrine-type smell, which every
Army man is familiar with."

The other big camp in the Hanoi area was nicknamed the
Zoo. It was on the edge of the city, and all kinds of farm
animals and fowl were around it—pigs, cows, chickens,
ducks and turkeys. Some of the POWs called it the Funny
Farm. Actually, it once had been a French movie studio. It
had roomfuls of film in it when the first POWs went there,
and the Vietnamese took the film out and threw it in a swim-
ming pool to make room for the prisoners. Then, they made
the prisoners gather the film up and roll it up again and they

moved it into some trees at the edge of the camp.

The camps outside Hanoi varied in size and construction. Son Tay, for example, had cells ranging in size from one-man solitary confinement types to big cells obviously designed for 13 Vietnamese prisoners, although no more than eight Americans were ever kept in them. The Briar Patch was made up of eight houses, each containing cells, and the houses were surrounded by walls in such a way that it was impossible to see from one to any other.

Many of the prisons were situated near military facilities, which protected them from aerial bombardment. From the Zoo, the POWs could see an antennae farm, an ammunition dump and an anti-aircraft battery. The Plantation was near a railway bridge. Dirty Bird was beside the thermal power plant.

One thing they all had in common was a public address system, variously described by the POWs as "the radio" or "the propaganda box." Over it, from morning 'til night, came a constant stream of propaganda, including material culled from American broadcasts—like the anti-war statements of Senators J. William Fulbright, Edward Kennedy and others. The propaganda also included anti-war statements and war crime "confessions" read by some of the prisoners. Of course, they had been *forced* to make such tapes for "the radio," but to a new prisoner it was somewhat disconcerting to hear the voice of an old and highly-respected Naval officer, for example, admitting to war crimes and thanking the people of the Democratic Republic of Viet Nam for their humane and lenient treatment.

One other thing the prison camps had in common was the smell of dirty male bodies. Dick Stratton says:

"I used to laugh at people who would say that a black man stinks. I don't think there's anyone who stinks any more than an unwashed Caucasian. In the winter, we froze. But in the summer, with the rooms boarded up and no air, and with the temperature going over 100, we just stunk. And if you were in bad trouble, which I usually was, you didn't get to wash. I've gone two hundred days without shaving or getting my hair cut, and bathing with a cupful of water. And boy, I was ripe.

"The stink was so bad that now, I find myself shaving my armpits and dousing myself with Right Guard, and, of course, I bathe every chance I get. And I use *gallons* of water."

There were no clocks, but the POWs learned to tell the time without them, relying on such things as the church bells in Hanoi and the regularity with which their food was served. In a larger sense, they found that time means nothing to the Vietnamese, as Rob Doremus points out in Chapter Four. Having spent a thousand years getting rid of the Chinese and 20 years getting rid of the French, the Vietnamese were prepared to struggle as long as necessary to get the Americans out.

There was no reading material, except for Communist propaganda documents and an occasional copy of the Soviet English-language magazine that can be bought in the United States. The senior officers asked for educational materials, and from time to time, in the "good guy" days, they might get one French textbook, to be shared among a couple of hundred men. So they relied on their own knowledge, teaching each other the things they could remember from their own school days.

They taught each other how to respond to interrogations, too. Initially, most men were tortured because they tried to refuse giving the Vietnamese anything more than their name, rank, serial number and date of birth, as specified under the Geneva Convention. But they soon learned that they could avoid torture by coming up with some answer, any answer—true or false—as long as they didn't get caught in an outright lie. Thereafter, torture was only what a man required of himself in order to maintain his sense of loyalty to his fellow POWs, although there were cases in which a senior ranking officer would order the men to take torture rather than provide the Vietnamese with specific information about the POW organization, communications, codes, and so forth.

Interrogations seemed to fall into three main categories. There was the initial intensive questioning, designed more to prove to a man that he could be broken, rather than to gain hard military information. There was the political quiz, in which a man was subjected to a propaganda lecture and asked to side with the Vietnamese. Sometimes, during this phase, he was required to write letters to the President, or other American officials, demanding amnesty for draft dodgers, for example. Then, there were routine interrogations: "How is your health? How are you sleeping?"

From time to time there were purges, designed to find out how the men were communicating, what code they were using, and what their senior officers were telling them to do. There also were special requirements. For example, at one point each man was required to write an autobiography detailing his background.

The interrogators and guards, like the camps, had nicknames. Again I'm indebted to Dick Stratton for this descriptive material:

"No two POWs could ever really agree on anything, not even the names of the guards. In fact we almost came to blows over whose name was going to reign for a new guard. For example, they got a new issue of Russian equipment including a fancy silver belt buckle, and, when we saw a new guard with this on, we called him Silver until about two days later, when every guard in the camp had the same belt buckle. My roommate was about to punch me in ths nose. He said, 'You see, I told you it was a stupid name.'

"One of my favorite names you probably won't be able to use. We had a guy named Dilligaf—D-I-L-L-I-G-A-F—**Do I Look Like I Give A Fuck?** And that was his attitude; so Dilligaf was his name. The favorite guard of all, whom I had sort of a stand-off with, was The Bastard, for obvious reasons. Certain basic names like that, I appreciated. Some people would get more poetic.

"The interrogators included The Bug—the most miserable and lowest of all creatures. He was given the name of an insect because he was, in fact, an insect; a madman as far as I'm concerned. The Cat got his name because he was so smooth and walked so quietly, but I called him Major Bai and that's his name. The Soft Soap Fairy was so named for obvious reasons. He was as queer as a three-dollar bill, and he was a soft soap artist. The Rabbit was so called because he looked like a rabbit—with long ears and teeth sticking out. When the Vietnamese tortured some guys and found out what names we were using, they got a chuckle out of that. They said: 'Oh, you mean the one with the big ears?'

"Straps and Bars was named because of his method of torture. Everybody who went through it knew exactly whom we meant. Vegetable Vic wore a hat with camouflage on it, even in prison where he didn't need it, and that's how he got his name.

"The Quiz Kids were enlisted men who tried to pass themselves off as officers. They did routine interrogations, and changed frequently. Marty Mouthful was a guy who had a mouthful of teeth and there was no way of closing his lips around them. He was a pimply-faced, pale, Chinese-looking guy who had nerve enough to refer to one of the other guards as a peasant, because he didn't have fair skin.

"By the way, they are extremely prejudiced people. They came around one time with a picture of Wilt Chamberlain, laughing and saying, 'He looks just like a monkey. Where does he ever find a woman to satisfy him?' Extremely prejudiced."

Some of the nicknames sounded almost affectionate, but there was no affection for the North Vietnamese prison personnel. Not one of the men to whom I spoke had a good word for any of them. But there appears to be no seething hatred of the Vietnamese people, even the North Vietnamese Communists. These are military men, and they realize that "war is hell." Their part of it was more hellish than most, but they're home now, and ready to move on to new challenges.

Some of the POWs died in North Vietnamese prisons. Hanoi listed 55 of them. The POWs believe the number may be considerably greater. They also believe that many hundreds of the 1,359 military men still listed as Missing In Action were captured alive but then put to death almot immediately by hate-filled local villagers.

But, of the known dead in prison, many could have survived with adequate medical treatment. A few simply lost the will to live in captivity. Only one or two are believed to have been tortured to death.

Once an American POW was put in a prison, he became a political pawn. He knew that his own government would do everything it could to keep him from dying. And he learned from experience that if he was basically healthy enough to survive under such rigorous prison camp conditions, the North Vietnamese government wouldn't let him die.

Surprisingly, the emotional horror of those years is fading quickly, and nothing but a few bad memories remain. Ned Shuman, who spent 17 months in solitary, told me he hasn't had one bad dream since he's been home.

Code of Conduct

For Members of the Armed Forces of the United States:

1. I am an American fighting man. I serve in the forces which guard my country and our way of life. I am prepared to give my life in their defense.
2. I will never surrender of my own free will. If in command I will never surrender my men while they still have the means to resist.
3. If I am captured I will continue to resist by all means available. I will make every effort to escape and aid others to escape. I will accept neither parole nor special favors from the enemy.
4. If I become a prisoner of war, I will keep faith with my fellow prisoners. I will give no information or take part in any action which might be harmful to my comrades. If I am senior, I will take command. If not, I will obey the lawful orders of those appointed over me and will back them up in every way.
5. When questioned, should I become a prisoner of war, I am bound to give only name, rank, service number, and date of birth. I will evade answering further questions to the utmost of my ability. I will make no oral or written statements disloyal to my country and its allies or harmful to their cause.
6. I will never forget that I am an American fighting man, responsible for my actions, and dedicated to the principles which made my country free. I will trust in my God and in the United States of America.

1

The Face of the Enemy

To most of the Air Force and Navy men who ended up in North Vietnamese prisons, the face of the enemy was just a set of map coordinates and some aerial reconnaissance photographs. To them the war was a succession of long, busy days flying out of bases in Thailand or off carriers of the 7th Fleet in the Gulf of Tonkin. They were "in the bombing business," as one of them put it later, and there was little time in their day-to-day existence to reveal any of their emotions.

The first time many of these men felt any real, emotional involvement in the war came at the moment of "shoot down." When they realized that their airplane had been fatally crippled over enemy territory, it struck them like a thunderbolt of terror.

Lieutenant Colonel Robert R. Craner of Cohoes, New York, was an exception to that rule. Bob is a tall, handsome man. He exudes a sense of inner peacefulness, a faith in himself that is as obvious as it is real. In his conversation with me, he was direct yet warm. Bob Craner is not the kind of man who goes along with the crowd, or "rides with the wave" as the Navy puts it. He accepts other viewpoints without criticism, and then states his own carefully thought out opinions clearly and gently. He does not have what the Air Force calls "a built-in head wind." In 1967, Craner was a

34-year-old Forward Air Controller, flying alone in an F-100, finding targets for Air Force fighter-bombers. He was shot down five days before Christmas, and he accepted his fate with equanimity—at least then.

Major Konrad W. Trautman of Steelton, Pennsylvania, like Bob Craner, is a family man, an Air Force pilot, and a '67 shoot-down. But there the similarity ends.

In 1967, Konnie Trautman was 40 years old. Because he had been out of the Air Force for a period of time, he had not attained the rank of other men his age, and this may have bothered him. But Konnie is a man of old-fashioned morality, and he would not have considered it proper to complain about his misfortunes. In fact, it was with obvious reluctance that he started talking about the torture he underwent in North Viet Nam, even though he suffered tremendous physical pain. When the dam of propriety broke, the emotions came flooding out, and I found myself holding on to my own emotions for dear life as I listened to him. He speaks softly, but you want to hear what he has to say. Konnie's F-105 was shot down on a bombing mission in October of 1967.

Colonel Thomas H. Kirk, Junior, of Portsmouth, Virginia, is more like everybody's concept of a fighter pilot: short, with lots of dark, wavy hair, "a crooked smile but straight teeth" as Shelly Berman once put it, a man of the world, married to a lovely Italian woman. There's a dynamic quality about Tom Kirk, and it's easy to see why he already had the command of a squadron of F-105s when he was shot down that same October, just five days before his 39th birthday.

Tom had set up the mission that day—48 planes instead of the normal force of 20. The North Vietnamese had been knocking down more and more F-105s, so Tom took along 16 planes to protect against surface-to-air missiles (SAMs) instead of the usual four, and 16 more planes to blast the conventional anti-aircraft guns on the ground. He led the flight of 16 planes that were going to do the actual bombing.

The 48 plane force—from two bases in Thailand—met over a tactical navigation station in northern Laos and headed for the target on the outskirts of Hanoi, the Canal des Rapides bridge—a vital link in the network of roads and rail lines down which supplies were flowing from China to the heart of North Viet Nam.

Tom told me the rest of the story as I met with the three of them at Andrews Air Force Base outside of Washington, D.C.

Kirk: Approaching the target, several missiles were fired at us, but these were not guided. That is to say, our SAM-suppression stuff was working and I just saw them come right up through the flight, and go right on in and explode up behind us—and then very light flak [anti-aircraft artillery] until roll-in. At roll-in, the flak was very intensive. I was going down and, just as I released my bombs, I felt a thump in the back end . . . just a mild thump, and I knew I was hit. I made my turn-off to the right, and back around, heading back out, and as I got leveled out, climbing and heading for home, my wing-man said I'd better drop my tanks . . . external fuel tanks. That's when I knew I was burning. Then, shortly after, I got the fire warning lights, and made about another 20 miles before the controls burned through.

That was probably the most terrified minute or two of my life. I'm sure Konnie felt the same thing.

Trautman: You've got that right.

Kirk: The airplane was burning, with almost no hope of making it out of enemy territory . . . with the full knowledge I'm going to have to try to get out of this thing or I'm going to be a prisoner, before it ever happens. And yet, there is the prayer that it will hold for another 30 miles, to get me over the mountains into the jungle, where I could probably be picked up. So, I'm talking about a space of three minutes, to save me from five years of prison. The airplane was burning —I didn't know the extent of my damage—and absolutely the only way to describe it is complete and utter fear . . . just terror.

Rowan: Tell me more about the thoughts going through your mind?

Kirk: The first thing was the reaction when I was hit. I didn't realize I was hit so bad. I was able to pull the airplane out. And all this time I was thinking, "Is it bad? Is it bad?" and I got it rolled out and when my wing-man said, "Punch off your tanks," well, that was all I needed to know. He wouldn't have had me push the button to release those tanks if I wasn't burning. And then the first light came on in the cockpit . . . fire warning light. Then, I was flying, hoping against hope that I'll be able to make it, and the controls started to get mushy in my hands. Then, they burned through. Then, the airplane just tucked over, and I had to eject.

By this time I was moving. I was really going fast. I ejected from the airplane, I'd estimate, when the airplane was going 500 to 550 knots [550 to 600 miles per hour]. I went out and I was flailed about and was unconscious. Then, coming down on the parachute, I came to, and when I came to, I was blind. That was the second time I was terrified . . . just totally lost . . . completely desolate. I said to myself—I remember it very vividly—"God, I'm a prisoner, and I'm blind." This was the most horrible moment of my life, even worse than the imprisonment. I was probably only conscious 10 seconds . . . 15 seconds. Then, I lapsed into unconsciousness, still on the parachute, and landed passed out. I came to in a plowed field, lying on my side, and there were a group of Vietnamese around me beating me with sticks, kicking me, throwing rocks at me. They were standing around just flailing me with sticks, and they'd run up and kick me and spit on me and so forth. And then a couple of Vietnamese militia came up and fired a gun and they captured me right then. I had no chance to evade or anything.

Rowan: You weren't blind, but other than that your worst fears had been realized.

Kirk: The traumatic experience came from the complete comfort and home of that cockpit . . . a minute later you're in a savage world . . . you know all is lost. In essence, that's the feeling. [You ask yourself]: "God, what can it be?" Then, I guess the old adrenalin starts pumping. I was terribly injured. I had been flailed about, and I just couldn't walk, and my knee was banged up, but nothing was broken. They dragged me to a farm house, and laid me on a bed in this farm house, and left me there for an hour while they got a truck. And I was completely lucid. I don't remember exactly what I was thinking, except that this can't be real . . . I'm dreaming this. I think I refused to permit myself to grasp the reality of the situation, at that hour. I just sort of lapsed into a sort-of nothing state of mind.

> Bob Craner joined us at this point, coming in from an appointment at the base hospital. I told him what Tom Kirk had said about the traumatic moment of shoot down and asked him for his story. He said he didn't mind sharing it with me, but warned me that I might find it uninteresting.

Craner: I was well prepared, and I anticipated being shot down, by virtue of the number of times I'd been hit before and the very, very close misses that I had encountered over a period of only four months prior to my shoot down. It seemed almost inevitable that I would be shot down, and the only question in my mind was what are the chances of survival and escape—the chances of being picked up. So, when that shell hit the tail of the aircraft, I found it no great surprise. It wasn't at all out of the ordinary.

Rowan: Did you punch out immediately, or did you try to make it over to the coast or back over the mountains?

Craner: This is what people up in the Wright-Patterson [Air Force Base] technical center call "a catastrophic failure." I had, I would say, something on the order of 45 seconds from the time I was hit until the aircraft was vertical, at a fairly low altitude, and a very high speed. Naturally, I would have elected to stay with that airplane no matter what condition it was in, assuming it was still controllable, but the controls froze. So it was all pretty much a panic-type situation, although I don't believe I experienced a great deal of panic. There wasn't time to make a great deal of my decision. I just found myself in a position where I had to punch, and I punched.

Rowan: Did you rate your chances of being picked up by the Jolly Greens? [Jolly Green Giants—Air Force rescue helicopters]

Craner: Yes, I did. The area where I was shot down was, to my eye, essentially jungle terrain, and looked very lightly inhabited. There were no other aircraft in the area. I was a solo ... a FAC [Forward Air Controller] and operating independently. But I figured I had a good chance of evading [the enemy] in this terrain, and being picked up within the next 24 or 48 hours. I held on to that line of reasoning right up until the time my parachute opened. And there I sat, suspended in the air, maybe a thousand feet above the ground. And from the ground all around me, from miles away, I could hear people screaming . . . just like at a Saturday afternoon college football game. They had witnessed the whole thing.

Rowan: And you knew what they were screaming for.

Craner: Right there, I got a chill, because I knew pretty much it was all over. Still, I was kind of surprised at myself. I kind of bucked up and said, "We've got to give it the old college try. We'll hit the ground and we'll see what happens." What happened was there were people waiting on the ground.

Rowan: What was their reaction to your arrival?

Craner: As their screams indicated, they were in pretty much of a frenzy. There were large multitudes of them, combing the area, and they were extremely excited. There was nothing professional about it. They were just a bunch of savages.

Rowan: Did they attack you?

Craner: Yes, but not in a method which indicated they were about to chop my head off or anything. But, as soon as it was clear that one fellow with a rifle had the drop on me and that I was not going to do anything violent, they became very aggressive. Then, there was just a general melee and pummelling session, and it simply resulted in them stripping all the equipment off me, and getting me well under control. Gradually, the hysteria subsided, and a leader came forward to take charge. I must have been surrounded by at least 75 to 100 people.

Rowan: What happened in the next few days, before you

got to Hanoi?

Craner: They followed a pretty classic procedure. I was bound and marched around, from village to hamlet to gun site, for exhibition. After a bit—maybe 24 hours—there were regular army people who had control of me, whereas previously, I suppose, they were militia.

Rowan: What happened after the soldiers took control?

Craner: They started marching me around to various spots, and it seemed like a dictated program that was to be carried out. The townsfolk, for their part, seemed to be quite willing to work themselves up to a hysterical pitch, and it looked to me as if they felt it was their duty to show that they had been caught up—had revolutionary consciousness, or whatever. And so they would gather in a crowd, and scream and holler and throw rocks and cry and roll on the ground and, in general, just create a hell of a bedlam. The bolder of them would try to get by the soldiers to me, to exhibit the fact that they had such hatred they were willing to throttle this guy on the spot, if they could.

Rowan: You sound as if you had no great sense of fear about this?

Craner: I thought it was pretty much a charade. I rather suspect that the hysteria was self-induced, perhaps as part of the program to show that they were in line with the government. At any rate, it was quite all right as long as it didn't get out of control. As for the soldiers who got hold of me, there were times when they were showing fear, indicating to me that there was a border-line situation, and they might, in fact, lose control, and that's the only thing I could be scared of.

Rowan: It's the belief of some POWs that such mobs did get out of control in a number of situations, and, as a result, some men were killed, men who are now listed as missing in action. You can see how that might have happened.

Craner: I can readily see that. For example, there were times when the soldiers were behind me, and I'd be passing —just a Joe, who happened to be standing there—and if the guy happened to have a machete in his hand, he might take a swipe, so I had my head on a swivel watching for this sort of thing. I was able to dodge them, but I can see where a guy who might be more befuddled mentally—not quite as alert, or have some injury—would be a fair game. And if a mob got out of hand, they could tear a guy to pieces, I suppose.

Rowan: Konnie, did you experience the same thing at the time of capture?

Trautman: I was captured by peasants, too, but fortunately there were four militia types there. And I believe I owe my life to those four men. Had they not been there with their rifles and bayonets, I think the local populace would have killed me. They had to strike their own people with their rifle butts, very forcefully, to keep them off me, yet they still kept charging in on me.

Kirk: I think that's a point that's very significant about this thing. There's a national will. Apparently their hatred of the American air pirates—what they called the American air pirates—is such that everybody, from kids to old people, men, women, and children, were beating on you. They hated us—there's no question about that.

Trautman: The civilians seemed to be so fired up, like they were on dope. Their eyes were just burning and glazed—fixed upon me. Just like they were doped.

Rowan: This was the first chance they'd had to strike back at an American.

Kirk: I think this is the key to a great deal of the bad treatment, mental anguish, as well as physical mistreatment. We were the only thing they had to take out their frustrations and hatred against.

Rowan: Is there a point that you can fix, Tom, when you came out of your relatively catatonic state, and said, "OK, I can hack it?"

Kirk: Well, I don't think so. I don't think that I ever felt up until October of '69 [when the policy of physical torture was changed], that there's no doubt in my mind that I'll hack this thing.

Rowan: How did you handle the first two years?

Kirk: My philosophy in prison camp from about the first

week there was: "I don't know if I can hack tomorrow. I'm not looking forward to next week, or next month. I'm looking forward to trying to get through this day . . . then I'll worry about tomorrow, tomorrow." I had no idea what day of the week it was, or anything, during the first month I was in prison. Then, I was moved in with people and I began to concern myself with days and dates and time. But, as long as I was living alone, I said: "I don't care about time. Time has stopped, and I've got to get through today and tonight, and then I'll worry tomorrow."

Rowan: How long did you think you might be there?"

Kirk: Until about 1972, I was of the considered opinion that we might be up there ten more years. I thought: "As long as they feed me like they're feeding me now, and keep me living like this, I can stay alive as long as my health will last." But health was a major factor. I wondered what would happen if I got cancer, or if any other sophisticated disease hit the camp. A thing like that could have wiped us out.

Rowan: Major Floyd Kushner, the only doctor who was a POW, said yesterday that there were a number of men who died in his arms within two weeks of saying to him, "It's just too tough, Doc. I can't hack it." And psychologists tell us that the same thing happened during World War II and the Korean War. What I'm trying to get at is, was there a point in time when you said: "I'm not gonna die?"

Kirk: There was never a point in time that I thought I was going to die, per se. I knew they would have to kill me. But I wasn't sure of whether they would do that, or not. I never for one minute lost the will to live, even in the darkest days. Did you Konnie? Boy, it never entered my mind, except in the parachute, when I came to consciousness and thought I was blind. I thought of taking my own life at that moment. That was more than I could hack, *I thought.* But in the prison camp, no matter what they did, I felt like, "Boy life is so great, I want to live. I want to hang on some way." There was no thought of ever giving up.

Trautman: You realize, once you've ejected and come down on the chute, that you're coming into a new world . . .

that is a tremendous change. I personally had the sensation after I was captured and made the trek through the villages, being stoned with small rocks and pebbles, and hit with the handles of farm tools, and spat upon, kicked . . . and after this initial shock, I felt like I had been through a time machine, from the year 2,000 back to the year maybe 1,000, perhaps 1,000 B.C. The people were that primitive and crude, both in appearance and their dress, their conduct especially, and the tools that they used to beat us with.

Rowan: Do you think at that time about survival, or is the horror of that moment so great that you just close your mind to what's going on and go blank?

Craner: I recall one thought which went through my mind as I was marching through the jungle right after I got picked up. I said to myself: "It looks pretty grim and there doesn't seem to be any end to this war in sight." I could psyche it out and say it would be an absolute minimum of two years from the time I was captured in December, 1967, until there would by any resolution of that affair over there. I figured, "Well, two years is within my capabilities, prepared as I am with the knowledge that I gained through survival school on what conditions will be like up here. More than two years, I am not at all sure that I will be able to exist." I thought at the time, "If it's five, I would rather die escaping than face five years." So, I pretty well rationalized myself to thinking, "We're putting in a big effort over here and two years is within reason, and it's possible it will be over in two years."

Kirk: I felt personally that I did no thinking beyond today. I stopped my mind, or maybe nature stopped it for me. I went into, not a regression syndrome, but I was in such a traumatic state about the whole thing, it was unreal. It was almost like a dream world. I was put in this truck, and blindfolded, and driven back to Hanoi, right to the Hanoi Hilton, arriving about an hour later. I was injured so bad, I was lapsing into unconsciousness most of the time. They laid me on a stretcher in a room, just a stone room, with not a piece of furniture in it, and I was the only thing in there, lying on this stretcher. And they left me there all day, from about 8 o'clock or 9 o'clock in the morning 'til that night. The combination of pain and the mental anguish—I think I retreated into myself. I don't recall a thought during that day. I must have just been in a state of shock, and complete oblivion.

Rowan: How did you react to the first time you got broken, the first time they wanted you to say something or do something and they tortured you or harassed you or coerced you into doing it? Had you told yourself: "No matter what they do to me, I am not going to do . . . (whatever it was)"?

Kirk: Oh no, I couldn't do that. Maybe there are people strong enough to do this. I am not going to be a hypocrite about that.

The toughest thing was the battle within myself as to how long I could hold out. Because I already knew that they were going to get it sooner or later.

Physical torture will achieve the desired effect in a *short* period of time. I don't care who you are. If I strap you up or rope you up, short of killing you, I can subject you to such pain that in a relatively short period of time your *mind* is going to overcome what you call your *will*, and you are going to give something to get out of this pain, short of dying. Because they will not let you die. At some point, you just don't care anymore, and then you will give them something.

Rowan: Did you hate yourself later for not having held out longer?

Kirk: I had no remorse for giving them something, once I had gone that far. On several occasions I felt later that I had not perhaps given my all. I think I rationalized that what they were asking for was not against my government, was not against my country, was of no value to anybody, but was pure out-and-out contrariness or vindictiveness on their part, to make me say something, and, as a result, to show me they were masters.

I've read stories about the great heroes who were subjected to all this punishment and torture for days and weeks at a time and never gave the enemy anything. I don't believe that anymore. I don't believe that at all. If you stand someone up in front of a firing squad and say, "Tell me this or I'll kill you," and he doesn't tell you and you kill him—that guy's not nearly the hero that a guy is who takes sustained torture for a week. That guy who takes sustained torture for a week, if he is allowed to live, either his mind's going to give way, or he's going to give something.

> The Air Force and the Navy run survival schools for their pilots. Details of what they teach are classified, but, generally speaking, there are two categories of training.
>
> First, the men learn how to survive in an unfriendly environment: which plants are safe to eat and which are poisonous; how to find water and purify it; how to administer morphine and bandage their injuries; how to plan a course of action to conserve available resources.
>
> Second, they learn what to expect from the enemy, if captured: what types of military information will be sought; what methods will be used to get it; what living conditions will be like as prisoners of war; what responsibilities they have to their fellow POWs under the Code of Conduct; and what responsibilities their captors have to them.
>
> Most of the POWs with whom I spoke were adequately trained to survive in the jungle or the sea, if that's where they got shot down. Most were *not* adequately prepared for the type of questioning and the brutality they faced in North Vietnamese prison camps. At survival school they had been questioned by highly skilled interrogators, and subjected to threats and some physical abuse, always with the knowledge that it would be over in a few days. In North Viet Nam, they were questioned endlessly about unimportant military matters, or told to make obviously false statements about their political beliefs, and then immediately tortured if they stood on their rights under the Geneva Convention.
>
> Those who kept up-to-date on survival training knew that it was advisable to give in and at least *pretend* to give the enemy some information of value, before they completely lost the use of their faculties and simply told everything they knew. This is called "adopting a fall-back position," or "setting up a second line of resistance." But some men found it difficult to decide when to fall back, and others didn't even know that they could.

Trautman: I want to add to what Colonel Kirk said. We all have that impression that we Americans, and especially fighter pilots, are real tigers, and damn it, I consider us to be tigers, but we're also humans, human beings. We're not supermen. We were all prepared to resist the enemy on capture and interrogation. I went through the old survival school back in 1959 that taught us just to give name, rank, serial number, and date of birth, period. When I was initially interrogated, I was in the interrogation room that they refer to as room 19 in the Heartbreak [Hotel section of the Hanoi Hilton] . . . the one with the green knobby walls. After name, rank, serial number, date of birth, the very next question that was asked of me was, "What type of aircraft did you fly?" I refused to tell them, simply stating, "I am not required to answer that question," and they asked me the *second* time. I said, "Under the Geneva Convention I am not required to give that information," and two minutes later I was in torture.

Kirk: That's exactly like me Konnie. *Exactly.*

Trautman: They didn't fool around, they didn't try to play games with me, or verbally force me, or go on to another question. They just repeated that question one time and I wound up in the ropes.

Kirk: That's exactly like me Konnie. When they brought me to that interrogation room they brought me on a stretcher. I couldn't walk. They sat me up with a box behind my back, and before they even started to question me, the first thing they said was, "You are not a prisoner of war. You are a *war criminal.*" And that was pretty traumatic. I'd never heard that before.

Trautman: I was aware of this to some extent. By the time I got shot down, the news media had circulated pictures of Dick Stratton bowing to his captors and of the other POWs being paraded through Hanoi. So I was aware that we were being treated as and called war criminals. But the physical torture came as a tremendous shock to me.

Rowan: Did it come as a surprise to you, Bob?

Craner: I had roughly 10 to 12 days of anticipation during my trip from the southernmost part of the country up to Hanoi. What we had been given in surival school in the way of physical preparation certainly was inadequate. We were not put through torture, but we were certainly made aware that it was possible that something like this would occur. I anticipated it, and approached Hanoi with a great deal of trepidation. When the event actually occurred, I knew pretty well what was coming; it was only a matter of degree that the physical torture reached.

Rowan: How many times were you put through the rope treatment?

Craner: Once on the way and once up there. Thereafter, not again.

Kirk: They put me in the ropes the second morning, for information. They got nothing that morning, and they took me out at noon for the siesta, and for food. That afternoon, back in the ropes again. I wouldn't give them anything, so they'd go out of the room and leave me there for some period of time, and then come back and take them off and say, "Now are you ready to talk?" I'd say, "No."

Back in!

They did not keep me in the ropes at night. I don't know whether the doctors told them not to do this or what. But, on the fourth morning after I got there, I finally gave them what they wanted to know. After that, I gave them enough that they didn't put me back in the ropes any more.

> At that point, according to many POWs, the North Vietnamese could have pried loose almost any military secret. But, they didn't know what questions to ask. They seemed satisfied that they had forced a man to answer more than the four questions permitted under the Geneva Convention, and the fifth question sometimes was nothing more than: "What type of aircraft were you flying?—a question to which they usually had the answer in the form of a wrecked airplane. As soon as the POWs caught on that the name of the game was "answer every question," they could save themselves from torture by making up answers, or by answering in vague generalities.
>
> But there were times when there was no way to avoid providing valid information, such as when one POW was being questioned about the activities of another. In those cases, the North Vietnamese had a way of checking the answers by torturing other men, if necessary. Konnie Trautman got caught in the middle of one situation when, to tell the truth about an escape attempt would have meant involving an ever-widening circle of men. He tried to resist.

Trautman: Let me try to tell you what it really feels like when they tightly bind your wrists and elbows behind your back with nylon straps—then take the strap and pull the arms up, up your back, to the back of your head. If you can remember when you were a little boy, the fooling around you did, and someone grabs your hand and just twists your arm up to your back, and says: "Say Uncle." He does it with just one hand. And this, as you remember, is a very severe pain. Well, imagine this with both arms tied tight together—elbow to elbow, wrist to wrist—and then, using the leverage of his feet planted between your shoulder blades, with both hands, he pulls with all his might, 'til your arms are up and back over your head, forcing your head down between your feet, where your legs are between iron bars. [Konnie was speaking in hushed tones—his voice cracking at times.] The pain is literally beyond description, but it was so excrutiating to me, that I let out a loud scream. And then, when I did, I learned that you are not allowed to scream when you are being tortured. You are not allowed to scream!

As soon as I screamed, the guard grabbed one of the shackles lying on the floor and he just rammed it in my mouth, and if I had not opened my mouth to absorb the impact, I would have lost all of my teeth. He said, "You are not allowed to make noise, you must not scream." If you scream, they pull the ropes even tighter. So you learn very quickly not to scream, and yet endure the pain. And the eeriest part of it all is that you know there are people in the room to the left of you, and to the right of you, undergoing the same excrutiating pain you are, and there is utter silence, just like a morgue or tomb. People are going through physical pain that's beyond description, yet you can't hear a sound. You can hear the irons drop, you can hear limbs being compressed and stretched. You can actually hear this, from one room to another. You can sense that another man is tensed up, and locking in all his emotions, just like you are, for fear of the deeper pain that would result from screaming.

Besides the pain itself, you are tied up so tight that your windpipe becomes pinched and you breathe in gasps. You're trying to gulp in air, because your wind passage is being shrunken. Your throat, in a matter of 30 seconds, becomes completely dry, like it's been swabbed with cotton, and you're gasping in air, and it feels like it's 110 degrees and dry as can be, and it's difficult to breathe. And it's difficult to even maintain a bit of rationale. At times I've gotten the urge to vomit, and I'd just feel so dry inside that just the dry heaves came up.

Rowan: How long can a man stand that kind of torture?

Trautman: Some people say they've had this for hours. I've been through this rope treatment 13 different times, and I've been in it no longer than about 15 minutes. However, sometimes I was fortunate. After about 10 or 15 minutes in this position, tied up so tightly, your nerves in your arms are pinched off, and then your whole upper torso becomes numb. It's a relief. You feel no more pain, and it's really a blessing. The breathing is still difficult, but the pain is gone. You've been anesthetized. However, when they release the ropes, the procedure works *completely* in reverse. It's almost like double jeopardy. You go through the same pain coming out of the ropes as you did going in. You almost think when you're tied up and the pain is gone, "Don't take the ropes off, because now there is no pain." But, they've got to come off sometime.

I would gladly spend six months in solitary confinement rather than go through one 15 minute rope session. I would gladly do that, although in 15 minutes it's all over. But I'm just trying to convey how great that torture with ropes is. I would personally take six months of isolation, minus pain, rather than 15 minutes in those straps.

> The "rope treatment" got its name from the ropes originally used by the North Vietnamese for this form of torture. By 1967, the ropes had been replaced with nylon straps from the parachutes of the downed airman.

Rowan: Was complete isolation worse than torture?

Trautman: When I was in isolation it was almost a blessing to be alone and not be beaten, and to have the guards off my back. I spent 141 continuous days in isolation and I was completely sealed off from all communication with anyone else. I was wearing leg irons, day and night. But it was a blessing not to go through those ropes.

Rowan: Knowing, as you all must have known, that sooner or later they're going to get this information, what is it that makes you hold out, that makes you decide that "they're not going to get it without torturing me to the point of collapse"?

Craner: The one thing that gave me strength up there was not what I've heard other people expressing so often since we got back: faith in God or a sense of duty to country. The thing that kept my endurance up, that kept me conscientious, was *my obligation to the other guys,* the people I was serving with, because I was reasonably aware of the lengths they were going to, and I was just trying to keep up with them.

Kirk: I agree with that a hundred percent. For me, personally, as a middle of the road type guy, religion was not a factor; faith in the Code of Conduct was not a factor. When it gets down to the bare facts, by God, I wanted to come out of there and look Bob Craner in the eye.

You live with another guy, and you go over there and you're tortured and you're brought back in that room and he says: "What happened?"

"They did this."

"What'd you tell them?"

"I told them this."

There's an element of fear in it, an element of fear of your fellow man, your fellow American. It's keeping faith with him, and the fact that you've got to face this guy. And tremendous strength derives therefrom.

They tried to keep us apart, keep us isolated. They knew this. There's strength in unity.

You've got to face this guy; you're going to have to tell him the truth. I wanted to keep faith so that I knew that when I stood up at the bar with somebody after the war, that, by God, I could look him in the eye and say, "We hacked it." And we know, everyone of us knows, we gave things that we should not have given, but I know these three men sitting right here did our best, and that's all you can do.

Rowan: That camaraderie gave you the strength you

needed.

Craner: I had an idealized concept of my military buddies up there, and the lengths they were going through to avoid giving the North Vietnamese what they wanted, and that was enough for me. I wouldn't call it strength on my part as much as just trying to hold up my end of the bargain.

Rowan: Konnie, you didn't mind solitary confinement, but Tom, you're perhaps a more gregarious individual. How did it affect you?

Kirk: To me, the first six months up there was terrible. After that, I was in communication with other people at the camp, and I began to look upon this as a way of life, and say to myself, "Hang on, because some day, you know, it's going to end." The first six months, "solo" was traumatic, because I didn't know what existed outside the walls of that room I was in. Once I was in communications, and after I was living with four guys, and then I went solo again for six or eight or ten months at a time, God, I didn't mind it at all. It was a piece of cake. Every day during the siesta I was up on the wall, bang! bang! bang! It was just like conversation; almost like living with the guys. And then you could turn it off.

> The principle means of communication throughout the Hanoi Hilton and other North Vietnamese prisons was a tap code, which is discussed in greater detail elsewhere in this book. Actually, any communication from one cell to another was forbidden, but the POWs soon learned that during the afternoon siesta period the guards left them alone, for the most part, and they could communicate. When they had cellmates, the POWs were allowed to talk, but even that presented something of a problem.

Kirk: When you're in the room with one other guy, you pretty soon run out of stuff to talk over with that guy. To me, being solo and being with one other man is damn near the same thing.

Craner: I agree wholeheartedly, and I would go a step further and say that, to me, solo is preferable to living with one other man. I don't think there's any combination less desirable than two men in one room. It works fine, depending on the individuals, for maybe two months, three months.

Then, after that, there would be a period of conflict which had to be resolved at some point. But that period of conflict can be a bitter thing. "Cabin Fever," it's been described as. Jack London did a fairly good study on it.

Rowan: When you were in solo, did the darkness bother you?

Kirk: I was never exposed to any solo where it was totally dark.

Craner: There was always light, 24 hours a day, from an electric light bulb.

Trautman: The solo I had, they would not turn on the lights until about 10 o'clock in the evening. I'm sure this was not normal throughout the remainder of the camp. This was just the room I was in. The darkness did not bother me, per se. What did bother me was that it gave free reign to the rats, and they would just run over my legs and across my bed and I was frightened more of them than just from the darkness itself.

> At this point in our discussion, Konnie Trautman left for an appointment at the hospital, promising to return, and Tom Kirk told me he would have to leave to round up his nephew, an active Italian lad of eight who spoke no English, and who had been left in the care of a somewhat confused young Air Force sergeant. Before Tom departed, the talk turned to what one does with one's mind when in solitary confinement. The men agreed that the first thing they did was review their lives up to the moment of shoot down. That usually led to guessing what life might have been like if certain decisions had been altered.

Rowan: When you thought back to your high school exploits or your sweethearts, did you extrapolate, and fantasize what might have happened if . . . ?

Craner: I did. But I was more concerned with reality in terms of the mistakes I had made or opportunities I had missed.

Kirk: Yeah. Why did I go this way?

Craner: Then, I would try to project a life from a certain crucial point in my past life, and see what might have happened.

Kirk: I did the same thing there. I had another thing. I'm a musician, and I spent up to eight hours a day on a bamboo stick about 10 inches long practicing my flute. I was amazed at the technical proficiency I was able to develop in prison on a bamboo stick. I had a routine, so that when the gong went at seven o'clock in the morning, I was going almost constantly until night, with something. I had a PT [physical training] program. A certain time of day was set aside for academics, for thinking, for walking. I could not walk a mile when I first started out. [Later] I would walk a mile every day and I built it up to five miles a day—hundred and hundreds of laps. That was the most ordered time of my entire life. I never had a problem with inactivity of the mind.

Rowan: Bob, with all the fantasizing you did in solitary, did it ever occur to you that you might be losing your mind?

Craner: Oh, I delved into the subject, but I don't know that I ever had any great fear of losing my mind.

After we all joined together in the later years, we used to banter back and forth about this, about who was crazier, and we'd assign "nutty levels" to all the individuals, and predict how difficult it would be for each man to be assimiliated back into a normal society.

I don't have a real good background in psychology, but I caught myself sometimes thinking, "Too much daydreaming is bad, and let's be a little more constructive." At those times I might shift to something like mathematics and puzzles and exercise, trying to recall certain tricks in algebra and calculus, and working with them for a few days or weeks.

Rowan: So there was no difficulty in separating the reality of that kind of mental activity and the fantasy of some other dream world.

Craner: Not a great difficulty. I think mental laziness or inactivity is the only criterion. If a guy is a little bit weak and given to self-pity, he might spend more time withdrawing into this fantasy world. It's a beautiful escape.

Rowan: What's it like? I'd like to get an example of where it took you at times.

Craner: Oh, picking a critical point, such as the woman I met and married. If I had never met her, if I had never married, this might have allowed me more latitude in the choice of jobs that I took . . . much more adventurous jobs, much more dangerous jobs, to which I probably would have gravitated, had I not had a more stabilizing influence in the family. And so I wound up in some fairly high blown espionage-type jobs, and soldier-of-fortune type things in my fantasies.

Rowan: On the limited diet of a POW camp, I imagine you had food fantasies?

Craner: Yeah! Those were unconquerable in the first four months. Even if I tried, I could not get away from food for more than the space of a minute. It was no effort on my part at all. It was just something that happened to me very naturally, and I coudn't conquer it for a long time. I assume that it was part of what was going on in me, and physically and psychologically, it showed. I think after I adjusted to the reduced quantity of food, my body adapted to that, and my mind did, also.

Rowan: Just what did you do, what did your mind do?

Craner: I started off reviewing. We are people who like to eat out, at least once a week, and we find restaurants quite exciting. So, I hopped and skipped around the restaurants in Asia and Europe and America that we had been to, and went through some of the more memorable meals I had had. I could pretty well see the inside of each restaurant and some of the fine meals that we had at home.

From that I kind of took off. I had no experience or adaptability or suitability to this sort of thing, but I fancied myself a chef, whipping up concoctions for each meal of the day, and they were unbelievably rich and heavy and packed with all kinds of nourishment that one couldn't possibly consume in an entire week.

Rowan: Was there any favorite that you kept going back to?

Craner: No, I can't really say there was any favorite. I would go from breakfast specialities, for hours on end, right on to lunch. Then, I would go on to dinner. Then, I would try little snacks, none of which I consume normally. There was

nothing very constructive about it. I didn't make any dis-
coveries about better nutrition in my daily diet or anything
like that. It was just wild stuff.

Rowan: Beginning in 1968, the Communists started to
send selected individuals home, usually as part of a
propaganda campaign associated with the visit to Hanoi of
anti-war delegations. Were you ever offered an opportunity
to go home as part of those early release programs?

Craner: Yes, the opportunity was presented in general
terms, not specific. I feel that whole subject is tied to the
loyalty I felt to the fellows around me, that it would have
been letting them down to accept an early release. One could
never be sure what the conditions were surrounding early
release.

Rowan: Is that whole early release thing a sore point?

Craner: There is a great deal of bitterness in people concerning this topic. I know some of them rather well, and I know
that some of them were offered, in very concrete terms, an
early release. My next-door-neighbor at the Plantation for
slightly over two years, John McCain, was in fact urged to
take an early release.

Rowan: That was about the time his father was to become
Commander-in-Chief of the Pacific.

Craner: Yes, it was in June or July of 1968. We became
very close, he and I, by virtue of the geography of the camp. I
was in an end room and he was in the room next to me. At
the time we were fairly effectivly cut off from the remainder
of the camp, except for sporadic contact, and so we relied on
each other. He asked for what advice I could offer on the
topic, after he came back from his little session. I'm afraid I
didn't have a heck of a lot to offer, except to say: "You might
progress a little further, and see just what they're going to try
to extract from you." But he said, "Look, I know, and you
know, what they're after, and we won't let it go any further."
And he just said "negative" right then. They lowered the
boom on him. But he stuck with that decision, and I am im-
mensely proud of him for that.

Rowan: If they had made an all-out effort, could they have forced him to go home?

Craner: There's little doubt in my mind that they could have tortured him right out of the country, but I'm sure that's not what they had in mind.

Rowan: In a situation like that, with no one else to talk with, did you find yourself sharing your emotions with McCain?

Craner: McCain and I leaned on each other a great deal. We were separated by about 18 inches of brick, and I never saw the guy for the longest time. I used to have dreams . . . we all did, of course, and they were sometimes nightmares . . . and my world had shrunk to a point where the figures in my dreams were myself, the guards, and a voice—and that was McCain. I didn't know what he looked like, so I could not visualize him in my dreams. Yet he was a very vital part of my dreams, because he became the guy—the only guy—I turned to, for a period of about two years.

We got to know each other, more intimately, I'm sure, than I will ever know my wife. We opened up and talked about damn near everything, besides our immediate problems—past life, and all the family things we never would have talked to anybody about. We derived a great deal of strength from this.

Rowan: What about contact with your family . . . did you finally get mail?

Craner: "Finally" is a good way to put it. It took just under five years, and it consisted of a packet of letters which dated back through those years. They were presented to me on the way out, within the last few days.

Rowan: Did you fear what might have happened at home?

Craner: No, I'm a pretty lucky guy, for this type of situation. I was well-equipped, in many respects, to endure something like this. I have seen other guys who were not, and my heart goes out to them. They had a much rougher time than I, because of this. I was essentially a family man, before I was shot down, to the detriment, perhaps, of my career and my social standing with my peers. I tended to shy away from outside contacts, and stay in the company of my family. And

I could not seriously envision any drifting away on their part. We were awfully close and tight, and I expected us to stay that way. At the same time, I reached a point where, after five years—which is a long time to wait for a guy to come back—I hoped that they had progressed, and led a full, rich life. And if that meant doing without me, that they'd proceed on that course. They certainly had to find somebody else, especially my son. I wanted more than anything else that he should be associated with *some man* who would take an interest in him, teach him things, and show him things that I should have been doing. I desperately wanted that. That's not to say I wanted another guy moving in and wearing my smoking jacket, sitting in my easy chair. But there had to be a replacement for me for certain things, and I wanted that very much.

Trautman: I think we all shared the same anxiety about who's filling the father role with the children. Where is the little boy going to run to when the wheel breaks off his fire truck? Who's going to fix this and fix that? These are things we take for granted just being around the house and being around the children.

Rowan: Were you able to envision your children growing?

Craner: I envisioned my kids pretty much as I left them. I couldn't conceive of them at the heights they are now, the mental and physical heights. In fact, most of the activities I planned, in getting reacquainted with my kids, were activities I engaged in six years ago with them, and they're not applicable at this time.

Trautman: I kept visualizing the same picture that I had retained the last time I saw them, and I could not forecast or extrapolate how they would look three inches taller, or five inches taller, or 20 pounds heavier. I preferred to retain the memories I last had of them, and carry them that way, until I received the first pictures of them, years later, showing a remarkable change in their appearance.

> In getting letters and pictures of his children, Konnie Trautman was one of the more fortunate POWs. Bob Craner had no mail for five years. Many other POWs were similarly isolated from their

families. Yet, some men were allowed to write home every month, and to receive letters and packages. The Communists seemed to have no clear-cut policy on mail, except to use it when they could as a propaganda device.

Rowan: You had mentioned that living by yourself is easier than living with one other person. What about living with 14 other people?

Craner: Picture a room just about this size.

Rowan: I think it's about 15 feet by 30 feet, maybe 40 feet.

Craner: I think that's just about the dimensions of Room 1, where I lived for this last two years in the company of up to 45 people, down to as low as maybe 20, at the very end. Well, if you pack 40 odd people in here 24 hours a day, with maybe a few people less at intervals, as they go out to wash and come back in, month after month and year after year, there is continuing bedlam. As different people pursue their different objectives, inevitably, there will be conflict, rarely ever resulting in anything approaching the physical; but nonetheless, there's plenty of time and opportunity for argumentation.

Rowan: What kind of an objective might someone have been pursuing that would cause such conflict?

Craner: If somebody set out to walk five miles a day, that obviously was going to be pretty troublesome. Naturally, guys are going to try to accomodate some fellow who's *got* to walk. So, one guy gets to march up and down, and then he is joined by two or three others, but then they start bumping into others. Well then, the people who want to go up to the other end of the room for a specific purpose, in order to relieve themselves, have got to fight the traffic. This is settled very quickly, but there is continually this problem. It flares up from time to time. There may be a group of four or five who are very interested in picking the brains of one fellow who knows how to speak Russian, and they want very much to gather in a small group, and have just a little bit of quiet, so they can talk back and forth and get a lesson across. But, there are maybe 15 others who want to engage in some kind of wild game, whether it be charades or one thing or another, which produces a lot of whooping and laughing. There's another major conflict. Then, there is a little shouting contest: "You guys are making too much noise." That all is part of a large mass of people jammed into a small place.

Rowan: How would you resolve those?

Craner: Oh, about like school boys do, I think. They have their verbal argument and there are bad feelings which may last for a day or two, and then it's all over.

Rowan: Is it difficult, in any sense, to leave that kind of environment? You had a pretty close-knit group, a loving and sharing group of people. What's it like to walk away from that and get back to the world?

Craner: Of course, getting out was what we had all anticipated and dreamed of and desired desperately for so many years. But I and everyone did establish friendships and very intimate personal relationships up there, which I don't believe any other set of circumstances would have allowed. And it was with just a little bit of melancholia that I finally said good-bye to John McCain at Clark [Air Base]. Even at Clark, we were still a group, and we were still talking to ourselves, and the outsiders were trying to butt in, but we weren't having too much of that. We were still a pretty tight-knit group. On the night before I was to get on an airplane at 8:00 o'clock the following morning, I could sense that here was the end. Now this group is going to be busted wide open and spread all over the United States. It may be a long time, years, before we rejoin, and when we do, it won't be the same.

2

The Cat and His Rabbit

The voice in Bob Craner's dreams for more than two years belonged to Navy Lieutenant Commander John S. McCain, III, of Orange Park, Florida, who, like Tom Kirk and Konnie Trautman, had been shot down in October of 1967.

McCain, then just 31 years old, was one of those who might have died for want of medical treatment. He had suffered two broken arms and a broken leg on shoot-down. He had been thrown in the cell next to Craner's in the Plantation, his injuries untreated. A few months later, the North Vietnamese started patching him up. They knew something he did not know. His father, an admiral, had just been designated by President Lyndon B. Johnson to be CINCPAC —Commander-in-Chief of the Pacific—the man with the technical responsibility for running the air war against North Viet Nam.

The North Vietnamese decided they didn't want young McCain. They wanted to send him home as an example of their "humane and lenient policy." But the POWs had established their own policy: that no one would accept release until the first man captured alive in the north, Everett Alvarez, shot down in 1964, was set free. Not everyone was strong enough to follow that policy, and some men went home with the "peace delegations" admitted to Hanoi.

Not John McCain.

When I met John in San Francisco he was walking with a slight limp, but walking very quickly. He had promised his wife, Carol, on that Sunday morning in April, that he would meet her at 10:30. It was almost 10:00 and we hadn't begun taping. He had promised to give me an hour or so of his time.

To add to that impossible time-bind, one of those once-in-a-lifetime problems developed with my tape recorder. I would have liked to blame it on the machine, but when I looked down at it I saw that I had simply forgotten to activate all the switches.

"Pilot error," I said, hoping to appeal to his aviator's instinct to protect the reputation of the man in the cockpit.

"Let's plow on," he replied with a boyish grin, leaving me to wonder whether he was implying that I was a clod.

In any case, we plowed on, and this time there was no mistake.

It was no great surprise to me that John would have little to say about his own heroism. In fact, he spent more time telling me about the pain his wife had suffered in a terrible automobile accident while he was in North Viet Nam than he did on the subject of his own torture.

That is the stuff of which heroes are made, and, to his buddies in the Plantation and the other prison camps, John McCain was a genuine hero.

Rowan: John, early in 1968 you were ill, you were down to a hundred pounds, you had dysentery, you had a leg broken, both arms were broken and you were in pretty bad shape. Why did you refuse an early release?

McCain: First of all, whether I could survive or not was the criterion. If I was sick or injured enough that I could not survive, then I felt that I should accept it. But I came to the conclusion that I could survive under conditions as they were. I felt that they were not offering it as a humane and lenient act. I felt that they were doing it for propaganda purposes, primarily.

This man we called "The Cat," who was the commanding officer of all the camps, said, "I can expel you." I said, "Yes, you can expel me. There's nothing I can do about it." But that wasn't what they wanted. What they wanted was for me to say, "Yes, I want to go home." Then, they would be able to say that this man asked to go home, so we allowed him, under our humane and lenient policy, to go home. If they had expelled me, and I later said I had told them I didn't want to go home, this would have destroyed all the propaganda value.

Rowan: Did you think you might take the chance of letting them have a small propaganda victory, but then come home and really blow the whistle on what they were doing to everyone else?

McCain: I didn't think so because, primarily, it would have been a great lever against other prisoners. They would have been able to tell the other prisoners, "We sent home the son of the Commander-in-Chief of the Pacific, and you still are here, because you don't mean anything."

Rowan: You did have a serious question in your own mind as to whether you could survive?

McCain: Yes, I did, because of the weakesss of my condition. But it's very hard to evaluate one's own self, particularly when you're living alone. It's hard to examine yourself and see exactly how well or how weak you are. I think sometimes you're affected with hypochondria, and other times I think you don't realize how badly off you are.

Rowan: Bob Craner, who was the only man with whom you were in contact at that time, said the only advice he could give you was that perhaps you might have played along with them for another few days to see what they were doing. But, you decided that you wanted to give them a flat rejection.

McCain: I didn't want to test my moral courage to the point where I'd play along with them, and it would become easier and easier, and more and more attractive, to just slip and say, "Yes." I felt that it was better, as I found in other experiences with them, to take as hard a line as possible . . .

although I certainly did not stand up and shake my fist in the camp commander's face, or argue, or anything like that. I just kept repeating I did not want to go. He said, "The doctors say you can't live." Of course I did not believe that. I hadn't seen a doctor in six months. He said: "Lyndon Johnson wants you home," and this kind of stuff.

They seemed to get more and more frantic about it. And so, the more important it seemed to them, the more important it seemed to me not to. At the final meeting we had, a fellow we named "The Rabbit" was supposedly interpreting for The Cat. The Cat was pretending he did not speak English, but I found out later on that he speaks very good English. The last meeting was the morning of the Fourth of July in 1968. The Rabbit said, "Our senior officer wants to know your final answer."

I said, "My final answer is the same."

The Cat was sitting next to him. He had an ink pen in his hand and a pile of papers. He broke the ink pen. Ink spurted out all over. He stood up and knocked his chair over backwards, and he said, "They taught you too well, they taught you too well."

He turned, walked out, and slammed the door, leaving The Rabbit sitting there. The Rabbit looked at me and said, "It's going to be very bad for you now. Go back to your room."

Rowan: When did it start getting very bad for you?

McCain: About a month later. I expected it immediately. However, it was not until that peace group had gone home.

Rowan: Were you living in fear?

McCain: No, not particularly. One of the things you have to guard against more than anything else is fear. As you know, the fear of beating is generally much worse than the actual beating.

Rowan: In this case, the beatings were pretty severe?

McCain: Yes, they were very severe. It was the first time that I had really been hammered. For a long period of time after that, until late '69, I was hammered periodically.

Rowan: In August of '68, when this started happening, how intense was it? And what do you mean by "hammered"?

McCain: I was beaten every two or three hours for four days, starting with a night of beating, and I was in the ropes that night.

Generally speaking, they did not use the ropes on me because of the condition of my arms and shoulders [broken at the time of his shoot-down]. They did not want to permanently injure me. Later, in May of '69, my leg had gotten so I didn't have to use a crutch, and my leg was reinjured, so I had to use a crutch again. Most of the time, though, things like that were accidental. They wanted to inflict pain without permanent injury.

Rowan: You obviously survived that with a pretty healthy mental attitude.

McCain: I owe a great deal of it to my friend Bob Craner. I consider his aid to me as the single most important factor. He's a very strong man and he's a man of principle. He is a much more calm individual than I am. Sometimes I would get very worried and he was a very stabilizing influence on me.

Sometimes I would say, "You know, Bob, I think that it's coming again." I knew that, when a purge would begin, they would not miss me. He, in his own way, would point out to me that, if it comes, it comes; if it doesn't, it doesn't and there's very little that we can do about it.

Being associated with a man of his calibre in a very close relationship was of great value to me. That is one reason why the Gooks try to keep people in solitary confinement, so you cannot have this. By having the ability to have long discussions with him, this helps us both a great deal.

Rowan: Has some of that stability that you learned from Bob Craner hung on since you've been home?

McCain: I feel that I have at least found what I want to do in life, which is to make a contribution to the betterment of this country, whether it be in or out of the military. I have lost a lot of personal ambition and it's been replaced by an ambition to make a contribution rather than to do something to improve my own status. I feel that I'm much better for the experience that I had.

Rowan: John, there were those *out* of the military who felt they were making a contribution to the betterment of this country by protesting against the war. How do you feel about them now?

McCain: I and most of the people that I know are not bitter against them, although there's no doubt that the North Vietnamese felt that they were going to win the war in the streets of the United States as opposed to South Viet Nam, as they won in Paris as opposed to Indo-China. But, I do not have bitterness towards them because, as you have already heard from other people, we were trying to defend the American way of life, the democratic way of life, and that sanctions the right of dissent. If we stifled all dissent in our country, then we would be as bad as the Communists are, and that's what it was all about.

I don't have a lot of bitterness towards peace groups that went to Hanoi. I feel that they were misguided. I also feel, to a degree, that they were dishonest. They knew how many of us were up there; at least they knew there were a big number of us there. However, after seeing seven or eight or nine POWs and not seeing any camps, or possibly one camp, they then made statements about how well we were being treated.

Why didn't they see our senior ranking officers? Why didn't they come to our rooms? Why didn't they tour all the other camps, and see everyone, rather than just seeing a select few?

I'm sure they have the intelligence to know that when you only see seven or eight out of a group of 500, you are not necessarily seeing the POWs. You're only seeing a few of them. I think that possibly because of the fact, as they stated, that they were on the side of the North Vietnamese, this had a great deal to do with their judgment as to some of the things that they were saying.

Rowan: Do you have any bitterness toward the North Vietnamese?

McCain: No. I think that their society is one which bred the behavior of the guards and the interrogators. They were taught to hate us and to believe that we had bombed their schools and hospitals.

As you know, one of our major complaints was the severe restrictions on what targets we could bomb. We didn't want to bomb churches and schools and hospitals, but some of the military targets that we could have destroyed were in populated areas, so therefore they were avoided. We couldn't hit any dams, even when they were used as roads. Where a bridge was down, you could see a road that went away from this bridge over to a dam and across the dam. The dam could not be hit. So, it was difficult to interdict their truck traffic.

But what I'm trying to say is that because of the way they are bred, that's the only reaction you can expect from them. I would like to see their leaders deposed, but the chances of that are very slim.

Rowan: Did you think of them as the enemy?

McCain: Oh yes, oh yes!

Rowan: Did you think of the Vietnamese people as the enemy?

McCain: Well, we thought of them as the enemy from a technical viewpoint, just like we thought of the German people as our enemies, although it was the leaders of the Germans in World War II who inspired them. But, in the ideological sense, I didn't think of the people themselves as our enemy. I thought of communism, the take-over of southeast Asia, and the leaders of North Viet Nam, as the enemy.

Rowan: When they questioned you prior to those discussions about the possibility of sending you home on an early release, they indicated to you they had larger plans.

McCain: Yes. These two discussions I had were not related to release. It was just because my father was a big man and they thought that possibly I had some inside information. They wanted to discuss the way our government runs; personalities like MacNamara and Westmoreland. Of course, I had no knowledge of anything except what I read in the papers—which they read also. Then, in a boastful manner, because of the tremendous boost which they got out of the Tet offensive in February of 1968, they said they were going to liberate South Viet Nam very soon and after that, they were going to liberate Laos and Cambodia. After that, they were going to liberate Thailand and Malaysia.

John McCain's apprehension about being tortured—that ". . . it's coming again"—was shared by most of the POWs. Dick Stratton lived at the other end of the same Warehouse cellblock in the Plantation, and he described the feeling to me in some detail:

Stratton: You'd hear those keys coming down the passageway, and it wasn't that you wished the next cell ill, but you sure prayed that it wasn't your cell that night.

We pulled an experiment recently. I maintained that I would wake up and bolt upright in my bed if someone rattled some keys. So we closed the doors in the hospital ward in Oakland and a guy came by after I was asleep and rattled some keys and I bolted upright.

Rowan: That's what happened when a guard came into the cellblock at night?

Stratton: Right. First of all, I'd be wide awake, and adrenalin would be pouring through me as if I was in the most extreme situation I'd ever been in as a flier. Then, the shakes, which I don't get in an airplane, thank God. But in that case, just absolutely uncontrollable quivering shakes.

Rowan: Could you hear the footsteps stop?

Stratton: No, because they wear those rubber-tire sandals. Sometimes a shuffle could be heard, and Bob Craner could identify a guard by his shuffle. He had very acute hearing— probably had never flown props in his life. Most of us who have flown props are slightly tone-deaf. He could pick up the footsteps and say it was one guy or another coming to get us, but I couldn't.

It was the keys. You'd hear them jingling. They always like to jingle things. They're like kids in many ways. Then, the next thing you'd hear is that the jingling would stop in front of your door and there would be some fumbling as everybody fumbles for a lock, drunk or sober.

You'd always hope you were hearing wrong, but then you heard the squeak of the door. There was no lubrication on the hinges, so it was "Inner Sanctum" all over again.

Rowan: Was that particular moment the worst, or was there a sense of relief that the waiting was all over?

Stratton: Right. My nagging doubts have always been over uncertainty. It's a psychological truth with most people. You can face the known. It's uncertainty that's most difficult to face. So, as soon as it was resolved: "It's my cell; it's my day in the barrel again," then, it becomes a matter of mustering what defenses you have left and meeting it head-on.

And perhaps there's a feeling of guilt about having been hoping it's not you, because you know if it's not you, it's going to be somebody else. So you really feel like a crumb.

Rowan: But then you're in it.

Stratton: Then you're off and running again, and then it depends on how much you've come back from the last time; how much basic physical strength you have; how your health is; how well you've done in bolstering your spirits with your little pep rallies; how good your com [communications] has been. Some days you do better than others.

Rowan: The other case is when the keys go by you, and you realize they're not after you.

Stratton: You start praying for the other guy. This was common with many people I talked to. Every night we said a prayer for the guy, whoever he was, who was in Room 18 after a raid. We prayed for that guy because we knew the hell he was going through. Another guy was taken out of his cell and you just started praying for him.

Rowan: Dick, while you were at the Plantation they subjected you to another kind of psychological pressure in a blacked-out room.

Stratton: Yes. That room was next to the Craner-McCain combination they've described to you. It appears to have been a dark room of some kind. It had a baffled doorway and you had to go through a sort of labyrinth passageway to get in. They had it boarded up. As they took me down there, someone was walking out with the light bulb.

What had happened is that they told me to copy some material that had been attributed to another American. They wanted it reproduced. I said: "No way." They said: "You will be punished. We will make you do what we want you to do. Well, by this time the charges of me being brainwashed had come out, and they couldn't afford to do too much more to me. They had already marked me. So, the blacked out room was their solution.

So now, I got into blackness. And, on the 25th day, I started getting a screw loose up here.

Fortunately, I had Jack van Loan, an Air Force Major, behind me. So I rapped him up on the wall and I told him the guard had come in to bring me lunch and I had started shoving the toilet bucket out the door. I said, "I don't know what time it is. I don't know where I've been. I don't know what's happened in the last 10 hours. For God's sake, help me." So he said, "Okay, fine, we'll give you a time hack. When we figure an hour's gone by, all day long, we'll give you a time hack." And he did. Even when the guards were in there, shaking down the room, he'd be there with his hands up against the wall and he'd be banging the wall with his head or his foot to give me the time hack, so I could get through the next hour. And that immediately solved the problem.

Then, I drilled some little holes in the boards so I could get some little pinpoints of light, so now I could walk, navigating like you do in a boat at night, between the lights.

Of course, I had crotch itch from my knees to my chest. And cockroaches would fight me for my bread, and the rats would come down out of the ceiling.

Rowan: Konnie Trautman found the rats terrifying in the darkness.

Stratton: Well, I had a *modus vivendi* with the rats. I'd take a little bread and shove it over in the corner and the rats were really nice. They'd go over there and eat their rations and leave me alone.

But the cockroaches . . . Actually, I had a piece of bread in my hand one day in that darkness, and a damn cockroach was up there punching me in the beak, wanting a piece of bread.

It reminded me that the only thing more disgusting than finding a cockroach in your soup is finding half a cockroach in your soup.

3

. . . but, "Whiz" Was Not Webb

Throughout the 1960's, the United States had hundreds of men working secretly throughout southeast Asia to prevent the so-called "liberation" of Laos, Cambodia, Thailand and Malaysia. One of them, Ernest Brace, ended up at the Plantation in a cell on the other side of John McCain.

Brace was a 34-year-old former Marine Corps pilot, working in cooperation with the Thai border police in northwest Laos, when he was captured by North Vietnamese troops in May of 1965. He had a legitimate cover. He had been hired as a civilian pilot by Bird and Son Aviation, under contract to the U.S. AID program, a State Department agency. But, I suspect he was a "spook"—working for the Central Intelligence Agency—reporting on the movement of North Vietnamese troops so as to help protect the neutralist government of Laos. His wife and four sons were at home in California.

Navy Commander Robert H. Shumaker had left his young wife of less than a year in La Jolla, California, when he steamed off aboard the *Coral Sea* in 1964. The United States had not yet started its all-out bonbing raids against North Viet Nam, and Everett Alvarez, at that time, was the only American imprisoned in Hanoi.

It was a different "POW war" in those days. For reasons known only to the North Vietnamese, Alvarez was being fed hamburgers and other western-style food. But all that was soon to change, and Shumaker was soon to become the first man to join him there.

On February 11th, 1965, during the second raid of the "Air War North," Shumaker's F-8 was shot down.

When I was setting up a discussion with these two long-time POWs, I asked that Lieutenant Commander David W. Hoffman of San Diego join in. Hoffman had bailed out of his F-4 over the southern panhandle of North Viet Nam on the second to last day of 1971—almost seven years after Bob Shumaker went to the Hanoi Hilton. Shumaker had spent three years in solitary confinement. Ernie Brace, held in a jungle camp, with not even a glimpse of another American for three-and-a-half years, had logged a record four years and seven months in solitary. Hoffman was to spend just 36 days by himself. Hoffman's radar-intercept officer, Norris Charles, also was captured that December 30th, but he went home a few months later in one of the controversial early release programs.

I was interested in talking with Hoffman because he was one of the prisoners "produced" by the North Vietnamese during a visit to Hanoi by Jane Fonda and Ramsey Clark. He obviously was nervous about discussing that subject, saying there might be an investigation of it, although the Navy later told me he was not suspected of any wrong-doing. Other than that, Hoffman was eager to join in the discussion with the two veterans of the POW war.

Shumaker was serious throughout the session. He was open and direct. Like many others who spent long years in North Vietnamese prisons, he obviously had hoped the war would end with a victory so that his sacrifice would have real meaning. Like many others, he was hurt by the fact that Jane Fonda and Ramsey Clark were even allowed to visit Hanoi, and angry that they were allowed to come back home and tell their story. For Shumaker and the other early shoot-downs, returning to an America which doesn't care much about things like that anymore obviously was something of a shock.

Ernie Brace was very much in sympathy with Shumaker's views, but he struck me as a somewhat different type of person, in many respects. Ernie is a soldier-of-fortune who seems to accept the bitter with the sweet. I was amazed at his obvious mental stability, knowing that he had been completely cut off from the sound or sight of his countrymen for such a long time. And, as we started our discussion at the San Diego Naval Hospital, I asked him about that period.

Brace: The first three-and-a-half years were spent in a jungle camp, near Dien Bien Phu. I did not see anybody. No Westerner, no English-speaking people, except an interrogator, in 1965. I had no news of the war. I didn't know what was going on.

They took me to Hanoi in October of 1968, and John McCain was the first man I made contact with.

Rowan: Can you go back to the beginning, and talk about what it was like? Was being alone torturous?

Brace: Well, I don't know if it really is torturous. I don't use the word "torture" in my own case, because I just wasn't in the position of Bob and Dave and these [military] guys. I was of no propaganda value to them. My name was always kept secret. I was never allowed to write home or anything. Some people would say that it was torture. I don't use the word torture in my own case. In fact, my punishment for escape attempts, I look upon as punishment. I could have lain there and not tried to escape. I do not consider my being buried in the hole for seven days, or my being in stocks [leg irons] for two-and-a-half years, as torture, although the period of time certainly would be torturous.

> The "hole" in which Ernie Brace was buried was an overflowing jungle latrine. This was a favorite torture method of some North Vietnamese army units, described in more detail by Ed Flora in the next chapter.
>
> Jungle camps varied in size and configuration. In North Viet Nam and Laos, they were relatively permanent facilities with camouflaged buildings, holding perhaps one thousand men and their equipment and supplies.

In South Viet Nam, NVA jungle camps often were underground facilities, complete with field hospitals, ammunition storage rooms and tunnel complexes.

In the Mekong Delta, Viet Cong camps were temporary installations, consisting of thatched huts and bamboo lean-tos, which could be evacuated, lock, stock and barrel, in a matter of minutes.

I had an advantage over most of these guys, I think, in the fact that I'd been working with the Thai border patrol for about six months prior to my capture. I had been in these villages, and lived under rice paddy conditions. I had taken prisoners off the hands of the border patrol, right after battles. In fact, we'd gone in several times while there was still shooting going on in the area. I had picked up prisoners and taken them to various collection points. I had walked the trails and hills before, and slept in the villages before, so from the time I was captured, it was like travelling with a different military unit, other than the fact that my elbows were tied behind my back and I had a rope around my neck.

Rowan: Did you speak Vietnamese?

Brace: No, I did not speak Vietnamese. I knew mostly Thai, and a little bit of Lao. But I was not fluent in them. I could make my wants known; that was about all. I picked up a little bit of Vietnamese, as a prisoner, mostly how to count and to make my wants known.

Rowan: But you did not consider your solitary confinement—out of touch with any other American for more than three-and-a-half years—to be torturous, per se?

Brace: No. I always found that I had plenty to occupy my mind. I used my mind all the time, out there, much of the time for introspection on my past life. I used many tricks, going back through the various crossroads of my life.

When I came back from Korea, I could have gotten out and gone with TWA. I had a friend who did exactly that, and he's a Captain on a 747 now, London to New York. He tried to talk me into going with him, when he went in '53. I said, "No, I'll just stay in the Marine Corps."

I'd go back to points like this in my life, where I could have made another decision, and I'd build up a whole life for myself, and sometimes this would take two or three days to do. This would occupy me for awhile.

The first cage I was in, in the jungle, I could not stand up. I was tied down, hands, feet, and neck every night, because the security was not too good. And I managed to remove myself, figuratively speaking, from that situation. I kept my mind occupied planning escapes, and figuring out what I was going to do, and how I was going to do it.

I ran through mathematical problems. I tried retelling old stories, books that I read, to myself. Finally, I ran out of those, so I started coming up with stories. I'd create a character, and build a story around him, and I'd last through these things for three and four days at a time.

Rowan: Bob, you also had a long period of isolation.

Shumaker: I was in solitary confinement for three years in a camp [in Hanoi] called Alcatraz. There were 11 of us. We were also in leg stocks for about half that period. And just sitting here listening to Ernie reminds me that a lot of the same thoughts went through my mind. I think in order to maintain sanity you have to keep your mind active.

I had a lot of training as an engineer in school. And so I spend a lot of time on mathematical problems, but with limitations. We didn't have any pencils or paper, and we couldn't even write with stones on the floor. That would incur the wrath of the guards. So you'd have to just work these problems in your own minds.

I went back to various departure points in my life, too, and played out what would have happened if I'd followed other options.

I became very materialistically-inclined in the first four or five years. I had been married for about a year when I was shot down, and we had a child who was about two weeks old when I left. I started thinking about all the things that I could buy to outfit a house, like refrigerators and washing machines and so forth. Anyway, I calculated how much money my wife might be saving, and I'd work on installments, buying these things. It was *quite* a list, and it would exercise my mind every day, running through lists like this, as the years went on.

Then, I started building a house in my mind. I'd buy all the lumber and materials and everything for it. It's almost embarrassing now to realize it, but I'd spend almost 12 hours a day, or 14 hours a day, on this thing. It would go on for months. At the end of this time, I thought I had the best house that man had ever devised.

But, then, I'd live with my house from day to day, and I'd make minor changes. I'd think: "What would happen if I moved the fireplace from that corner over to this corner?" This was a minor change, but then I'd live with that for a week or so, and then I'd make some other change, a staircase from here to there. Then, a couple of months later, I'd suddenly realize that this was an entirely different house! I think I went through about three of these permutations.

Rowan: Did you actually do the physical work in your mind? Did you saw the boards? Did you put the bricks up?

Shumaker: Oh, yes, every nail. I knew how many bricks were in it; how much it weighed; the square footage . . .

Brace: I was amazed to find the retention factor that we had in our minds while we were in solitary without any outside influence. I was able to do problems, binomial equations, where I would have to develop an answer and have to set it aside to get something else. And then, I'd be able to just kind of look over here to the left of my mind, as I was picturing it, and I'd be able to pick this up and plug it in.

Later on, the same type thing with the houses and the appliances. I ran through the same phase, figuring out exactly how much it was going to cost me to completely furnish a home after I got back, the drapes and everything else.

Shumaker: My point is that my initial thoughts were materialistic. I found that as the time went on, about the sixth year or so, these things lost their worth to me, and I put greater stress on human values, like friendship and things like that.

Rowan: Dave, you went down in '71, so you plugged into a fairly complete organization, I guess.

Hoffman: They made a pretty positive effort to make sure

that we *didn't* plug into that organization, to keep us *isolated* from that organization. I only spent about 36 days in solo, so when you compare it with these other two guys, it was nothing at all. But I went through just about the same thing in the 36 days as Bob was talking about, and Ernie's been talking about. The materialistic things: buying a car, deciding what equipment I wanted on that car, replacing things in the house, and so forth.

Rowan: Were you interrogated heavily when you were shot down?

Hoffman: Not for the first 10 days. I was shot down on the 30th of December, 1971, and that was kind of an interesting story, in itself. I was transported up to Hanoi, and got there the evening of the 31st of December. On the morning of the first of January, when the interrogator, the guy they called The Bug came in and gave me my morning meal, it was a little surprising because it was a New Year's Day meal, what they called a special meal. I figured, "Hell, if I'm going to eat like this the rest of the time up here, I'm going to go out of here fatter than when I came in."

Anyway, I got finished with this meal and he went through the normal things that he could get off your ID card, like your name, your rank, and then proceeded to tell me exactly where every member of my family was, and exactly what they were doing, told me what I'd been doing for the last couple of years, and told me the name of the thesis I'd written at Monterey, I'd just graduated from there in March of '71. He did all this. Then he got up, said, "We can get your family any time we want to," and walked out. And nobody said another word to me for 10 days. So while I was building cars in my mind, I also had this thing going through it the whole time. I wondered where they got that information, because it just plain wasn't available to them through my RO [radar intercept officer], who was flying with me for the first time, and didn't know me, and I sure didn't give it to them. And how did they get it within 48 hours of the time I was shot down?

By January the 1st, 1972, it was obvious that the North Vietnamese had acquired great quantities of information about the Naval units off their shores. They had lists of the members of every fighter-bomber squadron flying off each of the aircraft carriers assigned to "Yankee Station," which is what the Americans called that area in the Gulf of Tonkin. Hoffman's story indicates they also had additional material on many of the individual squadron members.

It's obvious that all of this material was gathered from unclassified sources. The military man's newspaper, *Stars and Stripes*, was printed in Tokyo and was available to the Communists there. It reported the movement of aircraft carriers for tours of duty on Yankee Station. Newspapers like the *Navy Times*—available to the North Vietnamese through the Soviet embassy in Washington, perhaps—carried other information about the squadrons, including the names of their ranking officers. The Home Town News Service run by the military provided newspapers in San Diego and elsewhere with details about each man's assignment, often mentioning his parents, wife, children and other pertinent details.

It would not have been difficult for any intelligence man to put all this material together and come up with dossiers on each of the members of a particular squadron.

As a result of this situation, some of the POWs think it is ridiculous to require a man to undergo torture rather than give his captors anything other than "name, rank, serial number and date of birth. Others think the Code of Conduct should remain as it is, but that information about the men and their families should not be provided to service or home town newspapers.

Knowing the nature of the American news media, it is my guess that the latter approach is unrealistic. In times of war, the newspapers, radio and television go to great lengths to humanize their stories about the fighting men, and the men themselves are only too eager to tell reporters about their families.

Brace: I was captured by North Vietnamese regulars in Laos, in 1965, and they were denying their presence in Laos in 1965. I was taken straight to North Viet Nam. For them to admit that they were holding me prisoner in North Viet Nam would have been to admit that they were in Laos in 1965. They denied this almost right up until the end.

I had no idea why they kept me alive at the time, other than my value after it was over, just another head for them. There were several times out in the jungle when I thought surely they'd just dump me in a hole. And when they brought me to Hanoi, in 1968, I'd been handed over from one unit to another so many times that they really didn't know what I'd been flying or what I'd been doing, at the time I was captured.

Rowan: Bob, we knew that from time to time, they'd exploit some of you by putting you out in front of anti-war groups, but, beyond that, we had no knowledge of what they were doing. It doesn't seem that they actually sent out many of the letters and the statements they got from you.

Shumaker: Of course, we had no knowledge of the extent to which they were being used. But, if this book has any one effect, I hope it will create an awareness among the public that they should take any statement made by a POW while over there with a grain of salt. It's hard to imagine, but any man can be reduced to a state of irrationality in an hour's time, and never bare scars to prove it.

I think 90% of the people up there wrote anti-war statements, most of them under great duress. These things can be used against the war effort, and also can be used to blackmail a POW.

> North Vietnamese interrogators would remind a POW that he had signed an anti-war statement, and that it was in his file in Hanoi. It would be released, they would threaten, unless the man agreed to do something else, like read his statement into a tape recorder for use on the camp public address system. The men feared that their families and friends back home would think them turncoats if the statements were sent to the United States. So this became another method of coercing them into further anti-American activity.

Brace: Some of the POWs who talked to peace-groups in Hanoi used the term "we." They'd say: "*We* get mail. *We* get six packages a year. *We* get a letter every month." And people at home think, "Everybody up there is getting mail." Well, there were 10 guys in my group, and not one of us was allowed to write, or get mail over the years.

Ramsey Clark and Jane Fonda visited specific camps, and got to see only specific people.

Hoffman: One specific camp, and one specific group of people, very carefully controlled. I know. I was in it.

Hoffman was reluctant at first to talk freely about the Clark-Fonda incidents and then had this to say, though in measured tones:

By the way, I've been quoted by the press as saying I was tortured to go see Jane Fonda and Ramsey Clark. I didn't say that at all. I said I had been tortured, but not specifically to go see Ramsey Clark or Jane Fonda.

The situation was such that these people wanted propaganda and they were going to get it, one way or another.

Hoffman was reluctant to go into details here.

Rowan: Suffice it to say, you were compelled to make that appearance.

Hoffman: The point is that that appearance was *by no means* voluntary, and was *extremely* well orchestrated, and scripted down to the point where we were told: "This is what you're going to say if they ask this question, and this is what you're going to do if they ask that." And if you deviate, then you know damn well that somebody is going to get hurt, and hurt rather badly.

Jane Fonda was not brought to one of the camps. She was downtown. I don't know where the story that she saw one of the camps got started. *It's wrong.* As far as I know, she never saw a camp. She saw five or six of the guys who were taken downtown to see her. Ramsey Clark was brought to a camp, and they spent 10 days before he got there, making that camp look like it was La Costa Country Club, so that when he walked in, it would look great.

The number of Vietnamese who were sitting right beside each of them, the number of Vietnamese who were around the people who were talking to them, I don't know *how* they could *possibly* think that the people they were talking to were able to say what they wanted to say. I don't understand that at all. They knew damn right well we were in jail. They knew damn right well we were going to stay in jail when they left there. And no matter what we did or said that night, the minute *they* left, we were back at the mercy of the people who had us. I just don't understand their logic.

Rowan: Should they have been allowed to go there?

Hoffman: I'm dead set against it. I think they did us more harm, as a group, and as a nation, than any potential good. I can't see what potential good they were going to accomplish.

Rowan: How did they do you harm?

Hoffman: Well, when some of these delegations came in, there were people who were physically tortured to go to see them. There were people who were beaten because they refused to go see them. So it's just plain and simple. There was physical harm caused to the prisoners, as a result of these people coming in wanting to see them.

Shumaker: And for the other 400 or so POWs, tapes of this stuff would be repeatedly played to them through loud speakers. It was morally depressing hearing that so-called Americans had come to Hanoi to meet a few selected prisoners and would carry back with them a story which misrepresented the actual state of affairs.

Rowan: What kind of misrepresentation?

Shumaker: For example: *mail.* They claimed that we were getting letters every month. Well, I didn't hear at all from my wife for the last two years. And they talked about receiving packages. I was cut off from packages for a two-year period. So it kind of hurts you when you think that the American public is getting these inputs from Ramsey Clark and Jane Fonda that everything was fine over there, when indeed it wasn't.

Brace: Pete Seeger was there for awhile, and he was running around singing songs about how grand and glorious the Vietnamese people were, and at the same time I was pulling a worm out of my roommate's rear.

Shumaker: I remember one guy told me he felt like he had a straw stuck in his throat, and he coughed a couple of times and out came a worm that was about 10 inches long.

Rowan: Is there an answer to this propaganda problem? For example, what would have happened if John McCain had taken an early release, and then blown the whistle on the North Vietnamese when he got home?

Brace: If he'd taken an early release, it would have put his father in disgrace, and he was Commander-in-Chief of the Pacific.

Shumaker: John McCain had a father in a fairly influential position, but all of us had families. We didn't want to put them in disgrace, and that was a factor with me. I certainly didn't want to fink out, and disgrace my family.

Rowan: But, wouldn't there have been a larger good served if someone had played their game, to the extent of getting an early release, and then come back and described in detail, for the public, the conditions under which you really were living.

Brace: One man did. Douglas Hegdahl was ordered by the Senior Ranking Officer in our camp [the Plantation], in 1969, to take release and blow the whistle.

Shumaker: Yes, and he did some very good work, He had a very good memory.

Brace: He was the only one of the early releases who was ordered to take release.

> Hegdahl's report of conditions in the North Vietnamese prison camps—including torture—never reached the public. The U.S. government was afraid to get into a propaganda war with the North Vietnamese, because the North Vietnamese still had the POWs.
>
> In any case, the idea of anyone accepting an early release jars the sensibilities of men like Bob Shumaker—who was second only to Everett Alvarez in terms of longevity as a POW in North Viet Nam.

Shumaker: In a subsequent war, that philosophy could be dangerous, because everybody could rationalize that they were carrying the "message from Garcia," and everybody would be flocking to the door.

> I probed this point further, but Shumaker felt that he didn't want to delve into the political rationale for the war from a philosophical point of view. I approached it from another angle.

Rowan: What was your own reaction to the split in this country that you found when you came back? Bob, you spent eight years in prison for what turned out to be not a very popular cause. How did that make you feel?

Shumaker: Well, I like black and white things. Personally, it would have been much more satisfying getting in there and getting the thing over with. I would have preferred a stronger military action. This is said now in retrospect, but I felt this way in 1965. The division in the country kind of disturbs me. But I get the idea that the anti-war group is more vocal than its size warrants. I've made a few trips around the country now, and talked to a lot of people. I see both extremes. The people whose opinions and values I cherished before my capture haven't changed. And I suspect that the great majority of Americans still feel a tingle in their hearts when thy hear the Star Spangled Banner.

Ironically, one of the reasons we fought this war was to give people the right to certain freedoms, like freedom of speech. I say "ironically" because some of our quote, "Americans," went and shot their mouths off in Hanoi and expected impunity when they got back. So I'm hopeful that Congress will enact some legislation which, while not preventing people from going into those countries, will at least place some restrictions on their return.

Rowan: Did you talk much among yourselves about propaganda?

Brace: Jim Bedinger, who joined me in 1969, had read the *Stars and Stripes* story about the November Moratorium, just prior to his capture. Over there, the North Vietnamese had blown it up to about four times its size. In order to put this thing in perspective, Jim and I put out the word that the peace movement is not as large as these people say it is. They did not have a-hundred-and-some-thousand in Washington. They had 40,000 and most of these were just onlookers.

Rowan: I take it the North Vietnamese did everything they could to discourage the flow of that kind of information.

Shumaker: The overall philosophy of the Vietnamese toward the POWs was to put a guy in isolation, and they would go to great efforts in blocking prisoner A from communicating with prisoner B.

Normally, Americans have great access to information. For example, this morning I read the newspaper, and watched television, and I'm now talking with you. We have a lot of contacts, and we don't realize how much information we get. But, when you take a guy and completely isolate him, it's a very frustrating experience. So you stew there for awhile, and then they very methodically try to influence your thoughts. They're clever in mixing some truths with lies, and it was very disconcerting.

For example, I was shot down on the second raid of the war. They told me they shot down 23 airplanes on that raid. Well, initially, that sounded ridiculous to me. But, as the days went on, I'd think: "I wonder if it's possible they could really have shot down that many." A week would go by and I'd start feeling sorry for the wives of all the men who "bought the farm."

Rowan: Did those kind of doubts lead some of you to question your own involvement in this war? Did you begin to wonder whether you were in the wrong profession?

Brace: I sent out messages about that to people who were newly captured. I said: "If you didn't think you were wrong at the time you were captured, don't base any action on what you are told up here, what you see up here, or what is passed on to you by these people up here, because it is highly edited, and you're only getting very selected pieces of information. Don't change your mind about the war based on what you hear up there."

Shumaker: That's right. It's like those 23 planes they said they'd shot down. I found, after I made contact with others, that that was hogwash. In my mind, if you establish a guy as a liar, you can discount everything he says. This is the way I treated their propaganda, and I think others did too. We just discounted everything they said. Now, I realize that's an extremist point of view. But I think, as Ernie suggested, that the right thing for us to do was to go to the extreme right and discount what the Gooks were telling us. Certainly if you didn't question the war before you got in trouble, you weren't in a good position to change your mind in Hanoi.

Rowan: Did you have any idea of what was going on in the Plantation, where there was a fairly active anti-war group?

Brace: I spent most of my time at the Plantation, and I was very aware of this anti-war group. I had run-ins with them a couple of times. They were very active. It was a bad situation for the rest of the prisoners in the camp. I don't want to go into any details. Colonel Theodore Guy over in Tucson, who was the SRO [senior ranking officer] in the camp at the time, is handling this himself. But these men were *definitely a bad influence,* and because of their actions, the rest of the camp did suffer.

Shumaker: I think they represented a minority. What hurt us in the majority was that they were misrepresenting the facts.

Brace: They talked like everybody in the camp was going along with this idea.

The Plantation, in '68 and '69, when it was making releases, was thought of by the other POWs as a political camp, an easy camp. It was the camp, at that time, that delegations were visiting. We had a row of cells we called "The Show Place." The delegations were shown some very model cells that were fairly large, and had good ventilation, and all. They were not shown the "Gun Shed," or the back side of the "Warehouse," or any of the other places in that camp. They were shown "The Show Place," which had four rooms in it.

Rowan: How big was that anti-war group? I'm told that initially it was rather large.

Brace: You're under a misconception there. It was rather insignificant. There were eight hard core members in it. They were joined by four in 1971, who later on got out of the group, for a total of 12. This is among the enlisted men captured in South Viet Nam. I can't speak for the officers and others caught in North Viet Nam.

The anti-war group was able to roam around the camp, at will. They were allowed to talk to the other prisoners, if they wanted to talk to them, and other prisoners did talk to them, at times, but it generally meant trouble for you if you did get involved with them.

> Charges of misconduct and collaborating with the enemy were preferred against the eight so-called "hard core" members of the anti-war group—Army and Marine Corps enlisted men—by Air

Force Colonel Ted Guy, who claimed they had given the North Vietnamese certain information about the POW organizational structure and communications. A month later, one of the eight, Marine Sergeant Abel Larry Kavanaugh, shot himself to death in his father-in-law's home in a suburb of Denver. The day after the funeral service, the Secretaries of the Army and the Navy announed that charges against the remaining seven men were being dropped because of insufficient evidence. The two Secretaries also cited as mitigating circumstances the hardship suffered by the enlisted men in the North Vietnamese prisons for many years.

Generally, the POWs I talked with were more reluctant to talk about those POWs who cooperated with the Vietnamese— apparently because of pending litigation. There was some concern that this book *not* give the impression that there were any great numbers of men who cooperated with the Vietnamese.

Shumaker: Ninety-five percent of the guys up there were "Jack Armstrong" types. Now, perhaps there are a few who didn't do a creditable job. But, I think there is a great tendency in the press to exploit these few.

Brace: There were only eight out of 130 men at the Plantation. But, just like in the peace movement, *their* voices were publicized, and what *they* were doing was blown out of proportion, so it began to look as if they were a much larger influence than they were.

Rowan: Could you accept the fact that they, perhaps, were honestly motivated?

Brace: I can only agree with what Colonel Guy said in his press conference, that most of these men were not highly motivated in their anti-war statements, other than the fact that they were getting a bottle of beer a week, and a few things like that.

Rowan: Do you have any bitterness now about these people?

Brace: No, I have no personal bitterness, other than about one specific incident, which I would rather not go into right now.

Rowan: I'd like to go back, Ernie, to what it was like to get into communication after four years and seven months in a jungle camp near Dien Bien Phu. Was that an emotional time?

Brace: Well, I had not seen any Americans, nor did I know what was going on in the war. In fact, I thought the war was over when they took me to Hanoi, because Lyndon Johnson had gone to limited bombing in April of '68. On the way in, we were driving down the road in broad daylight, and there was heavy truck traffic. Then, we got to the Plantation and they put me in a room on the back side of John McCain. He made contact with me on the second day in the room, and, talking through the wall, he brought me up to date on the war. He told me funny little stories about sports incidents. He told me about the Six-Day War in Israel, and that the Suez Canal was closed.

I could not talk back to him, because I did not have the apparatus [for voice communication through the wall] at that time. So I was just tapping back to him, and I could only tap, "Yes," "No," or "I don't know." Perhaps he overestimated my emotional reaction to being back in touch with Americans, but he kept asking me: "Am I helping you, Ernie?" I'd tap, "Yes," but I didn't feel I was that much out of it emotionally. He kept asking that question over and over, for the first week, "Am I helping you get along here?" I'd say, "Yes, Yes" [just to make him feel good].

Shumaker: I think communication is the key to sanity out there. Every guy's an individual, and I'm kind of reserved by nature, and I think I'd be happy tapping with a guy maybe 15 minutes a day, just knowing that there's some other guy experiencing the same thing you are. There are other guys, friends of mine, who wouldn't be happy unless they were on the wall four or five hours a day.

You might be interested in how this code came about. When I was shot down, I was living in a section of the Hilton, and the place was getting kind of crowded, and so they moved in three other guys with me, and that was a really joyous day in my life. But then we realized that subsequently we might get split up. So, I suggested that we work out some way of communicating, like beating the wall or doing something like that. By good fortune, one fellow there, Air Force Captain Smitty Harris, remembered from survival school a coffee break conversation where the same question was brought up. He remembered the tapping system that was worked out in that conversation, and so we adopted it, and it just spread like wild fire.

The tap code went as follows:

A	B	C	D	E
• •	• ••	• •••	• ••••	• •••••
F	**G**	**H**	**I**	**J**
•• •	•• ••	•• •••	•• ••••	•• •••••
L	**M**	**N**	**O**	**P**
••• •	••• ••	••• •••	••• ••••	••• •••••
Q	**R**	**S**	**T**	**U**
•••• •	•••• ••	•••• •••	•••• ••••	•••• •••••
V	**W**	**X**	**Y**	**Z**
••••• •	••••• ••	••••• •••	••••• ••••	••••• •••••

The letter K was omitted to make the code mathematically symmetrical and because its function can be performed by the letter C or—in the case of plurals—the letter X.

From those days, in 1965, when there were only a few POWs in the Hanoi Hilton, the tap code spread throughout the prison camp system in North Viet Nam.

Other methods of communicating also were devised. For example, the men noted that there were slots in the bottom of their "buckets"—the only lavatory facilities they had—so when they were out emptying a bucket, a note written on toilet paper with the head of a burnt match could be passed to a man from another cell, or the buckets themselves surreptitiously exchanged.

The "apparatus" for voice communication could be a cup, or even a towel twisted around in the shape of a cone—anything a POW could use to keep his voice focused on one spot on the 18-inch concrete wall, and at the same time muffle it so that the guards outside didn't know he was shouting. "You'd be surprised at how well it worked," Rob Doremus later told me. Since Ernie Brace didn't have anything to use in his first days at the Plantation, he could only signal "Yes" or "No" to John McCain's questions, by banging once or twice on the wall.

Brace: The tap code came to be the basic pinpoint around which almost all communications were focused.

Hoffman: One of the first things, when I was moved out to

the Zoo after my initial solitary, one of the interrogators called me out and said, "Now you will have a roommate, but you must not communicate with the other people. However, if you do communicate, this is how they do it, and if you don't remember, ask any of the guards." (*Laughter*) This is an *interrogator* telling me this.

Shumaker: Yes, but, by the time you got there, the Vietnamese had very severely tortured Bob Lilly and Dick Bolstad, back in the summer of '66, to get the code.

Brace: Even later, if you were caught "on the wall," they dragged you in and said, "What were you doing?" and you denied doing anything. They'd go ahead and bust you until you gave them the tap code again, and then you thought you were a real dog for doing it.

Rowan: How about the first moment when you give them information. What's your reaction to that?

Shumaker: When you're initially broken, and forced to give something against your will, it's a horrible blow to your psychology. You feel as if you're in company with Benedict Arnold.

Rowan: Could you give me an example?

Shumaker: For me, the first 10 months of captivity [in 1965] mostly involved threats of torture. They hadn't started hammering guys real heavily. But, they got real nasty, in '66, '67, and '68. I guess my last torture session was in '69. I won't go into all the gory details, but the first session, what they wanted was for us to choose one of two paths. We were going to 1) continue to support the warmongering imperialist American government, or 2) cross over to the people's side and join the Vietnamese. In the camp where I was located, in the Briar Patch, all the 60 some people chose the first way, and they got hammered very hard for the thing. Eventually, all of them wrote confessions and apologies to the Vietnamese people. And it's a terrible blow to realize you can be forced to do something like that. I still bear the scars. My hands, seven years after, are still a little bit numb as a result.

But, then, you build up experience. You go through that thing, and you learn that they didn't really kill you, and they probably have an interest in keeping you alive. And this makes you a little stronger to hack it the next time.

Rowan: Bob, what was your initial reaction to first being broken.

Shumaker: I just completely broke down and cried. It was the most horrible experience of my life. I think what separated the men from the boys at this stage of the game was that you've just got to come off the canvas and come back for the second round. If you give up at that point, you're in bad shape.

Brace: John McCain, because of his father, was under a lot of pressure to see delegations. He constantly refused. He constantly was being dragged up there and pounded around for two or three days. And the next time a delegation would come, he would still refuse. So, finally, they gave up on him. They would go after those who were easier to get to see the delegations. The same thing happened over the business of reading on the camp radio [public address system which all camps had]. I know Dick Stratton was constantly being forced to read on the camp radio. He was taking beatings for it. But every time he was told to read on the camp radio, he took a beating before he agreed. So, finally, they gave up on him. They had guys who would do it without having to go through the beatings.

Shumaker: I discovered something up there when I stopped to analyze who I was trying to satisfy. Was I trying to satisfy the demands of the President of the United States? The Secretary of the Navy? Was I trying to satisfy the demands of my wife? In the final analysis it was myself I had to satisfy, myself I have to live with the rest of my days. I've got a little home town in western Pennsylvania, and I just wanted to go back to that home town and walk down the main street and be able to look at people in the eyes, and not be ashamed of what I did.

Brace: I remember one specific incident. Mel Pollack picked up a note one day that did not belong to him, with the code name "Whiz" on it. He had a man living in the room with him by the name of Webb [Ron Webb]. But,

"Whiz" was not Webb. So they hid the note in their room. They were going to try to pass it along the next day. Then, Mel got caught with the note, in a room inspection.

They took him up, and laid him down on the floor, and said: "Say that 'Whiz' is Webb." Well, Mel didn't even know who "Whiz" was. He didn't know who the note was supposed to go to, or who it was coming from. He had just picked it up. So he went through three days of being pounded around on the floor, with his arms behind him in the straps. And finally he said, "Okay, 'Whiz' is Webb."

So they dragged Webb out and pounded him around for being "Whiz." And Webb didn't know who the hell "Whiz" was either.

Mel felt really bad because now Webb was taking a beating because he had broken down and said that "Whiz" was Webb.

Rowan: It sounds like a Catch 22 situation—damned if you do; damned if you don't.

Shumaker: I was hammered, tortured, five times. But I would rather go through torture than listen to a friend screaming in torture, and suffer the frustrations of not being able to do anything for him, knowing if you did try to do anything for him that you would just aggravate his problems.

Brace: We tried to protest one time against solitary confinement. We staged a 14 day fast. We started out with three guys in solitary confinement and at the end of the 14 days, we had about 10 guys in solitary confinement in the camp.

The thing about the fast is it's not going to work if you don't get any publicity outside the camp. And of course there was not going to be any publicity outside the camp.

Rowan: One of the things the Code of Conduct encourages is escape. Ernie, you planned escapes. Did you actually get away at any point?

Brace: I got away for four days in April of '66, I was recaptured on the fifth night by a different unit. I was in a village trying to steal some food. But, it was a mistake to go into a village.

I spent two days up on a mountain trying to signal aircraft.

No success. So I had to come down to get some food. I was irrational at the time.

But, as far as escape from within the Hanoi area, you're in the center of a town of three-and-a-half million people, and they all had black hair and brown eyes and were about five feet, four inches tall. They don't change. (*Chuckle*) So, to escape from Hanoi without outside help was absolutely impossible, and I would recommend, "Don't try it."

There were two escapes from prisons in Hanoi, but, in both cases, the POWs were quickly recaptured. One of them, in May of 1969, sparked so much controversy that the entire matter of escapes now is being studied at the Pentagon.

The Code of Conduct states unequivocally: "I will make every effort to escape and aid others to escape." Nothing is said about the consequences of such escape attempts.

A prisoner who contemplates escape has to face many questions: Will I get out of the prison? Will I escape detection outside the prison? Will I get to the coast? Will I be able to signal an American plane? Will I get picked up?

But, the most important question he has to pose to himself is: Whether I succeed or fail, what will happen to all those who remain in prison?

In a news conference on March 30th, 1973, one of the men involved in the May '69 escape, Air Force Lieutenant Colonel John A. Dramesi, talked about going over the wall with Edwin Atterbury, then an Air Force Captain:

"When we went over the wall Ed and myself had skin coloring. We had surgical masks which you see many Orientals wearing during times when they are struck with flu and such diseases. We had a carrying pole and baskets. We had conical hats which we fabricated. We had another hat that Ed made which was similar to those worn by the natives. We had clothes that were very much like the North Vietnamese . . . sandals.

"We actually walked through the town right outside of the prison, walking by . . . policemen on bicycles and people who were no more than three feet away from us.

"We were caught the following morning . . . by an intensive search.

"We were unable to get out of what we referred to as a security circle of five miles around the camp.

"Our biggest problem was to attempt to determine how much time we had used in finding our hiding place. We stopped too soon and neglected to . . . get out of this circle.

"The next morning we saw people going by us all morning with machine guns, in groups of 15 to 17, headed by officers. Later that morning, they overran us and did find us. But not until one of the North Vietnamese guards, or soldiers, was actually within three or four feet of us and he recognized that we were, in fact, what he was looking for.

"As far as the aftermath is concerned . . . the torture which occurred at that time over a 30-day period, and later the harassment over an extended period of six months in most cases, was unbelievable, even sometimes when I described it to those who had actually experienced torture in the camp."

Atterbury may have been tortured to death. He was not repatriated.

The escape resulted in torture for many others in the camp (the Zoo and Zoo Annex) as well. Some men felt it was perhaps 18 months before the situation returned to "normal" (i.e. what it had been prior to May 10, 1969).

As Ernie Brace said: ". . . escape from Hanoi without outside help was absolutely impossible. . ." But the Code of Conduct says: "I will make every effort to escape . . ."

This conflict has yet to be resolved.

Rowan: I've read in some of the news conference reports that many of the fantasies you experienced dealt with sex. Will you elaborate on this?

Shumaker: Well, I can contribute this much, from a negative angle: In my experience, there was never any case of homosexuality there. People, I suppose, would think that in a situation like that, it would develop. And I was a little surprised.

Of course, the American military has been very quick to weed out any homosexuals from normal service life.

Brace: We got into a discussion of that in our group one time because we had a man, Captain Steve Long, who had been a psychology major and had worked around the state prison in Oregon. He said that in any prison study, the question of homosexuality always raised its head, sooner or later. And he said that usually it started out either among the extremely low educated people, who were depraved in their minds in some way or other before they became prisoners, or else it was among the super-intellectuals, who wanted to go the other way.

As far as our group went, we had people who were not extremely highly educated. We didn't have any Ph.D.s up there, and very few Masters, but almost eveybody had been a college graduate. And because they were a stable group to begin with, this question of homosexuality in the camps never came to be a problem.

I've been in the Briar Patch, the Plantation, Vegas, and Unity. I never came across any incident of homosexuality.

Hoffman: On the other side of the coin, I think the biggest thing we saw, particularly toward the end, when we knew the peace agreement had been signed and we were probably coming home, was that everybody was overestimating his own capability when he got home. We were going to go on forever.

When I first moved into the Zoo, most of the guys who were there had been there for four years, and had no contact with anybody. All of a sudden there were these four or five new guys. One of the first questions that came across was: "When was the last time you got laid?" We sent them back a date. And they came right back with: *"Describe in detail."* It was the normal, typical American reaction to the thing; nothing unhealthy about it at all.

Rowan: You shared a great deal of your intimate lives with each other, talking with your roommates.

Shumaker: That's true, but we made a pact that when we crossed the International Date Line, we had sealed lips. (*Laughter*)

Brace: Jim Bedinger lived with me longer than he lived with his wife before he was captured. As you say, you get to know each other extremely intimately, as far as everything in your background goes. But, as for discussions on sex, I'd say that matter was rather insignificant. We had other things on our minds, particularly in Hanoi, where daily efforts at communication were required. In my particular case, anyway, in Hanoi, most of my waking hours were devoted to efforts to communicate. Jim Bedinger even went to the extent of writing a little newspaper. We had about three editions of it out, it was called the *Vegas Gambler.*

Rowan: What was it printed on?

Shumaker: Toilet paper.

Brace: That's right. You got a copy of it, over at the other end of the camp one time.

Shumaker: We had different writing implements, like a burnt match, or some ink made out of cigarette ashes, and brick dust.

Rowan: Let's get back to the sex situation. Did you dream about your wives?

Shumaker: Oh, sure. I relived every experience I'd ever had with my wife.

I'm getting in an area where I'm going to get in trouble. (*Laughter*)

Brace: I think that nature has a way of providing relief in such cases. I'm sure that most guys were having wet dreams, about every six or eight weeks.

Rowan: What about masturbation?

Brace: That reminds me of a rather humorous exchange I heard about.

We had a very badly wounded man in the Plantation, who had stepped on a land mine. Then, Doc Kushner moved in next door, with a group of men. And one day, Dennis Tellier, an enlisted man, was calling over to Captain Kushner, telling him about the injured man's medical problems, and trying to find out how they could help him.

Finally, they got down to the point of describing all the symptoms, like his not being able to control his bowels. Then, he added, "He can't jack off either." Doc Kushner said: "What?" Dennis said: "He can't jack off either." Doc said: "I don't understand." And Dennis turned to the injured man and said: "What's another word for jack off?" (*Laughter*)

That was the communications gap. Doc Kushner was so naive he had never heard that term, and the enlisted man didn't think to use the term "masturbate" either.

Hoffman: I don't think anybody was what you'd call preoccupied with sex. I think we were all smart enough to realize that you could drive yourself nuts if you allowed yourself to become preoccupied.

Rowan: And of course you didn't have very much stimulation in the way of female companionship.

Hoffman: When the best thing you've seen in a long while is Jane Fonda, you haven't seen much.

Brace: We had a gal over at the Plantation we called "Queenie." One time John McCain was taking a bath. He was all soaped up and Queenie came through the courtyard. He was leaning against the door, taking a look at her through a crack in the door, and he fell out. He was slithering around there in the soap, and the guard was kicking him, trying to make him go back in the room. Queenie screamed and dropped what she was carrying and ran out of the courtyard.

Rowan: Did other things get an exaggerated value, for instance, when you got a chance to see the stars or the moon?

Brace: Oh yes. We moved up to the Briar Patch from Camp Unity in February of 1971, and there was a window that came down to about waist-level or a little bit below, and went almost up to the ceiling, and we could stand there and see the moon and the stars. We had not seen them for years. All of us just stood there and looked at the stars for hours, during the first few weeks there. We even saw satellites, which was a big thing. Everyone was trying to spot these things.

Rowan: Greenery, flowers, things that you normally wouldn't have seen?

Brace: There was a group of cucumbers growing in one corner of our little compound in the Briar Patch when we we got there. There were only six plants, but we weeded them and spent more time on those cucumbers than we would have on a whole garden any place else. We fertilized them with some of the stuff from our buckets, and in the next few months we started getting cucumbers off of them. We had a tremendous argument with the guards about whose cucumbers they were.

Shumaker: I was something of a horticulturist up there. Rarely, but occasionally, we would get fruit, and I'd save the seeds. I remember we got 12 oranges in 1967, and I saved the seeds. I was in Vegas at this time. We'd sweep up our floors, and I'd save all the dirt and put it up on a window that was at about a nine-foot level. I suppose there were about two handfuls of dirt up there. I'd plant these seeds, and I'd water them twice a day. But, as soon as they'd spring up, the rats would wipe me out. There were all kinds of rats in the Hilton. Huge things.

Rowan: Who won the argument about whose cucumbers they were?

Brace: We won the argument. It was in 1971, and things were not too bad. The guards wanted them, but we knew they had cucumber patches outside the place. So we got the cucumbers.

Rowan: Gardening must have made you think of home. Did you worry about what was happening at home? Did you think that after five or six or seven or eight years, your wives might have divorced you and married someone else?

Brace: Well, I rather hoped, especially after the second or third year, that my wife had remarried to provide a father for my four boys, because one woman with four boys is really in a tough situation, and sure enough she had. She had remarried. But the man she married died a couple of years later in an accident.

I'd gone over almost every situation in my mind. That's another thing during solitary. You go over everything introspectively, and look back at your family life and so on. I'd gone over the possibility that my wife had remarried, and I had come to accept it. So, when I came back to find out that she had, I accepted it.

Shumaker: I think I would have been shattered if my wife had divorced me. Of course, I was only married about a year before I was shot down.

I think my wife had the experience of having more longevity than any other POW wife. Most of the other early guys have lost their wives. Mine was raised a Catholic, and has very strong moral principles, and I'm very pleased with the way she not only conducted her personal affairs, but that she did such a good job with her finances.

Rowan: Did you ever consider it possible, though, that she had divorced you?

Shumaker: Really, the hardest time up there in eight years was the last three years, because there was so much frustration. I think the Vietnamese played on this with me in restricting mail. And I'd seen other guys who stopped getting letters from their wives, and then eventually wound up in a divorce. I stopped getting letters from my wife, through no fault of hers, but because of the Vietnamese. It bothered me. I thought that I might be heading in that direction.

Rowan: In addition to those periods of doubt, were there times of really deep depression, when you wondered what the hell life was all about?

Shumaker: Well, in the summer of '67 I think it was the worst for me. There was a lot of torturing going on. I was forced to make a movie and play the role of a wounded American. I refused to do this thing, although to induce me to make it, they had said I'd be made up, and my identity wouldn't be recognized. Anyway, I got hammered pretty hard. So I made the movie, and ironically, I did their makeup work for them. They wanted a wounded American and I produced one.

Rowan: In the torture session?

Shumaker: Right. I went through the ropes, and the guards stood on my knees with my arms tied at the elbow, thumbs tied together with a string, and they bent my head down, 'til I touched my feet. To keep me from screaming, they had a rag on a long metal rod that they shoved down my throat. You know, these guys are just not skilled at this thing. They did some damage to the extent that I have a little trouble swallowing now. They did some nerve damage. It was a bad summer. I can recall praying for death on a number of occasions, and finding myself a little envious of my buddies who had been killed.

Brace: Well, the worst period for me was in the winter of '67-'68. In September of '67, I took a pretty bad beating, because they caught me untied.

I'd been in stocks in the cage since April of '66, 24 hours a day. I'd get out once in the morning and once in the evening. But, I was in the habit of untying my wrists and loosening up my neck rope at night, and then retying them in the morning, before they came to check me. I was not trying to escape. I did not have the legs to make an escape, to begin with. They caught me untied in September, and I went through a pretty bad beating because of it. And, within the period of the next few weeks, I started to develop paralysis. It was more a lack of motor coordination, than paralysis. I could not move where I wanted to move. It went through my bowels, and I lost control of my bowel movement. By the middle of October, I was just a vegetable. I was crawling on the ground. I went through the month of November like that, and on into December. It got to the point where I wasn't even using the hole anymore. I was just going in my pants. I did not have a bath or a shave for this entire period. My last bath was in early October.

On the night of December 10th, which I marked because it was my son's birthday, I actually tried to strangle myself, with the neck rope.

I just got a warm feeling after awhile, pulling this thing, and trying to strangle myself with it. And I fell asleep. I woke up a few hours later urinating on myself again.

I came to realize, through this experience, that *God* had not put me there, and God was not going to get me out of it. If I wanted to get out of this mess I was in, *I* was going to have to get myself out of it, somehow.

I was eating like a dog, by pushing my face into the food. And gradually, on through December, January and February, I started being able to walk a little.

In March, a new unit took over, and they cleaned up the cage, and they gave me a haircut, and a bath, cut my beard off, and got rid of the lice and bugs that were crawling all over me.

I guess that was the lowest point I had. In the spring of '68, I recovered from that particular illness, and then, in October of '68, I was taken to Hanoi.

Rowan: What's the biggest shock about coming home?

Shumaker: I was initially disturbed about some superficial things, like long hair and strange-looking clothes and things. But I've sort of adapted to those. The thing that bothers me is the change in the moral fibre of the country. I think we've taken a couple of steps backwards. And the attitude of people, which existed to some extent before, but is more prevalent now: "What's in it for me?" Those things bother me.

Brace: I was amazed by the divorce rate. I've been in Los Angeles visiting friends and most everybody is divorced. They're either with their second wife, or perhaps they've dumped their second wife and are with the third. As for me, even though my wife went through another marriage and we're separated now, I'm trying to get back together with her.

4

Breakfast at Brennan's

Like Ernie Brace, Army Sergeant First Class Carroll Edward Flora, Jr., of Walkersville, Maryland, was captured by North Vietnamese troops in Laos (although the Pentagon still insists on describing the location at which he disappeared as "a hostile area").

Ed Flora was a tough 25-year-old Green Beret working on a secret mission—possibly checking on the movement of NVA troops—in July of 1967. He knew what to expect if the enemy found out who he was and what he was doing.

Navy Commander Robert B. Doremus, of Montclair, New Jersey, knew what to expect, too. As a "backseater" in an F-4 in June of 1965, he and a pilot, Lieutenant David Batson of Buffalo, New York, had shot down the second North Vietnamese Mig of the war. Two months later, in August, Doremus and another pilot, Fred A.W. Franke, Jr.—now a Navy Captain—found themselves on the ground in North Viet Nam—the 18th and 19th men to join Ev Alvarez at the Hanoi Hilton.

Rob Doremus devised a cover story, and it worked. Ed Flora devised a cover story, and it didn't. Like so many others, Flora wanted the North Vietnamese to kill him.

Rob and I drove out to the Valley Forge Army Hospital in Pennsylvania on April 10th, 1973, to meet with Ed, who was undergoing extensive surgery for the repair of the bones in his arm.

This pair of men was of great interest to me. Rob is a warm and friendly young man. He was 41 years old when he got out of North Viet Nam, though he looks even younger than 34, the age he was when he went in. His marriage had been in trouble before he went to Viet Nam, and now it was on the rocks, despite some warm letters that had come from his wife while he was in prison, and despite *his* determination to be a better husband. Rob is well-educated, something of a sophisticate, a Naval officer. He is interested in people, and seemed immediately at ease with Ed Flora, despite the differences in their background.

Ed is "salt of the earth"—his voice is soft but there's still a trace of hillbilly twang that suggests his native West Virginia. Ed is proud to be a member of the United States Army; prouder still that he made it into the toughest and best-trained part of that Army—the Special Forces. His respect for Rob's status as an officer made it a little more difficult for him to relax, but he settled down as we went along.

It should be noted that Ed was suffering considerable pain as the result of surgery that had been performed a few days earlier. But then, I soon learned that Ed was capable of withstanding a lot of pain. I asked him about the day he was captured.

Flora: I was wounded. One of our helicopters was trying to extract me. They were hovering about the trees, and they had lowered a jungle seat to me. Then, as I came up through the trees, a vine wrapped around the seat. I was quite high, two or three hundred feet. The seat broke, and I fell, and I was knocked unconscious for awhile. I came to a couple of times that night. I knew our guys were looking for me; I could see flares in the air. But I couldn't move and I didn't have a radio.

The next morning I saw the North Vietnamese Army move up. I was lying there semi-conscious. They thought I was unconscious. They saw our rescue unit looking for me, and they were using me as bait. They set up an ambush around me. I saw the rescue party go about 150 or 200 yards up the side of the hill. But, at the time all I could do was say, "help." I couldn't have said much of anything else, because of my condition. So I just laid there and watched them go. And once they went past, the NVA [North Vietnamese army troops] came down.

The only weapon I had was a small pen flare, and I fired four rounds of that, which didn't impress them too much. Then, they came up, and took it away from me. If I had a rifle they wouldn't have captured me. Either I'd have gotten them, which would have been impossible, or they'd have gotten me.

I wasn't really afraid at the time, I was probably too darn weak to be afraid.

Rowan: Did you feel helpless?

Flora: Helpless more than anything. I had no weapon, I couldn't run. I couldn't get up. I couldn't move. They came up and stuck a bayonet in my throat. Then, they noticed I was wounded.

They couldn't decide at that time where I had come from. They tied me up and tried to make me walk. I couldn't walk. I kept passing out, and when I'd pass out, or at least pretend to pass out, they'd stick me with a bayonet and try to make me walk. I couldn't walk. They'd kick me a few times. Still, I couldn't walk.

Then, American planes started bombing in the area and, when that started, they panicked and they tied me to a tree. Then, they left. That night I got loose. I don't know how far I went, maybe a half mile, maybe less. I was semi-conscious all the time.

The next morning they found me. They picked me up. I would have preferred that they shot me at the time; that's what I was hoping they'd do.

Rowan: Why would you have preferred that?

Flora: I knew I'd be tortured, and, rather than go through torture, in the condition I was in—I didn't think I was going to live anyway—I'd rather have them shoot me, and get it over with. I figured once they had tortured me, and got what information they could get out of me, they were going to kill me anyway.

Rowan: Rob, you were an early shoot-down—before the message had gone out from Hanoi to take as many prisoners as possible. Did you expect death at the hands of your captors?

Doremus: I guess the first look I had at the enemy close-hand was from the parachute. When I landed, they were coming from at least four directions across the dykes, which, like roads, surrounded the rice paddies. And, as I saw them coming, I realized there was no chance of me being picked up [by a search and rescue helicopter] without them dragging at least three or four dozen Vietnamese with them. I knew that many people would be hanging on to me by the time the chopper arrived. I couldn't tell whether they were armed or not, although, as I got closer, I could see that some of them had rudimentary weapons, pitchforks and the things like that.

We had heard stories of the North Vietnamese in the south not taking prisoners, but ending up doing all sorts of things, including torture and dismemberment. I knew that to be a fact. But, the only thing I could figure was, "If that comes, let it come. Right now, I want to keep my wits about me, and get through today."

I look back at that moment now as being the beginning of seven-and-a-half years of frustration. The frustration first came because I couldn't even contact the other airplanes, to tell them that I was alive. They were not able to ascertain that either one of us, the pilot or myself, had gotten on the ground, alive, and therefore, as I later learned, we were declared dead. And because of that, this frustration built and built over the years.

Was I or was I not considered dead? I never got a clear-cut answer to that. I was told by some later shoot-downs that I had been declared missing; others said that I had been declared killed; then even later, I was told that they really didn't know about me, but they knew my pilot was declared killed. I never knew what I was, until I came home. At Clark [Air Base in the Philippines] I found out I had been officially dead for the first 16 months, then transferred to the POW list.

Rowan: Ed, how did you know that you would be tortured?

Flora: I know that there were three Special Forces men who were found hanging upside down. Gasoline had been poured all over them while they were alive and lit. I know of another man, captured in a Montagnard village. They took the man, and while he was still alive, nailed his beret to his head. Cute little things like that. I expected to be kept alive for a couple of weeks, but I didn't expect to live too long.

Doremus: In the early days up north, when someone dropped out of the sky into an outlying district, the village people got into quite a frenzy, and one way or another killed their captives. As soon as the high command found that out, there was, in fact, a price put on our heads. And those people began to look for that reward. But, that was after I was shot down, perhaps a year later.

Rowan: Did you think that you could hold out against giving information, assuming you were going to be tortured?

Flora: It's hard to explain. I thought I could, to a point. I knew I'd have to tell them something eventually, but I figured I could get by with a lie. At that time I *couldn't* tell anything, just because of certain things [classified information].

> Some of this information remains classified and Flora was unable to go into it.

At first they told me that in order to get medical care, I would have to fill out a piece of paper. Well, I couldn't remain conscious long enough to fill out the whole piece of paper. So I gave them my name, rank, and service number, and then I passed out. When I came to, I gave them my date of birth, and then, just like in the book, I put an X on the rest of the paper, and nobody seemed to get extremely upset about this.

Rowan: What was on the rest of the paper?

Flora: Questions about what I was doing, my unit commander, other personnel who were with me, the size of the unit, the destination of the unit, the home base of the unit. Other things like that. There was a girl involved in this. She was the translator.

Rowan: What happened when you refused to answer those questions?

Flora: Well, their lavatories over there were made out of bamboo and mud. This particular one had caved in. So they took me out and they set me in that. The next day or the day after, whenever it was—I never was conscious long enough to get my time oriented—I noticed little fuzzy balls all over me. And then, hours later, I came to, and had a burning sensation in my arm pits and around my groin. I put my hand under my arm pits, and there were maggots. And then it dawned on me what they were doing. As long as I had blood all over me, the flies would be attracted to me, and lay their eggs, and the eggs would hatch. I've got scars to prove it, under my arm pits and in my groin, where the maggots were "eating" me.

I decided that I just couldn't take much more of that, so I told them I changed my mind, that I'd tell them what they wanted to know. So they got me out and they cleaned me all up. They went through the trouble of taking off all my bloody clothes. They put black pajamas on me, changed my bandages, took me and sat me down.

Then, I was feeling a little better, and I told them I had changed my mind again. And that's what worried me. Nobody appeared to get mad. Nobody really appeared to be upset about it at all. They just sort of shrugged their shoulders, changed all my clothing again, took me out, and set me back down again.

If I could have just forced them to kill me right away, it wouldn't have been so bad. The way they acted, I knew they would have let me sit down there 'til I was down to about five ounces of flesh left. Psychologically, that's when they started getting to me.

So I told them I had changed my mind. They said, "Are you sure this time?" I told them, yes, I was sure this time. They came and went through the whole process again, changed all my clothes, took me in and sat me down. That's when I told them the fictitious story about getting lost on patrol. They took it, but I don't think they believed it. They didn't believe anything I put down, because they knew it couldn't be true. But, for some reason, it seemed like they were satisfied that they had gotten something.

Doremus: That's a big point. A lot of times these guys were filling squares. They had to show something to their superiors. They got something. Whether it's right or not, may never be proven anyhow. And, as long as this guy could save face, and fill his square, and pass that thing on, somebody else can verify it, or believe it, or not, whatever the hell he cares. And that's the way they'd do it.

Flora: That's the way it was with just about everyone I talked to.

Doremus: Most of us, with our busy schedule, and running between coffee breaks, don't ever really seem to comprehend that time is not important to those people. That whole war should have proven that. It wouldn't have mattered to them if it went on for another four years.

And, when it came to them looking for something, they never seemed to be in a hurry for it. It was never the kind of stuff that you need today. Granted, there were probably a few instances where they wanted some military information they had to have *now.* [Like, when] a guy just got shot down, and they wanted to know what he knows about tomorrow's operation. I think those cases were so few they were almost negligible. But most of the stuff they were after was of the political and semi-political type.

They'd sit you in a room and let you think about it. In fact, even when you told them you were ready to talk, they would take their time before they got somebody to come in and talk to you about it. Maybe tomorrow. They took time to wash you up, and clean you up, and let you have your food, and make you believe you were being treated like a king. Well, you are, when you get a meal after you haven't had one for two days.

Rowan: What was your cover story Ed? What did you tell them?

Flora: I told them I was in the 199th Light Infantry Brigade, and I was on patrol, and that we got lost, and got separated from our unit, and I was captured, and that the rest of the unit had gone on.

Rowan: Of course the 199th wasn't operating in that area.

Flora: The 199th was south of Saigon at the time, hundreds of miles away. But that was the only unit that I knew anything about, at the time. I had been in it for a very short time.

After I filled this paper out as much as I could, they took me to a field hospital. My arm was pretty messed up. They cut some bone out, cut some meat out, put splints on it, wrapped it up, and gave me a shot of penicillin. I stayed there in the hospital for, I guess, about a week, then they started marching me north.

The first thing they did was take away my boots. They know that Americans, unlike the Vietnamese, are not the best walkers without boots. And they kept my boots away, figuring I couldn't escape. They walked me 38, 39 days, off and on.

Everything was going along fine. I got to my first camp on October 5th of '67. For some reason, which they never explained to me yet, they put me in a small cage, almost 6 feet long, and about 2½ feet wide by about 2½ feet high, and I was allowed out of there twice a day. They just stuck me in there, and they gave me two cups of rice and two spoonfuls of salt a day. They left me in there 30 days; no explanation, no reason. And then, one day, they just came in and picked me up and moved me up to what we called the "Telephone Booths."

Now, during all this time, I'd escaped three times. When I left the hospital, this girl had handed me this little sack of papers, and she told me that that was to be my death certificate in Hanoi, because of all my "lies," and she said, "We allow you to carry it." So I put it in my shirt pocket. The first time I escaped, the first thing I did was bury that. I knew the guards had other papers too, but they also had my watch. And this one guard was pretty greedy. When they changed guards, just as I got to North Viet Nam, he kept the watch, but in order to keep the watch, he apparently had to keep the other paper work, too.

Rowan: But, your cover story was still sticking?

Flora: My story stuck up until April of 1968, when my little world caved in on me. I don't know *how*; I don't know *why*. They had some information, and I just don't see how they got it. Now, up until then, I had been beaten around a little bit, and, when I escaped the third time, they put all these scars on me, knocked my teeth out, things like that. But then, they started on mental and physical torture. That went on for about a month and a half.

One day, I was just about to give up. I couldn't see whereas I was accomplishing anything. And this old man came in there, and he spoke pretty good English. He said, "Eventually you're going to have to tell me. You know we have places for people like you." So I had one last try. I said, "Look, if I was in the type of a unit you say I'm in, do you think I could possibly have any information that I could give you? Do you think it's possible that the unit that you think I'm in would give me the information, knowing there's a possibility I could be captured? Don't you think that all I would know is just the few things I needed to know as I went ahead on this operation?"

And do you know, they never questioned me about it again!

Rowan: What kind of punishment did the North Vietnamese dish out?

Flora: The one they used the most at our camp was kneeling down on the floor with your arms extended over your head. And when you couldn't take that anymore, they'd stand you up at attention with your arms over your head. They'd put you in leg irons and put a rope around them and pull your legs up towards the ceiling so you'd be resting on your shoulders and your head.

At first, all they used to do would be to interrogate us. But, there would be three interrogators there, one questioning us and two watching. If they said something that obviously made you mad, they'd write it down.

All the guys were treated differently. We had one man, and if you talked about his family, he'd get very upset. On him that's what they worked on. For instance, they'd ask him: "What did your mother eat to beget you?" Me, they called a coward, a dog man, and a few other choice morsels, and I'd just laugh at them.

Doremus: That's a very serious thing for a Vietnamese, to call you an animal.

Rowan: What was the kind of thing that they *could* get to you with, Ed?

Flora: They would torture other men and I could hear them screaming through the compound, and that got to me more than anything else. I don't know if they knew it or not, but they moved me and another guy up next to the interrogation building. And, as the guys were being interrogated sometimes, they would actually go temporarily out of their minds, and they'd start hollering and screaming. That got to me more than anything else, and I think they knew it. I think that's why I was in that room. I would have much rather been over there, having it done to me, than to sit there and listen to somebody else going through it.

Rowan: Rob, you had greater success with your cover story. What was it?

Doremus: I didn't really think about a cover story before I got there, because I didn't think I was going to be there . . . it always happens to the other guy. But, before I was captured, our unit, which was an F-4B squadron, had played host to a group of newsmen and a practicing minister, who had some connection with President Johnson. And, because of this connection, he had permission to fly a combat mission in an F-4B, into South Viet Nam. Our skipper had taken him on a ride. Because that had occurred, perhaps, the idea popped into my head that if I could make then believe I didn't know anything, then they probably wouldn't ask me anything. And even if they did, my answer could always be, believably, that I didn't know anything, and that anything I said would be all guesswork on my part. So, to lay the ground work, I told them that I was strictly a passenger on the airplane, that I was really a member of the ship's company, and not a normal fly boy.

Rowan: Did you think that would be believable to them?

Doremus: I knew that minister's picture had been in *Stars and Stripes,* and hoped they would remember it—although I didn't want to tell them to go back and look at their newspapers, because I was on the front page on one of those papers, myself, as a MIG-killer in June. But, when I finally told them something, I went ahead and told them I wasn't a crew member and I don't know anything about the airplane. They asked me how fast it was going, and I said, "I don't know. I don't know which dials to look at for that. I was just up there looking around. I wanted to see what Viet Nam looked like in war time, and we were looking at the weather."

They did and they didn't believe that, over the years. No matter what your story was, they would question you, and I just *had* to stick fast with it. I did, for seven-and-a-half years. And it seemed to work.

Rowan: Were you tortured, initially?

Doremus: No, not in the accepted sense of the word. They did in fact cuff me on the head. I thought they were going to break my ear drum. They hurt my hand when I tried to protect my ears. They threatened me with no medical attention for my badly burned hands.

The way they were doing it at that time was that they would put us solo, and try to work on the pressures that we had within ourselves. Time was our worst enemy. We're not used to having a whole day to do nothing but sit in a cell that's seven by seven, with a concrete bed and no furnishings —mosquitoes, filth, rats running in and out. All of those conditions were prevalent the whole time I was there.

Rowan: What were some of the things you were thinking about during the initial time you were there, out of touch, I presume, with other Americans?

Doremus: I was out of touch as far as the Vietnamese were

concerned, but I was not out of touch in reality. There was a total of eight cells in that block. One of them was empty, and was used as a shower. There were people close enough who could talk to me occasionally. A sentence in an hour. A sentence in a day, sometimes. They kept looking out to see when it was clear. If there was no guard around, or at least if we thought there was no guard, they'd call over and say, "OK, you can talk now. What's your name?" But, in fact, 23 out of 24 hours every day, I was alone, and I had no contact with those people who I knew were close to me but there was a 10-12 inch wall between us.

Rowan: What were the first things that you wanted to find out?

Doremus: Well, you got to find what your status is there. What do they do there? What's the routine? If you can find out the routine, you got a good handle on what's gonna go on. If you *know* that every day they have certain times for feeding and you do get out to wash your hands, your clothes or that they do or do not interrogate you a lot—is there in fact torture—if you can find out those things you can at least prepare for them or not worry about them so much.

Rowan: Did you find out that your pilot was captured alive?

Doremus: I was very lucky in that respect. They kept me in an interrogation room by myself. I was there overnight and, while I was there, I heard one of the interrogators questioning another POW about me—because this guy was from my ship—and about Commander Franke. Because they were asking about him, I felt that they at least had his wallet or something like that, his identification, and they probably had him. When they finally put me in that cell, I found that my skipper was holed up two doors away from me, but that he was out in interrogation at the time. And so, within 48 hours, we had contact with each other. We were able to make a rudimentary story consolidation between us.

Flora: For the first eight months, I never saw another American. They kept me in strict solitary. While I was in that cage, most of the time I spent trying to keep my story straight, trying to get everything in my mind so that I wouldn't make any mistakes later in interrogation. The biggest problem I had is that they wouldn't let me out of the cage. I was let out only twice a day, and the cage had no lavatory facilities or anything.

Solitary is not bad for the first three months, because you can always think about home, your family, things like that. After three months, you start running out, and then you have to go to fictitious stories.

At first I had a spider over the door. And I played with the spider. I'd catch flies and feed him. Believe me, that spider kept me busy for about two weeks. I used to play with my food, too.

Doremus: Yes, they'd bring you a meal which you could finish in about 15 minutes. But, instead of eating it all, you'd take half of it and decide how you were going to eat the rest. You could even make a sandwich out of rice, roll it in a ball, and divide it. You'd take about half an hour playing around with it before you'd even eat it. Then, you'd chew it very slowly watching for the rocks in it. The Vietnamese, they couldn't believe the way we played around with our food. You could string that whole thing out to about an hour-and-a-half. And that's an hour-and-a-half of your time that's gone.

Flora: That's right. I used to make little snowmen out of my rice, 'cause I despised rice anyway.

But most of the time I watched ants. I couldn't see out of the room at all. But the ants would come in. In fact, I would leave food there to bring the ants in. I'd watch the ants taking the food out, watch a spider, watch a chameleon.

Then, I went back to as young a time as I could remember, and thought what would have happened if I had done things differently. That kept me busy for almost a year. Then, I went to the future, what I'd do when I got out. I had a plan, even if they cut my arms off, which I didn't think they would, but I had a plan for that. And that took about a year.

Then, I spent about a week being a millionaire, but found I didn't make a very good millionaire. I had a million dollars, and no matter how much of it I spent, I still had a million dollars. I was a million dollar bum, because I just don't like doing things millionaires are supposed to do.

Rowan: How did you see yourself spending it?

Flora: First, I bought me a boat, and then a nice house up in the mountains, then a car, and in about a week I had bought everything I ever wanted, and I still had a million dollars. It just got boring to me. I just couldn't picture how a person could have a million dollars all the time and be happy with it. So I just gave up on that idea.

Then, I started building roads. I built a road from Brazil to Argentina. I don't know a thing about building roads. That took me about 30 days. When we were doing these little projects, we would get so meticulous with details, that, like one time I had to build this bridge, but I had to blow away some dirt before I could do it. I think I was in Venezuela then. So I tore the whole road apart and went back to Brazil and started all over again, got enough dynamite, and things I needed. It took me almost three months to build that road, and then I started drilling oil wells, although I knew absolutely nothing about oil.

Doremus: You didn't try to retain the stuff in your mind, after you'd done the project, because if you didn't retain it, you could do it again some day.

I would rebuild and restore cars. And there was a time when I could have told you about the color-coding I would have had for every nut, pulley, accessory underneath the hood of that car. All the things that revolve were going to be red. All the headers were going to be silver. One time it would be a Porsche, another day a Mustang. The more meticulous you got, the more time it would consume.

Flora: I'll tell you how important this got to us. We'd get on these little projects, and they'd call us over for interrogation, and we'd be infuriated, just because they'd stopped us in the middle of our little project. I'd be mad for three or four days, because I'd have to go back about two or three days to start all over again, and get myself caught back up again. These things really got important to us.

I did notice one thing. Along about 1969 or 1970, which were our worst years as far as torture was concerned, I started losing confidence in myself. I'd be building this road and I'd be frustrated, because I'd run into something I couldn't cope with. I started thinking real things, things that I'd done before and that I might want to do when I got out, and I'd notice even then that I'd be losing confidence. So I stopped that.

Doremus: We used to refer to it as "being squirrely," but I think that rather than the normal sense of losing touch with reality was that we were losing our sense of time and we were getting stale. Everything that we talked about would be circa 1965 or before, because that was when we were "alive." If somebody new came in and started talking about an Oldsmobile Toronado, why I just couldn't picture that car. The more the years went on, the longer the time hung heavy, because we didn't know what was going on, and we thought we'd never be able to catch up. It's going to take years. As much as I think I'm abreast of things, it's vivid in my mind as soon as I go out on the street and look at a car, and I don't even know what car it is; what brand it is or what year it is. There was a time when I could have told you any car, the model, the name, the year and all the rest of the stuff. This goes for your children, your wife, your parents. You remember them the way they *were.* When you come home, they're going to be completely different. The more the years went on, the more you realized the world is going on. You hope it does go on without you. But, in fact, you're "out of it."

Flora: Getting "stale" was a big problem. Of all the men we had in our camp up until 1971, the latest one captured was captured in the Tet offensive of 1968. We had nothing in the way of contact with the outside world after February of '68. We knew *absolutely nothing,* except what the Communists wanted us to hear from our propaganda box.

Doremus: And if you ever did get some little bit of news from a new guy, that was of paramount importance to pass on, and this could be so infinitesimally small, that at home you would think nothing of it. It could be anything. It could be that somebody's wife had darned a pair of stockings, and wrote about it in her letter. And that's news. That's something big. We'd pass that on.

Flora: Remember when Jacqueline Kennedy married Onassis? That went through camp like wildfire. That was the greatest thing we'd heard because that was the first news we got in 1971.

Doremus: We'd go six months, and there would be no input of news, whatsoever, even from the quizzes [the interrogation sessions]. The quizzes would stop. And sometimes we used to think, "Maybe it would be a good idea if we had a quiz." They'd always drop something [in giving us a quiz]. They'd have to say something in order to debunk it. And after six months of having nothing, not even a quiz with the interrogators, we'd have nothing to say.

Rowan: So then, what did you talk about?

Doremus: Every morning, we'd get up, and we'd sweep out in front of our room [sending messages in code]. There was a solo in the room next to us, and there were two of us in our room. When the door was closed during the day, we tapped on the walls. But, in the morning, for something to say, we'd give a breakfast menu. We'd make one up every day and it would be grandiose. Breakfast at Brennan's [in New Orleans] is great, but it never approached what we used to have. It included about everything you can imagine. We also had a booze of the week. This week it was Scotch. One morning we'd be talking about Johnny Walker, and tomorrow it was Chivas Regal. You had to think about seven different kinds of Scotch. Then, when you got to rum, you had to think of seven different kinds of rum. And that was the thing we put on as a tag, after we gave the breakfast menu.

The breakfast menu would start out with fruit and cereal; and we had a different cereal every morning. It might be Rice Krispies today, and Grapenuts or Grapenut Flakes the next day. All you had to do was have it different every morning. It was a big criticism if you had the same thing twice. The guy in the next room would say: "Hey, you 'swept out'

Grapenuts. We had that yesterday."

We'd sign it off with the regular sign off, which was "God bless you," and the guy in the next room would cough, to say that he had gotten it.

> As our discussion continued, I noticed that Ed Flora was shifting around on the couch, trying to get comfortable. I asked him if he wanted to take a break, or get a pill, but he said no, it was okay to continue. However, he pointed out one other difficulty he'd been having, of which I was not aware.

Flora: A thing I've had problems with since I was released is concentration. In that 1968-70 period, we had to sit on our beds, at attention, with all our clothes on, from seven in the morning 'til nine at night. They gave us propaganda books, and they would have one man reading them aloud to the other two men. I don't care who you are, eventually some of it's going to start sinking in. But, we got so that the two men listening had no trouble ignoring it and we even got so good that the man who was reading it could read out loud, and concentrate on something else. We did that for almost six months. But, then, when a book came in we really *did* want to read, we couldn't concentrate on it. If there was something over the radio, you know, like some American Senator making a statement, and if it was over 20 words long, we couldn't concentrate on it. Ever since we were released, that's been one of my biggest problems. I can't concentrate on anything.

Doremus: I find that when TV is on, I pick up a magazine and I don't read the magazine or watch the TV.

Rowan: How did you get along with your fellow inmates? Did you find that some guys would do things that would drive you nuts?

Flora: Well, the first six months I was in a cell with other men, it wasn't bad, because we all had our life stories we could tell each other. After that, there was nothing else to talk about so we started telling our life stories all over again. And six months later, all over again. And it got so bad that, if someone forgot something, the other guys could tell him what it was: "Well, his name was such-and-such," or "You forgot about when you went over there." We used to get on each others nerves this way. So the way we broke that up is by having our little projects going. From early in the morning, until after what we called "pot time," which was two o'clock, we'd get up and say "Good morning" and exchange a few words and go our own way in a manner of speaking. Then, in the evening we'd talk.

There was never a period when we couldn't get along. Sure, we got mad at each other once in a while. Some guy would say something about somebody else and they'd have a few words. You had to make sure that you didn't say something that would hurt the other man to the point that he'd never forget.

Rowan: You were away from women for six or seven years. What effect did that have on your views about such things as masturbation or homosexuality?

Flora: The third time I was recaptured, I was recaptured by five women, and that's how I got all the scars. They kept me for two days, and during that two days, every time I'd go to sleep they'd kick me in the groin. For almost a whole year I hated women, Vietnamese women. I couldn't stand the sight of one. I had no sexual desires whatsoever, during that first year. After that, I had normal sexual desires. I still enjoyed women, even though up until 1972 I never saw a woman, not even a Vietnamese woman.

We talked about it quite a bit among ourselves. It seemed like the younger guys, the guys who were captured at from 18 to 22 years of age, seemed to be bothered more than anybody else. The married men, it didn't seem to bother quite as much.

Everybody in the camp masturbated. But, there again, how much depended on the age. I know some guys who masturbated twice a day. Other guys masturbated once a month. Very seldom did I ever masturbate.

Wet dreams, we all had them. In fact, most of the guys were pretty proud of them. They would wake up the next morning and tell us exactly what they were dreaming about.

But as to the question of homosexuality, in our camp, I don't know of one man who had any homosexual tendencies at all. It surprised me, because I figured over that length of time there would be guys who would turn homosexual. But, after we all got together in 1971, I talked to all the rest of the NCOs [non-commissioned officers] and most of the officers, and they also had no problems with homosexuality.

Doremus: I think for me and probably for a lot of other guys there was just a resignation on that whole subject of sex. You realized that was not one of those things that were going to be afforded you. Even in the most "good guy" days, you weren't going to have a woman brought in on a tray, and I don't think I looked for that. Certainly I missed the companionship and all the rest that goes with the feminine world, but it was something we just kind of put out of our minds.

However, the mind is a tricky thing. I dreamed more in Viet Nam probably than ever before. I'd have vivid dreams, about many things of course, but especially about women. I could picture women I had known, and I would have had many different relationships with. It might have been like getting a book from a library, but I'd put a face on that librarian, whereas, normally you'd check out and never notice that it was a gal. There'd be vivid recollections when you woke up in the morning that it was a woman, to the point where you'd think you could have smelled the perfume.

I certainly dreamed about the women that I knew the best, and my wife would be the prime example. I could have told you exactly what she looked like. If I were an artist I could have painted her picture. There *were* artists who *did* paint pictures of their own wives. And when I saw photographs of them, later, I recognized them from those pictures that had been sketched with a brick on the floor, or with a tooth paste tube to make a pencil (because of the lead in it) on a piece of toilet paper.

Women certainly were a topic with us. There were no restraints. Jokes were quite often about women, or the relationships between men and women, They ran the gamut from the sublime to the ridiculous.

Flora: We used to get a Soviet magazine about once a

month and you'd see some Caucasian gals in there. And guys would go wild. Everybody's sexual desire was still there, but we just put it in the backs of our minds. I used to have dreams. I dreamed about women I knew before I met my wife, girls I'd known in school and my wife. I even dreamed about girls I'd never met.

Doremus: One time, as a project, I tried to picture all the girls who had been in any way prominent in my life. The ones I'd dated steadily, or had gone with for more than one or two dates, to see if I could put a face, or a figure, on those girls and I found in a large sense that I could.

Flora: We had a Special Forces medic in our camp and he actually suggested masturbation, monthly, because of the danger of sterility. Most of the guys took it seriously, and, even though there was really no desire, they'd do it.

Doremus: There was an article [in *Life* magazine] that, for many reasons incensed us, quoting Valerie Kushner, the doctor's wife (he was a captain at the time he was captured). I don't want to go into any of the political stuff about her, but one of the things that got to more people and prompted more comments was something that she said, in an offhand way, I suppose. She said she had been advised by army doctors and other wives that, when these men come home, you must be prepared for changes, and one of the things that you are probably going to find out is that they're going to be impotent. Well, that incensed everybody in the room. Even if he was going to be, he wasn't going to admit it, and he certainly wanted to find out, first. And I remember one of the guys told me at Clark that in his first phone call home he told his wife that when he got home he was going to show her that "Valerie's wrong" and I think that *she* knew what he was talking about as well as *he* knew what he was talking about.

Rowan: So your feelings about sex remained the same. Did your views about God, religion, your place in the scheme of things, change in any way?

This question provoked a lot of thought and a period of silence elapsed before Ed Flora offered his views.

Flora: I never was religious before. I believed in God, but as far as going to church and praying and things like that, I just didn't do it. When I was first captured, I used to pray for all kinds of things, to get home and all this other stuff. And then I got to thinking it was ridiculous. So I started being thankful for what I had. It helped. It helped a whole lot. I talked to other guys and found out they were exactly the same way. They gave up on praying: "Give me better food; keep me alive; get me medical care," and prayer became just a day by day thing. They would be thankful for everything they got that day, no matter what it was. It helped. It helped all of us. We weren't religious fanatics or anything like that. Most of the guys said silent prayers to themselves when they went to bed. Guys like me, who weren't overly religious, changed quite a bit.

Rowan: Is it a change that will last?

Flora: Oh, yes. Oh, yes.

Doremus: We had a common signal, and it was a *V* in our tap code that we would give. The senior man would call the time, on Sunday morning. He would give this signal and that was the impetus for everybody, no matter where he was at that particular time, to have a common church time. Church services consisted of saying "The Lord's Prayer" and the "Pledge of Allegiance" to the flag. If we were within earshot of each other, we would be saying it loud enough for everybody to hear. But we didn't want to get caught doing it because it would sound like we were communicating. In fact, we were. But, it wasn't the kind of communicating they were talking about.

Right from the beginning, people had been doing this before I got to Heartbreak Hotel. And we continued that in every camp that I knew of, for the entire time that I was there. On Sunday morning, the signal was given and everybody knew about it. If they were out of ear range of that signal, they had their own time for doing it, and they did it as if we were all together. It was something that gave us a little togetherness.

I prayed at other times, too. I can remember that, as a solo, another "thing to do" before each meal was to give thanks. It was a quiet little thing. It was a prayer that I learned from my wife. I felt that that was a little togetherness with home to do that. When I moved in with some other people, another fellow noticed that I would also hesitate before the meal, and he assumed I was praying, although I did not cross myself, not being a Catholic, which he would do. He said, "Look, you're praying before a meal and I am too. Would you like to do it together? You could do it one time and I could do it the next." I said, "Sure." And it was just one of those things that brought us closer together. We had something in common again. Perhaps, had we been looking for friends, we never would have found each other, because we had completely different backgrounds, different mentalities. This guy was a genius. We had very little in common, but we found common grounds to talk about. He had to come down some, and I had to go up some, in many cases. I was mechanically inclined and he was academically inclined. But, we found something between those roads to talk about.

He was a very religious, devout Catholic, who had had some kind of religious experience almost every day of his life. But we both also found respect for those who did not want to attend the services—agnostics and atheists—and they would tell you so. And they would respect the time for our church services, and they'd go down to the other end of the room, and just be away from us.

Rowan: What about your feelings about other races? Did you find yourself looking past the black face or looking past the Polish surname to find out what the man was like?

Flora: I didn't have much experience with that until 1972 because I was with two Caucasians all the time. One was Irish, the other was German, and I'm a mixture of English, Irish and German (*Laughter*). I had no problem. I did get in with three Negroes, and actually, we had no problems. We had no problems whatsoever.

Doremus: I knew of no problems.

Flora: In fact, one [black guy], Cordine McMurray, he and I became best of friends. We talked about what we heard over the propaganda box, about the NAACP, and the Black Panthers. He explained it to me from his people's viewpoint. I would explain to him why I didn't think it would work. He would explain to me why they thought it would work, even though he didn't think it would work. We came to understand each other. Same way with the other three, younger guys. We'd get outside periodically and we'd be able to talk, and we found that we actually became closer by bringing this stuff out, sitting down and talking about it like men. Nobody would get mad, because nobody was trying to push it on the other guy. We were just trying to find out each other's viewpoints. We found that there is no problem between the Negro and the white man.

Doremus: The Vietnamese, however, tried everything they could to alienate one from the other. If you have something that is black and something that is white, you have something that you can start putting the needle in between. Anything they could use that way was something they worked on, and of course that was the reason for their propaganda, and all the Black Panther stuff they gave us. It was to infuriate us, and to separate us, and to alienate one from another.

There were, I'm certain, people who had basic prejudices before they got in there, but they swallowed them. I know that for a fact. They swallowed them. Now the guy who all his life has been traveling in one circle and making little prejudiced-type remarks, the nicknames people have used over the years, once in a while you're going to let something like that slip, and certainly in the close quarters we had, that can make for some pretty blue air. I know that things like that happened, but they were able to patch that up.

Flora: I can give you a good example of that. We had a kid from Georgia, a Caucasian, and we had a black guy from Detroit. They were sharing cigarettes because we weren't getting that many, so they would smoke half apiece. This guy from Georgia handed one to the other guy and said: "Hey, I nigger-lipped it." Then, the black guy took the cigarette and didn't say anything. This kid stood there and he went white. He turned around and said: "I want to apologize for that. I didn't mean it the way I said it. It was the way I was brought up. I hope you understand." And the guy said: "Yeah, I understand." They were best of friends. They just got to the point where they knew they were going to slip and it was overlooked, just like that. "You said it and I know you didn't mean it."

We considered ourselves all Americans, and we were damn proud to be Americans. We kept it that way. We didn't care what color we were, or anything else. We were all Americans.

5

Waiting for the Jolly Greens

After years in prison many of the men said they felt closer to God, country, and their fellow man.

Commander Eugene B. "Red" McDaniel was a 35-year-old North Carolinian who had raised his share of hell before he was shot down on May 19th, 1967. Red calls that day "Black Friday," because six other Navy planes and two Air Force planes also were lost. He and his "right-seater"—bombardier navigator—in the A-6 bailed out about 30 miles southwest of Hanoi. The other man is known to have survived for four days on the ground, but has never been heard from since—another of the mysteries of the MIAs. Red believes *he* survived those first days, and the next five-and-a-half years, largely on the strength of his faith in God, and his optimism.

Commander Edwin A. Shuman III is the same age as Red. Ned too was an A-6 driver, and an optimist. He and his right-seater, Dale Doss, parachuted just 10 miles north of Hanoi on March 17th, 1968, and were captured immediately.

Commander Kenneth L. Coskey, another A-6 pilot, admits to being less of an optimist, and perhaps with reason. He was shot down in September of 1968 in the southern panhandle of North Viet Nam. His plane was close enough to the Gulf of Tonkin for the rescue helicopters to get to his right-seater, Dick McKee, but not to Ken.

All three of these men now live with their wives and

families in Virginia Beach, Virginia. When they came to my hotel room for this discussion, it appeared obvious that they were good friends. Red and Ken kidded Ned about the boat he's equipping—a project he had dreamed about for years as a POW. Ned answered with the same kind of humor, complaining that he had already, that very day, spent $500.00 on things for his boat, but hadn't had a chance to go down to the water and feast his eyes on it. He said that in prison he had expected the boat to cost about $12,000.00—in 1968 dollars. Now, he was going to have to spend twice that much on it.

There also was a good deal of eyebrow lifting, winking, and silent laughter when the talk turned to such things as sexual fantasies, and we joked about what people would have thought if they saw the discussion on television, rather than reading the words in a book.

It was an extremely revealing discussion—and the two hours we had planned to spend together stretched unnoticed into three.

The conversation started with a question about how close Red McDaniel had come to being picked up by the Jolly Greens Giants—the rescue helicopters.

McDaniel: I was shot down on May 19th, in 1967, the day after we hit the Hanoi area for the first time in almost six months.

Someone had jokingly written on the ready-room blackboard, "Make sure you have a shave and a haircut for Ho Chi Minh's parade, because it's his birthday." I was with a flight of 26 aircraft. We were hit at 12,000 feet. I was hit by the fifth of five SAMs. I was dodging the fourth SAM, when I was hit by the fifth. My BN [bombardier-navigator], James Kelly Patterson, wanted to get out at that time, wanted to blow the canopy. I told him to just stay with it, and get over the hills, and I made this transmission: "Lost both hydraulic systems and we're heading for the hills."

Actually, we were heading for wherever the aircraft took us, but there were hills ahead, and, at this point, we were over the valley, the Red River Delta. So, we stayed with the aircraft for more than a minute, to get over those hills, and consequently we got out quite low. We got out about 2,000 feet above the terrain, and we were going pretty fast, about 500 knots [550 miles per hour], because we had no speed brakes. We went out about a second apart. He blew the canopy, even though you're not supposed to blow the canopy above 300 knots. The danger is that if you blow it at high speeds and it doesn't come all the way off, you're screwed. You can't get out. We elected to blow it and it came away clear. My BN went. Then I went. I remember that I had a tremendous pain in my left leg. I wrenched my left knee quite badly.

Coming down I was able to see the plane crash, and my thoughts on the way down were, "Boy you've had it. You've gone from a white knuckle combat pilot to a disabled airman over enemy territory." At that moment, I started thinking two years into the future, figuring I was going to be out of circulation that long.

I got a little encouragement, though, shortly after getting on the ground, thinking about being able to see the people I knew who had been shot down, Jerry Denton, Jack Fellowes, people like that. Little did I know that I wouldn't get to see them, that I would be in solitary for a number of months.

On the way down, I looked up at my 'chute, and saw that a panel was ripped. So, even though I had never jumped before, I felt that I was coming down fairly fast, faster than you should be. So, as I came through the jungle canopy, I intentionally tried to grab a limb, to slow my rate of descent. I grabbed, but I didn't grab anything, and my 'chute caught the limb as I came down, and I was suspended about 30 or 40 feet in the air, in my parachute.

I had two survival radios. One had ripped off in the ejection and one remained. And the antenna had deployed. But, rather than talk while I was hanging in the tree, I was going to try and get back up the parachute, climb the risers, get up to the limb, come down the trunk. But, on the way back up to get to the limb, the limb broke, so I fell 30 to 40 feet, down about a 60 degree mountain, kind of a glancing blow. And, when I hit the ground, I was paralyzed. I could not move. I was later to find out, I had a broken vertebra in my back. It was a pretty bad break, but it healed itself properly over the years, so the doctors now say.

But, even though I was paralyzed from the waist down, I could still move my upper body. I pulled out the radio and told them I had an injured back. I'd forgotten about my knee, which had been creating all the pain. I told them I had an injured back, and a plane was circling overhead.

After a period of time, probably about an hour, I was able to move. So I took my survival packet and charted my survival situation. I put the pack on my back. I took my parachute and hid it, and started trying to get up to the top of the mountain, and to get in contact with my BN. I tried to contact him for about five minutes every hour, but I got nothing. I heard no sounds, except jungle sounds, monkeys frolicking around fruit trees, and stuff like that. So I kept climbing up the hill, trying to get to the top which was about 900 feet away.

I had landed about 2,000 feet up a 3,000 foot mountain, so I had roughly about a thousand feet to get to the top. It was thick jungle growth, and damn near impossible to climb. But, as I looked down at the valley, I could see cultivated crops, so I knew there were people living nearby. Then, I saw what appeared to be a hamlet down in a valley. But, I felt it would take about two hours for the people to get from the bottom up there, to get to me. I was still trying to get to the top, so I could transmit to my BN who could be on the other side. I needed line-of-sight to communicate with him. So my intention was to get up there. Well, I had been shot down at 10, and I worked all afternoon, and finally, at about four o'clock, I heard a whistle, like a cop's whistle, and for the first time I realized there was activity in the area. So I stopped and hid for the time being. Apparently, they left the mountain, because it was going to take them some time to get down, so they left early, prior to sundown. They probably came within 20 or 30 feet of me. I never saw them, but I heard the sounds.

Rowan: That must have been a pretty scary moment.

McDaniel: It's frightening, but I was kind of in a state of shock.

Rowan: How did you hide?

McDaniel: I just let the bushes in front of me go. I was in completely dense foliage, these big jungle trees and plants and bamboo. The only thing that bothered me was that along the distance I'd made, which by this time was about 200 feet, there was a pathway where I had just kind of beaten the bushes down, crawling and walking up the mountain. So I was afraid they might be able to see that. But, they passed uphill from me, so they did not see it. Then they left.

I continued to try to get up the top of the mountain, and I got about another 100 feet, probably, maybe half way to the top. Then, nightfall set in, so I decided to camp out for the night. I was still on a real steep mountainside, but I had a tree there, so I put it between my crotch, to support me so I wouldn't fall back down. That's the way I stayed for the rest of the night.

One of the most frightening things that happened though was something that we experience every day, but I didn't recognize. I heard this damn loud noise coming through the jungle. It sounded like a herd of elephants, just thousands of elephants, coming through the jungle, and I had no idea of what it could be. It turned out to be rain, falling on the dense, jungle canopy. It was the most frightening sound I've ever heard. Here we don't hear it, because we don't have all that foliage.

Rowan: Was that triple canopy—three layered jungle?

McDaniel: Yes. It was very, very thick.

Rowan: So what you were hearing was the rain hitting the uppermost level of foliage.

McDaniel: Yes, and it was really frightening. It was not raining where I was, and I hadn't seen any clouds, so I had no idea what the sound was.

When the water started coming through the trees, I realized it was rain. I was happy then, because I was very thirsty. I only had one little bottle of water with me, and I'd used that earlier in the day. So I took my tarpaulin out. It's treated with some kind of powder, but hell, I didn't even bother to wash it off, I just caught water, and started drinking it, 'cause I was so thirsty.

I did a lot of praying throughout the night. And I heard the damn monkeys singing, playing and frolicking around, *all night long,* within probably a hundred feet of me.

Rowan: Did you sleep?

McDaniel: Not a bit. As the dark set in, I took my netting out. We had netting for the hands, and for the face, and I put that on. Earlier in the day, I'd taken the mosquito repellent and put it on my body, but I still had a lot of insects and a lot of leeches on me. They say, take a lighted cigarette, and burn them off, and I had two cigarette lighters with me for this purpose, but I just took the damn things and *pulled* them off.

Just before sundown, an aircraft flew overhead. I think it was an A-6. I was still trying to contact my BN, every hour. I was very conscious of trying to conserve battery power, but yet, I tried to get in touch with him. That night, about 10 o'clock, an aircraft flew over, with lights on. I knew that was a bad sign, because I knew anybody who came in after me would not have lights on. I made a call to him anyway. I told him, "This is a downed American airman." It was probably the ICC bird [International Control Commission passenger plane] going from Vientiane to Hanoi. He was probably on VHF, so he didn't hear me.

That night I kept thinking, planning, wondering whether a 2,000 foot jungle penetrator could get down from a rescue helicopter to where I was. I felt that the next morning somebody would be there at first light. So, through the night, I just kept praying, and finally it was light, six o'clock, and there was an A-6 overhead. It was Nick Carpenter, who is since missing over there. I asked him: "Is Jolly Green coming in?" He said, "Wait one," and he went to another frequency, and came back in about five minutes and said, "They'll be here in 45 minutes." I said, "Okay Nick, I'm going to run down and get my parachute."

I went back down the hill, and it was very easy going back down. I went back down to get my parachute, got it out of hiding, spread it out. He flew over-head and saw my parachute, and dipped his wing. I said, "Nick, I'm going to try to conserve power." He said, "I'll see you back on the ship," and I said: "Outstanding!"

So I was waiting to be rescued.

Six forty-five—nothing; seven o'clock—nothing; seven-thirty—nothing; eight o'clock—nothing.

Rowan: No sound of the choppers?

McDaniel: The only sound I heard were VC coming up the hill. I had heard a search party that appeared to be 15 or 20 people. I kept hearing these voices, calling from one point on the mountain to the other. So I knew they were en route, but they didn't seem to be very close.

About 7:30, I gave up on the rescue, and I put my parachute down in a little ravine, so it could be seen from directly overhead, but hopefully not from the mountainside. Then, I began to panic, and I gathered the parachute up again, and hid it. Then, about eight o'clock, I decided to move again, so now I had to go back up to where I'd already been. It was fairly easy getting back up, that two or three hundred feet.

I was still trying to get my BN. But, in the conversation with Nick Carpenter, I was told that my BN had a badly broken leg. Between 12 noon and one o'clock, I was making it up the mountain, and all of a sudden I heard a shot whiz by. I pretended I didn't see it, but I knew damn well it had to come from a rifle. I had a pistol with me, and I threw my pistol in the bushes, and I took my radio and threw it in the bushes, to get rid of it. I knew I'd been captured. When I did this, they fired a second shot and it whizzed by. I threw my hands up, and they came over, and when they got to me, they fired a third shot. The third shot was a signal to have the other parties come, apparently.

One of the guys had black teeth. They'd been chewing bee-tle nuts. His damn teeth were just completely black. And his feet were bleeding. He was barefooted, and his feet had been cut and scratched coming through the jungle and were bleeding. But that didn't bother him at all.

They tied me up. I tried to show them my swollen leg and my back, to get a little sympathy from them, but they weren't very sympathetic. They just continued to tie me up, completely unemotional. I didn't think I could walk and I continued to sit there and told them I'd have to be carried, but they would not carry me. They kept beating me with a rifle butt, about the shoulders, until finally I moved. And, as we started down, within 50 feet of where I was captured, they had a foxhole that had been dug the night before. So, apparently they had come pretty close to me the night before, and had dug in and made a fort that was about five feet deep and about that wide, that they could get down into, freshly dug. They apparently had come very close to where I was and had dug in, in case they had to shoot it out.

Rowan: Were these guys bounty hunters?

McDaniel: Oh, I'm sure they were given so much rice per capture.

Coskey: I think the guy who captured me, his main incentive was to get to Hanoi. I could just tell by the look on his face when we got up there. That guy hadn't been there in a long time, and he was *dying* to get there. The only way to get there, I guess, was with me. I don't know what else he got, but he sure enjoyed that.

Rowan: Ned, your capture was pretty close to Hanoi.

Shuman: Yes, it was about three o'clock in the morning. We were getting pretty close to Hanoi, and we were picking up a lot of flak [anti-aircraft fire]. I hadn't had any SAMs shot at me, but I didn't want any shot at me, because, at night, if they start shooting SAMs at you, it ruins your run. The lower you stay, the better chance you have, so I got down pretty low. I was at 200 feet and I'd just broken out of bad weather and we were in the clear at 200 feet. A nice moonlit night. I could see the moon shining off the rice paddies. There was "no sweat" flying down there, but there was a lot of stuff coming at us. As usual, it seemed to be going behind us, but I could hear it going off and it was pretty big stuff. I could see the muzzle flashes of the guns, because they were fairly close on the ground. And I could hear the things going off. And it did bounce the plane around quite a bit. And then the wind screen shattered, and we took a big jolt.

I got completely disoriented. I didn't know if we were right side up or upside down. I couldn't see the instruments. I didn't even know if the lights were on or off. So I keyed the mike to try to tell my crewman [Dale Doss] to get out, but I couldn't talk. He got the message soon after, 'cause *I* went out.

Rowan: You couldn't talk? You were in a state of shock?

Shuman: You'd better believe it. I wasn't capable of flying the machine. I don't know whether the machine was capable of flying me or not. I don't know how badly we were damaged, I just don't know. I went out, took one somersault, took a couple of small swings on the 'chute, and hit the ground. I landed right in the middle of a soft, plowed field. I could have landed standing up, except that I had the seat pack on, and I fell back down on my butt.

It was a "no sweat " landing; it wasn't too hard. But I'd broken my shoulder getting out and had some cuts on my hands, because I went through the canopy. Other than the broken shoulder, which was giving me a considerable amount of pain, I was in pretty good shape. I could walk and run pretty good. So I landed in that field and nobody was around. It was, of course, dark, but I was right close to Hanoi and it was very flat.

I looked around and in the bright moonlight I couldn't see anything to hide behind. I took off the 'chute and I did look over and see one group of trees, maybe two or three or four trees. I started running down this paddy dyke toward those trees. Just as I got there, there were a couple of houses, built underneath those trees, and a couple of dogs started barking, so I started running back in the other direction. Then, I saw a big hole in the ground. It looked like a bomb hole or something, and I jumped in that. I tried to collect my thoughts. I didn't have many thoughts.

Rowan: What *were* you thinking?

Shuman: I guess I was thinking that I was in deep trouble. I can't remember exactly what I was thinking, but it wasn't happy. I knew I was had. There was no way of being rescued. They don't send anybody to rescue you when you're that close to Hanoi. There was no way, and I just wondered how and when they were going to get me.

I hid out down there for a while. I was hurting pretty badly and I had a survival kit with me and I had some morphine in there, so I said, "What the hell, they're going to take it away from me pretty soon, so I may as well ease the pain." So I took a shot. Felt pretty good. Then I heard them coming, after about a half hour. They were all around me, but they never did see me down there. I just kind of ducked my head down. They were going all around and jabbering and hollering.

All this time, I had two survival radios, and I'm alternating from one to the other, transmitting "in the blind," saying what had happened, and I'm still trying to contact my crewman. I never heard anything and, to my knowledge, no one ever heard me.

Voices started getting closer and closer, and I said, "Well, I'm going to be had." So I took *another* shot of morphine.

By now, I'm not feeling too bad. I'm quite lethargic, as a matter of fact. I knew they were going to get me. I had two guns with me. One of them I had in my armpit, a little .25 caliber Beretta. I thought, if they find that, they're really going to give it to me. So I got rid of that. Buried it. I had my .38, and I kind of put that off to the side, close enough so I could grab it if I had to, but far enough away where it looked like I wasn't going to go and get it.

About five, five-thirty in the morning, just before it started to get light, they found me . . . about four what I would call militia types. They weren't in uniform, but they all had rifles. They came and they picked me up, took all my clothes off me, except my underwear, and tied me up. I pointed to my broken shoulder, indicating it was kind of hurting, and, to my great surprise, they showed a little compassion. They didn't tie me up very tight, particularly on the right arm.

They didn't rough me up at all. I mean they weren't tender, but they weren't nearly as bad as I thought they'd be. They started marching me down a paddy dyke, and a crowd—I can't imagine where all those people came from, because I didn't see any houses, except for the couple in the trees— but, boy there were just all kinds of people around by then. They were throwing rocks and sticks, and smashing me. But these guys were doing their best to keep them away.

They took me, we walked away, and there was a little, very low-ceilinged, one-room school house that I had not seen coming in. They put me in and locked me in with yet another militia man. I indicated I was thirsty, and they gave me a drink of water, which was the last one I was going to get for a long time. I stayed there for about 20 minutes and they opened the front door of the school, and in the school yard, there must have been *a thousand* of them out there, women and kids and old people, just jabbering, all of them jabbering like hell. I thought, "This is it, they're just drawing a crowd, and they're going to take me out and shoot me."

They marched me up to this paddy dyke and I thought, "This is where they're going to execute me, and it's all over now." But, I got up on top of the paddy dyke and looked down and there was a jeep coming down the road. They turned me over to a couple of guys in uniform, with guns, and then they threw me in the back of that jeep.

They were not too tender. They were pretty rough, smacked me around a little bit, threw me back there, blind-folded me. We drove for about five minutes and the next thing I knew, another body landed on top of me. It was Doss. They had stopped, and picked him up.

Rowan: Could you talk to each other at that point?

Shuman: Yes. I said, "How are you doing?" He said, "I've got a broken arm." And I said, "I do too." And they smacked us. I said, "Sorry about that Dale," And he said, "That's okay," and they started smacking us around again, in-dicating we shouldn't talk to each other. We didn't say much more; there wasn't much more to say. We drove, and it didn't take long before we were in the Hanoi Hilton.

me because I was alone. So, the next time I went out to wash, they said, "Are you by yourself?" I said, "No." So they started talking. They gave me the code. I gave them my name, my ship, and a little news about the world. After about a minute we got caught.

They knew better than I, because I was a novice at the game. They knew we had to have two people to clear [one to watch and listen for the guards]. Well, I wasn't clearing. But I lied to them and told them I was with somebody, to get them to talk to me.

They were taken out for interrogation. So was I. I was asked to write down what we were talking about, and I told them I thought I heard a Vietnamese next door and I was trying to ask a question about the wash area. I got off scot free, but they didn't.

I found out about three-and-a-half years later what had happened.

I'd given them my name, but I'd not gotten their names. One of them sent a note to my cell years later, when things had eased up. His name was Ensign Ralph Gaither. He said: "You owe me a steak dinner, because I spent 17 days in irons for giving you the code."

Rowan: At least you had communications.

McDaniel: Yes, I took that code and I went back to the room that afternoon and I was using it, and, in the process of using it, I got caught again. I was tapping on the wall very loudly, and I kept getting these loud thumps on the other end. Well, I thought they were "Rogering," but it was a danger signal. I was later to learn that every time there's danger you hit the wall very hard.

I kept beating away on the wall. I gave my name, my ship, and I just continued right on through, with my BN, and that I'd been severly tortured. And I kept getting these thumps.

About this time, a guard stuck his head in the peep hole. He apparently heard me out in the courtyard, beating the wall. That afternoon I went back out for interrogation again, and this time I was only there for about six hours. I was put on my knees, but not tortured. I was given a couple of severe

Rowan: What happened to all of you, when you got to the prison?

Shuman: That's where the fun started.

Rowan: The initial interrogation—what was it like?

Coskey: Mine was a little different, I think. I had my initial interrogation down [in the Panhandle area] where I was captured. I got what I expected. I pulled the name, rank, serial number, date of birth type of thing.

They had me in a quonset hut off the side of the road. They had let me sleep for a couple of hours. I guess they were digging up an English speaker. Finally, they got one and he was as bad as any I've ever heard. He just was terrible. He could just *barely* make himself understood. He asked me questions, like who was the commanding officer of the ship. I said I was only allowed to give name, rank, serial number.

I knew it was going to happen, because there were two guys standing on both sides of me, and pretty soon, *wham*, a fist or something. Then, he'd ask again, and then they'd hit me again. Then, they brought out a club, and hit me with that on the back of the head, and again on the back of the head.

I was sitting on a stool. I still wasn't in any real pain. I didn't know how far they were going to go, this was the thing that bothered me. How far were they going to take this thing? I was holding my arm all this time, and they took my arms and put them behind me and tied them. Of course, my elbow was broken, and they started pulling up, pulling up, jerking up. I could feel the bones back there, getting all screwed up. Finally, I said, "Okay, okay, okay, I'm off the Constellation." Then, I gave him a bunch of phoney names and that's all he wanted, that's all he wanted.

He wanted the name of the operation officer, the commanding officer, the CAG [Commander of the Air Group]. I told him I was an administrative officer, attached to the ship, not operational. I didn't know anything. The English was so bad, I don't think he understood what I was saying, but he did write down the names. He made me spell each name I gave him. I got on an Irish name kick, so I thought maybe I'd have to remember them later, but I never did. After about a half hour of this, of just trying to get names over to him—he'd write them all down, that's all he wanted—that was the end of it. Then, they let me go back to sleep again, and gave me some water. I got other interrogations later on in a man's house. I lived with him for six days. During this time, three interrogators came in from Hanoi, and worked me over for about three days—military questions. I got some beatings, knees, bricks under the knees, trying to get me to give them better answers than what I was giving. That was about it. They didn't get a hell of a lot out of me. You couldn't get away with saying nothing. They were going to make you talk.

Rowan: Did you have the feeling you could tell them almost anything?

Coskey: Well, not these guys. The first guy, yes, but these guys were a little better than that. I couldn't get away with a bunch of crap. They had my helmet, with CO [commanding officer] written right on it, and *U.S.S. America.* The cat was out of the bag as far as that was concerned. But, *yeah,* I could tell them things that were just inconsequential.

After I stayed there six days, they moved me on up to Hanoi, where I went into solo.

Rowan: Were you in communication with the other guys, as soon as you got inside?

Coskey: I was lucky. I was in *instant* communication. The first day I was in the bath stall, I got my name into the system. I was given the information that "they're pretty much on the soft sell now. They've pretty much stopped the torturing." Wes Schierman gave me the "Back US," which was a code that the prisoners were using at this time—guide lines, as to how to behave, which was very helpful. Then I got a map. They threw me a map. All this was very dangerous, I realized, and I destroyed it after I looked at it. But I got a map of the whole area where we were living, which was very invaluable. And the most important thing, I got the tap code. Once I had that, I was in the system—in communication.

Rowan: What did you want to know? What was it important for you to find out?

McDaniel: What was coming next. I'd just gone through many days of torture, ropes, beatings, leg irons, wrist irons. And I'd lost the use of my hands and my leg. You're wondering if you can take it again. You wonder what's coming next. So it's so important to get to talk to people, to find out what their pattern is, what comes next, when's the next torture session coming. Because, in my particular case, I was going to take some kind of action. I don't know what that action was going to be. I never decided. But I was going to do something. If I was told I was going to go through the same thing I'd just experienced, I was going to do something. I had no idea what—probably commit suicide. I just never expected it to be like it was. It was damn brutal.

Rowan: That all happened during your initial interrogation?

McDaniel: I was interrogated by some professionals. They were very concerned because Hanoi was again being attacked for the first time in six months. They were concerned about what targets we were going to hit next. We didn't know any targets because we had a policy on the ship that only the skipper knew.

I went through the ropes four times in a two-and-a-half day period, and I remained in leg irons for the entire time . . . and wrist irons. I was blindfolded a lot of the time, and I was beaten. During the second day, I had to tell them something. I had to give them names. I gave them names of people who had been deceased, people who had gotten out of the Navy, false squadrons. I told them I was an EA-1F pilot. We had been flying A-6s in there at night so often, and we had been told to expect the worst if we got caught.

Rowan: Did they believe you?

McDaniel: They did, they believed it. They accepted it until the third day. Then, they walked in with my A-6 knee-board. A knee-board carries a list of all procedures; it's a checklist. They came in with this, and they apparently had recovered it from the crash sight. So they said, "This is yours." I said, "Yes, well I've flown that aircraft in the past, and I just happened to have that on me." Well, to this day

I'm not sure they know. I told them I'd flown an A-6, but my missions were all EA-1F, over the beach. They seemed to buy that.

They got off into other areas; they really weren't concerned with the type of aircraft. They wanted to know about the Walleye, which was a new missile we had. That was their main concern. We had a few pilots who were shot down around then, men who had been involved with that program, and they had disappeared. They were very concerned about the Walleye. About the Walleye, and targets in Hanoi. It was almost as if they were trying to protect their own ass. Not the country, but where *they* were. They never got into any other areas, just those two, and they were things I really didn't know.

Rowan: What can you do in a situation like that?

McDaniel: Finally, I had to make up a target. I knew Hanoi has a couple of rivers running by it, and it must have some bridges, so I told them we were going to bomb a bridge. I knew nothing about the bridges, the sizes or locations, but I said, "They are going to bomb the Hanoi bridge." He broke out a chart and he pointed to the long Doumer bridge, and he said, "This one?" and I said, "Yes."

He said, "When are you going to hit it?"

And I said, "Well, as soon as we can."

He said, "What kind of tactics are you going to use to get there."

I said, "We're going to come in direct."

He said, "Why don't you go this way, and make turns?"

I said, "Well, your flak is so good here, it doesn't make any difference. We'll just come in straight, the shortest route, because it doesn't make any difference where we go, you have guns there."

Shuman: (*With a laugh*) It was true wasn't it?

McDaniel: They seemed to accept this as a compliment, and they kind of backed off.

Still, at the time, I was in pretty bad shape. I'd lost the use of my hands. My hands were swollen quite badly. My right leg was swollen, and I had no use of my **right** foot. It was really kind of pathetic. I didn't have to write anything, because they had gone to the point where I couldn't write. I had no food, no water, no sleep. They had had me in what we called the Blue Room, which was not a normal torture room, for those three days. Then, they took me out of there and threw me into a shower stall, for about six or eight hours, tied my legs and hands, and I got to sleep for the first time in about four days.

I slept, and after eight hours they took me and put me solo in a room, and at this point I was trying to get in touch with people. I got one guy to "come up" [answer] very briefly. I just kept saying, "I'm a new prisoner. Are there any Americans here?" Finally, one guy "came up" and started to say something and he was caught, and he was placed in irons. I could hear him being put in irons.

I wasn't able to get anybody up for about seven days. I did see, on my wall, a block code, the alphabet, which we used as a tap code, missing the letter K. I knew it had some significance, but I didn't know how to use it.

Up to this point I had no medical treatment. I had a badly swollen knee, which was obvious, and a broken back. I had no use of my hands and the leg, and I had developed a heat rash and boils all over my body, and the boils had begun to get infected. They became concerned, so they decided to give me some medical treatment. They allowed me to wash for the first time, and they gave me a razor, but I wasn't able to use the razor because of my hands. They gave me at that time one change of clothing: one long sleeve shirt, one long trousers, one short trousers, one short shirt. The shorts I had on were so soiled because during the three days of torture I had lost control over my bowels and my kidneys, and I really just smelled like hell. In fact, when the guard came to the door, he'd take a handkerchief and put it over his nose because the stench was so bad. I was living with it so it didn't bother me at that point.

Rowan: How did you go about making contact?

McDaniel: The first couple of times I went to the shower, I could hear Americans next door, but they wouldn't talk to lectures. They kind of felt I was still a new guy, and a novice to the game, and I wasn't too dangerous.

Rowan: Ned, did you have just about the same experiences?

Shuman: I really didn't know what to expect. I kind of thought from my survival training that they may not torture me. I was kind of hopeful. But, in any event, I was not going to say any more than I had to. They got me in there at about six in the morning. They spent the next several hours with the most God-awful threats you could imagine.

I said, "I want medical attention, my arm is broken."

One of them said: "Good, we will cut it off."

When I didn't respond to that, they said: "We will just not fix it; no medical attention until you see the truth."

Then, they were going to kill me. That didn't seem to bother me. "We're not going to kill you. We're going to punish you."

They didn't use the word "torture." Usually, they used the word "beat." They liked that word better than punish.

Rowan: How long did that go on?

Shuman: They kept that up most of the day, threatening me. Then they went out for their lunch. They gave me a bunch of garbage to read about my position in the camp, and this explained that I was a criminal and I would be treated like a criminal. However, I would be allowed to enjoy the humane and lenient policy of the DRVN [Democratic Republic of Viet Nam] should I cooperate. Then, they showed me some statements written by other previously captured people, indicating that I probably should cooperate with them. I was to find out later how they got things like that. A bunch of garbage. A lot of it was mimeographed, and some of it was hand written.

Rowan: Did you believe that some people had voluntarily written the statements?

Shuman: I didn't think they did, but I wasn't positive. One of them, and I won't give any names here, was written by a very highly respected guy whom I'd heard of before.

Coskey: I know who you're talking about and I saw the

same thing.

Shuman: I just couldn't imagine he would do a thing like that. The handwriting was just a little bit shaky, and the wording was not too believable.

Coskey: There was one other thing that we faced at this time; that's that the voice over the radio was an American, reading this stuff. And this, coupled with those statements written by Americans, was disconcerting.

Shuman: In the afternoon, they started the same old thing with threats. I still gave name, rank and serial number. Then, a bunch of them came in, and they had some straps and some ropes, and a metal bar. I thought: "They're probably going to do something now."

A couple of them jumped me and they put me on the floor and they put this metal pipe in my mouth, and they had a line attached to it and they pulled that behind my head and tightened it down. It wasn't extremely painful, but I was wondering what they were going to do with it. I didn't know if it's supposed to break your jaw, or take your teeth out. As it turns out, I think it's to keep you from hollering—making too much noise. So then they put me down on the deck, and they put ropes around my arms, and tightened them, and pulled them up. This was the broken one, they started on that, and they had that thing coming right over my head. It was pretty bad. The morphine, unfortunately, had worn off, and that one was pretty bad. But, they seemed to be able to do what they wanted to it, because the bone was broken. Then, they stopped, after awhile, and they'd ask questions. I'd still give name, rank and serial number. And then they started on the other arm.

This went on for quite some time. It's very easy to exaggerate things like that. Pain comes fast. I have no idea how long it was before it felt like the arm was ripped right out of the socket. I thought they had taken it right off. Gosh, I was hoping they'd shoot me.

Rowan: You were actually wishing for death at that point?

Shuman: Oh yes. I was just hoping like hell somebody would shoot me, but of course they wouldn't. Once, I passed out. Another time, I pretended to pass out, and they relaxed a little bit. But, the minute they detected any sign of life, I was right back in it again. These guys were not really sophisticated interrogators, but they weren't real dummies either. The one in charge, The Bug, was a fairly good English speaker, but he was a cruel son of a bitch, and he'd done this many, many times before. Finally, I said: "Okay, what do you want to know?"

Rowan: Did you have a cover story?

Shuman: No, I didn't, and that was one of the worst mistakes I ever made. In a two-place airplane you're really in trouble if you don't have one, because I'd give them an answer and they'd go check with Dale; then they'd come back and say: "That's not right," and bang me around. And I guess they were doing the same thing to Dale. We didn't have a cover story. I was kind of an optimist in a way. I never thought we'd get shot down. Anyway, it was pretty tough to give them lies. They wanted to know about future targets. They were very interested in what targets we were going to hit, in Hanoi, in particular. To tell the truth, although I was Exec [Executive Officer] of the squadron, I still didn't know exactly what targets were in the planning stages. All I knew is that we hit several targets there, and, with a certain amount of reluctance, I told them we're going to hit the same ones again. They bought that.

Pretty soon, I passed out. And the next thing I knew, I was on the floor in the Riviera section of Vegas, with a blanket over me. And *I'm some hurtin'*. They break me out about six the next morning, and I can't use my hands. I'm in bad shape. And they move me back, and they continue this for about four days. But I did not take any more heavy torture. After that, I came up with something when they asked me a question.

I was on a stool facing the interrogator, and another guy, Big Ugh was his name, was behind me, and they'd ask me a question, and if I was a little bit slow in coming up with an answer, the guy would . . . *WHOP* . . . hit me with his fist, and I'd go off onto the deck. They had to pick me up, 'cause I couldn't get up. They broke an ear drum doing that, but I usually came up with *some* answer.

After about four days of that, I guess they were satisfied that either they'd gotten all that I was going to tell them or all that I knew. They moved me into a regular cell, and gave me my issue of clothes like we all got. From then on, they interrogated me twice a day for the next two weeks and then it kind of slowed down a little bit, after that.

Rowan: Everyone says the important thing to do at that point was to get into communication with other POWs. Did you succeed in doing that?

Shuman: No, I didn't have any contact with any other POW for some time. I wasn't as adventurous as Red, and I didn't recognize the value of this. Nobody ever tried to contact me the whole time I was there, that I know of. After I'd been there about two weeks, I got a note in my slop bucket from my BN, Doss, and he was trying to find out if that was me over there. He wanted me to cough at a certain time if that was me, so I did. And the next day I got another big note from him, and he told me some of the stuff he had told them, to keep our stories straight. They wanted to know a lot about anti-radiation missiles, and we didn't tell them anything. We kind of skirted that. Another thing they wanted to know about was CBUs [cluster bomb units—a weapon considered particularly horrible because it is designed to kill people, not destroy targets] and napalm. They wanted to know how many churches and schools and stuff like that we'd hit; how many war crimes we'd committed. Of course we told them we'd never dropped CBUs or napalm, and we'd never bombed anything but bridges and military targets, which was, in essence, true. We were never assigned to bomb anything but those things, despite what some of the peaceniks might say. Everything we aimed at was a military target, to our way of thinking. Not that some of them didn't do some collateral damage, of course. We did carry CBUs on one occasion, but since they were so interested in those things, I didn't think we'd better tell them about that.

Doss and I started banging on the wall. We didn't know

the tap code, so we just started banging. I don't know, just for morale, I guess. And they heard us, and they moved him.

Rowan: You were out of touch for two weeks. How did you feel?

Shuman: I felt terrible. I've never been able to express it. I hadn't thought I was the toughest guy in the world, but I thought I was better than average, and I found that I wasn't. And it's a very, very bad feeling. I thought I was a coward and that I'd betrayed my country. I had lost all my self-respect, and I just felt like a worm.

Rowan: Did you do any thinking about home?

Shuman: That's all I thought about, how ashamed they would have been if they had seen me; and wondering how much more I should have taken.

Rowan: Knowing that they've broken you once, what gives you the strength to go back and resist again?

Shuman: In my case, it took a long time before I could bounce back, because I didn't have contact with anybody for a long time. When I finally did get contact with somebody, and talked with somebody, I bounced back, just like that. But, as Ken was saying, you're listening to all this garbage on the radio, and there are voices in English—they're making these guys read these tapes. God, it's terrible stuff. And you're listening to all this all the time, and then you're going out to get interrogated by Gooks. And you say, "Gee, I'm trying to hold out. Am I doing the right thing?" You know you're doing right, and you've got to do your best, but there's always that little element of doubt there.

Coskey: If you're not in com, it's doubly tough. If you're in communications, every time you go to a quiz you come back and you tell what was on that quiz and what you said. So this, alone, is enough to give you the strength to do it right, because, if nothing else, you've got to go back and explain to your compatriots what went on in that quiz.

Rowan: How would you go about explaining what happened?

Coskey: Oh, you had a shorthand type of way to say, "It was a normal type of quiz, same old stuff, political, no pressure." Or, "They're asking for something. They're being hard-nosed," or whatever. You'd give them an idea of what the next guy could expect.

Rowan: What was their response, if you told them that you had agreed to sign a statement or to read something over their public address system?

Coskey: I should let someone else handle this because I was never forced to make a tape on the radio. I was never asked to make an amnesty statement. But I know that when this program was on, one of our Senior Ranking Officers ordered us to "take four days in irons before you read on the radio." There were rules, and the guys had to do it. Otherwise they would lose face.

McDaniel: Normally, when they went after these things, they were after the entire group, and if you were in communications, the "system" would support you, because you would be operating under ground rules laid down by your seniors. When you stood your ground, and didn't do it, if they still wanted it, they would remove you from the system, so you wouldn't have this support.

I was never asked to do any of these things either, make tapes or sign things, but I feel that if they had wanted me to do it, they would not have left me in the system, because I got strength from the system.

Rowan: Ned, when you finally got into the system, what happened to those guilt feelings?

Shuman: I spent 17 months in solitary the first time. Half that time I had no contact with anybody.

I was trying to resist as best I could, on my own. I never made any confessions or signed any amnesty statements or read any tapes on the radio. During this time, I wasn't tortured. However, I was always getting slapped around, and threatened and kicked in the ass. Your ears pulled. Degrading stuff. Nothing with real pain. Just enough to keep you right on edge, if you're already down.

They sent me to a church service at Christmas, the year after I was shot down, and I talked to a couple of guys out there, and from then on I was OK. I said, "I hear this stuff on the radio, I hear these confessions." And they said, "Don't listen to that crap. These guys are all being tortured to do it."

I just wanted to have somebody else confirm that what I thought was right was, *indeed*, right. And, from then on, I had no problem at all. I went back and they told me the tap code and I was so excited I didn't get it right, so it took me some more months before I could do that, but I talked to a few guys, and everything was OK after that.

Rowan: What happens to time when you're in solo?

Shuman: I don't know, but it sure went fast. Each day was kind of slow, but hell, when you look back it was gone in no time.

Coskey: The days pass slow, but the years pass quickly.

Shuman: That's what we used to say. I can't imagine what a guy does sitting in his room. Why, hell, some guys were there for years. I don't think 17 months are any big deal.

Rowan: Ken, you're disagreeing. What did time seem like for you?

Coskey: Time . . . that just drove me crazy . . . time. There was a period from after the evening meal about 4 o'clock, until we went to bed, which was about 9 o'clock, they didn't allow you to lie down. You had to sit up or walk. This was the longest part of every day. It was an *eternity*—to try to kill this six hours. Nothing happened. You just sat there. And this went on day after day, week after week and it never got better for me.

Rowan: What did you do with your mind?

Coskey: I relived my life a hundred times, with a lot of regrets, a lot of mistakes. For some reason, I would dwell on the mistakes that I had made instead of the things that I had accomplished. And, I would kick myself for things I had done, *even when I was 10 years old,* and go over this again and again. I eventually got to like to do interest problems. So I got to thinking, "My gosh, if my wife saves umpty-ump amount every month, let's see how that would build up." And I'd compute the interest and use a straw [to keep track] and this took a lot, a *lot* of time to detail. Communications with other prisoners also took a lot of time.

Rowan: You wanted to keep your mind active, I take it?

Coskey: Sometimes you just couldn't.

Shuman: You looked forward to things. The evening "radio" programs. It was a lot of propaganda and a lot of garbage but you looked forward to it because it was a change and right after that you could go to bed. It all seems ridiculous now, but, then it was important.

Rowan: I think the interesting thing is what happens to a man's mind in this environment.

Shuman: Like I said, I wasn't anxious to get a roommate, although sometimes I was, sometimes I prayed for someone to talk to. Other times I thought: What would it be like to have a bowel movement in front of another guy, right there in this same room? Well, this is hilarious. We used to have bowel movements in front of each other playing bridge and eating lunch. (*Laughter*) These are the kind of things you thought about.

Rowan: What happened to your sex drive? Did sex remain a matter of some concern to any of you while you were there?

Coskey: It does for a period of months after you're shot down and then you completely suppress it. You have an occasional wet dream, maybe every two months, but you learn to completely forget about it and then you realize at some point that you've got to do something about it. You've got to keep this alive too. I believe, personally, that you've got to exercise every part of the body, mentally and physically, and you've got to start thinking in this vein. Then, when you're coming home, you have to get in the right mental state. Sex is never a big thing up there, though. You learn to suppress it, keep it in the background, except enough to keep it alive, I think.

Rowan: I heard that in some of the other camps, medics recommended that guys masturbate once a month.

Shuman: We didn't have anyone to make that recommendation. I can state from my own personal experience that I hardly ever thought about it the first couple of years. I was interested in food, and I was wondering when they were going to pound me next. That's all I thought about except when I day-dreamed about my boat. Sex . . . it used to be a big part of my life . . . *I thought* . . . but I realized how insignificant it can be.

McDaniel: You almost suppress it completely. It's not a big factor at all because it's such a desperate situation, the sex drive is . . .

Shuman: You need a little stimulation. The most stimulating thing that I can remember back in those days of solo was Ponytail, the little cook that used to swing by, and she wasn't too bad looking. That was the only stimulation you got. There wasn't anything else.

Later on, when we were living together for a while, guys would have a wet dream, get up the next morning, and laugh about it. One guy would kid the other guy and say: "You sure you didn't help that?"

Rowan: When you were discussing *everything* with each other, and I guess you reached a point where you discussed everything, would you discuss sex just as openly as you discussed other things?

McDaniel: Yes, I think so. I think *more* so. That *is* your sex life, the things you talk about. A few guys will tell sex stories occasionally, those that have them.

Rowan: It's interesting whether your *attitudes* towards sex change. Whether any of you can look back and think that perhaps you had a hang-up about masturbation, or a hang-up about wet dreams, or a hang-up about discussing sex with other people.

Shuman: I think sex was grossly over-rated as regards any of us. It's just something that almost isn't there.

McDaniel: It just doesn't exist.

Coskey: There are a couple of guys who lived together and they were discussing minute details of almost every sexual activity they had ever participated in with or without their wife for their whole life. And they enjoyed this. The group I was with, the three of us . . .

Shuman: The old guys.

Coskey: . . . we didn't talk about our extra-curricular activities.

Rowan: Did faith in God help you to stay OK?

Coskey: I was a semi-agnostic. I hardly ever attended church. But I have fallen on my knees, in the cell, and prayed to God, on several occasions, because of desperation, just sheer desperation, and the loneliness and fear of these interrogations. I asked to give me strength to resist them. *I really did.* I asked to take care of my family. I don't know who I was asking. I was asking God. I don't know the motivation. I had nobody else to talk to, nobody to turn to. And I guess, when you get to this point, you turn to God, or you turn to something.

Then, when we all got together, and things got easy, I forgot about it again. And Chuck Gillespie, who was our chaplain, would remind us about every other week. He'd say, "Look, remember how it was when things were tough. You should be thinking of God this same way now, when things are easy."

Rowan: Did your attitudes toward religion change?

Coskey: Yes, I have more respect for religion now. I am attending church now, and want my kids to go to church, because I want them to get a better education about Christ than I had. I wasn't converted into a religious person, no, but I have a deep regard for it now, and I know what it means when you're in trouble. I know what religion can do.

McDaniel: When I went to college, I met my wife, whose father was a Baptist minister. I became a Baptist right quick, and developed that through the years, out of respect for her, because I have great admiration for her father. I had always believed in God, and I was a *fair* Christian before I was shot down, even though I'd been pretty much of a "boomer" in every thing I do. I'll work hard, I'll play hard. I'll go to church hard.

When I went to Hanoi, the most available source of strength was God, because it's a pretty desperate situation.

Rowan: Was that a *real* source of strength?

McDaniel: Oh, yes. You start asking yourself, when you first get there, "Why me? Why am I here?" You think back, "Well, I've done so damn many things that are bad, perhaps I *should* be here." But then you look next door, and here's a guy who's never done a damn thing that's bad, and he's here. So you start saying, "Why was I spared? Why did I make it here?" My right-seater hasn't shown up, and a lot of other men were killed in combat, and a lot of other men were killed in operational accidents. So perhaps there's a reason for my being here.

I took this approach and developed that, and developed a lot of strength. I moved in with a young man [Bill Metzger] who was critically wounded. He had a broken leg, his arm was completely ripped open, he had a 10 inch gash in his leg about six or seven inches deep, a two pound piece of shrapnel in his leg, and they put him in a room to live or to die. He had been a real hell-raising guy, who prided himself that he couldn't cry. No God.

So we talked a little bit and decided that we had to have something. Your government's not there to help you right now. You've got to have faith in your government, but right there with you, you've got God, and through God you've got strength. So we started having church services, just the two of us. We got a third roommate and a fourth roommate and every Sunday we'd have a church service. It was not permitted by the VC, but we had it. And I said daily prayers. It developed into pretty much of a standard prayer. You pray for your family, and friends, relatives, your leaders, for our country, and that God will give our President strength to make the right decisions to bring the war to a speedy and honorable end. And to me it was a great source of strength.

Shuman: I was born and reared as a Catholic. I went to Episcopal school and I was confirmed as an Episcopalian, but I gave it up shortly after that. I've been agnostic most of my life. Then, I got over there and things got *pretty rough,* and I just couldn't handle it all by myself, so I reverted back to my old ways. And I was kind of ashamed of that, too, because I had *wanted* to be an agnostic. I thought, "Well, what a hypocrite you are." It was very hard for me, because I really didn't believe it, but I prayed it anyway. When things got rough, I really prayed hard. I don't know why, because, when I thought about it, I still didn't believe it, but I prayed anyway. I'd pray for strength, to be able to hold out against those guys, more than anything else, and for my family, of course.

I can't analyze it. I know that I don't believe in the mechanics of the religion any more now than I did before, but I just had to have something to lean on. I couldn't do it by myself.

Rowan: Some guys were wounded so badly nothing helped them. How did you feel when somebody close to you died?

McDaniel: You become very callous to situations involving a roommate. You live with him for month after month. You see his injuries. You see his wounds drain. The blowflies get in. The maggots go to work. You become callous to it.

Most men are very stoic, they don't complain. But, they have to complain sometimes, and you listen to this. You listen to it, but you kind of let it go. You really don't have enough strength to sympathize wth him. But you accept it, and you try to help him in whatever small way you can, and try to keep him clean. You become very callous to death and injuries because you see so much of it.

Rowan: Did you ever think, "I just can't hack it anymore?"

McDaniel: No. I always felt I had a little left. I know that at times I would have accepted death. It was the easy way out, and I would have preferred death to the pain. Many times during torture, I would try to transfer the pain from one place to another, biting myself. I really don't think I ever gave up. I would have accepted death, yes, and I looked for ways to take my life, if I had to, but only if I had to. But, I always felt that I had a little bit left.

Rowan: Ned, did you think about making that decision?

Coskey: I can remember one time, sitting in one of the cells when I first got there, after several weeks, and these were the really tough times of getting adjusted to this thing. I looked at the light bulb and I thought, "If I stood in water and shoved my thumb up that thing, I could probably commit suicide, if I wanted to." But I never had any desire to. I had a feeling I was going to make it. Once I got to Hanoi, and was in that prison, I had a feeling I was going to make it home.

Rowan: That brings up the question of—what did you call them—the gastro-politicians?

Shuman: In survival school, they always told us, "Watch the food, because that's a sure indicator." Well, in general, I think it is. When good things were happening for *them*, I think *we* ate a little better. Now, we couldn't translate this to going home tomorrow. But, at the time, things were looking good.

"We had peanut candy today. It can't be long now." That's what we'd say. We said that for the whole time I was there.

McDaniel: I thought the food was geared to the international situation. If things were going good for them, as Ned said, the food would improve. Of course, there it's a hand-to-mouth operation. You get what they grow.

Coskey: Well, I'm in disagreement. When I was solo, I used to agree with this. But, when we got together, Carl Crumpler and Byron Fuller and I, we had many many hours of talking about this, and we decided that the kitchen did not know what was going on in Paris.

We "rang in" on the spring of 1973, sometime back around 1970 or 1971, with no knowledge, other than the fact that President Nixon was in office. We knew he was a hard Communist-fighter and always had been. We felt that that guy was going to stay tough with these people, all the way. Carl, who was a Democrat, kind of wanted a change. He emphasized the fact that as long as President Nixon was in office it didn't look as if we were going to go anywhere. And it kind of looked as if this was an obvious way to think. So we rang in on the spring of '73, thinking that perhaps there would be a change of administration.

Rowan: What do you think about the war, now?

McDaniel: I believe that it will prove to be one of our best wars. I think it was long, costly, and very difficult, but I think the ARVN [Army of the Republic of (South) Viet Nam] needed time to strengthen itself. I think the division in our country prolonged the war. At the same time, it gave the ARVN time to strengthen. Now, they are strong enough to defend themselves and strong enough to maintain the stability in Indo-China that is necessary, so I think it has been a good war, and will prove to be one of our best wars.

Rowan: What was your reaction to those whose minds *were* changed? Did you lose respect for men like Navy Captain Gene Wilber, for example, who takes the position that America was wrong, and that we shouldn't have been there?

Coskey: I always sincerely felt that he's entitled to his viewpoint. But I did feel he's in the wrong business. I expected him, when he did get out, to get into some other business.

McDaniel: I feel the same way. I think it's his decision to make, and we had people in the U.S. who made that same decision. But, I find it strange that a man would make that decision just after he's captured. I hope some of the men were not being opportunists. But, if they really believed it, I have respect for them for saying so.

Shuman: I don't have any respect for him at all, because I figure that he's there getting paid *not* to say that kind of crap. I have absolutely no respect for him *whatsoever*. If he wants to be a minister, let him be a minister, and stay home. If he wants to turn all his pay back that he got for the time he was in there, he can do that.

Rowan: I was wondering what living in such close confines, sometimes 40 to a room, does to your tolerance toward each other.

McDaniel: If you're in a room with 40 people, you're gonna go with the wave. You're gonna think alike. That's the way we were. We didn't have any weak ones. If they were *weak* ones, they became *strong* ones.

Rowan: What about your personal reaction to people. Do you find yourself getting bugged by a guy because he always picks his nose? What do you do with that kind of a feeling? (*Laughter*)

Coskey: You look at yourself for one thing. You say: "He picks his nose, but maybe I scratch my ass." You learn tolerance. You learn a *lot* of tolerance.

Shuman: (Kiddingly) Being a Polack from Detroit, you did all those things. *(Laughter)*

Rowan: Did you learn to like each other?

Coskey: We learned to *love* each other.

Shuman: You do. Literally. There are little conflicts, you know . . .

McDaniel: You have problems. Really. The amazing part is that you live with a guy so long and you can get so mad at him that you just *hate his guts.* But, you leave him for two nights and you miss him. In fact, I know guys who lived together for 46 months and they separated and a couple nights later a message came through: "I miss you." I respect every guy I ever lived with up there and I've been so damn mad with some . . . I've developed a lot of dislike for their personal habits but I find that when you separate, you forget those small things.

6

A Prisoner from the Zoo

Navy Captain Walter Eugene Wilber was out to kill a Mig when he was shot down on Father's Day in June of 1968.

On the face of it, Gene Wilber, at the age of 38, was perhaps the last man you would have suspected of harboring anti-war sympathies. He had enlisted in the Navy 20 years before, an eager 18-year-old who wanted to fly. He had been commissioned an officer before his 21st birthday. He had served as an A-1 pilot over Korea at the end of the war there. He had risen to the rank of Commander and had been given a fighter-bomber squadron, equipped with the newest model of the Navy's hottest plane: the F-4J, flying off the aircraft carrier *U.S.S. America.*

His mission that day, in 1968, was to fly inland just south of the 19th parallel, the northernmost point for American fighter bombers in those days, and to look for North Vietnamese Mig jet fighters. If he found any, he was to intercept them, and shoot them down. A Mig was there to meet him as he flew over the beach that Sunday afternoon.

But there's another Gene Wilber, known to only a few. He's a soft-spoken man who married his childhood sweetheart and kept her radiantly happy over the years as their children grew up; he's a man from the quiet hill country of north-central Pennsylvania—an area almost as far from the everyday life of most Naval officers as it is from the sea; he's a man of peace and a deep faith in God.

What was he doing trying to shoot down a North Vietnamese Mig? That's what Gene Wilber was wondering about that Sunday.

I talked with him at the beautiful country home he and his wife, Jean, bought near the tiny community of Columbia Crossroads, Pennsylvania, just before he went to Viet Nam.

In one of his early letters from North Viet Nam, Gene told his wife to sell their home in Virginia Beach, Virginia, where they were surrounded by Navy families, and move to their country home to be near his parents and hers. Jean had no way of knowing it then, but the move actually represented her husband's resignation from the Navy.

He had made up his mind shortly after being shot down that America's involvement in the war in Viet Nam was illegal and immoral. At that point in time he had done what only one or two other officers did voluntarily—writing statements urging that the United States get out of the war.

Upon his return to this country, he was not given what other men received: an extensive debriefing that usually took several days and covered every aspect of each man's period of captivity. The Navy's apparent unwillingness to listen to *his* story seemed ominous, and Gene Wilber was prepared for the worst.

As we chatted, Jean baked a coffee cake and made a pot of coffee for us. Gene appeared sincere about his anti-war beliefs, but nervous about what his opposition to U.S. participation in the fighting would mean to his future. He was not yet ready to announce his resignation from the Navy, but it seemed certain that he would have to take that step.

Like anti-war activists in the United States, Gene Wilber thought the torture stories of some of his fellow POWs were overstatements. He believed there had been little or no torture after 1967. He also thought that many of the "horror stories" the POWs told each other after coming back from "quizzes" with the North Vietnamese interrogators were less than truthful. In his view, most of the men were asked nothing more than how they were sleeping, whether they had any medical problems, or what they thought of the food.

It seemed to me that Gene held back from telling me all that he knew. He answered a number of my questions by saying that he couldn't recall the specifics. I found that surprising, in view of the fact that all the others to whom I had spoken were able to tell me about their experiences in great detail. But, I accepted his position, realizing that he had no desire to tell me things that might later be used to support charges against him.

One thing he remembered vividly was what happened that Father's Day in 1968, when his plane was shot down.

Wilber: We went through some flak, a barrage of flak, as soon as we crossed the beach. It bounced the airplane around pretty heavily.

Nothing seemed to happen to the airplane. We kept on going. And Bernie, my RIO [radar intercept officer] and I were talking. We had the Mig on the radar and we were trying to get clearance to intercept it and to launch our Sparrow missiles. It was a pretty busy time and we were talking constantly with each other.

Suddenly, we lost our oxygen system. Then, we lost our inter-communication system. Then, the throttles were sticking and I couldn't move them. Everything on the left side of the airplane started going bad. Then, some fire lights started coming on.

In a jet airplane loaded with 10,000 pounds of fuel you worry a little bit about fire.

Anyway, we rapidly lost control of the airplane—within a minute. We were way inland. I could see a spot over there called a "safe area"—a hilly spot—and we were trying to get there with the idea that we could eject and get picked up by helicopter.

Rowan: You were out of contact with the man in the back seat. Did you signal him to get out?

Wilber: At the last moment, I gave him the signal to get out. He could see me through a little hole between the cockpits. I could see him in my mirror. When he didn't get out, I initiated the ejection myself. At this time, the airplane had just about given up the ghost.

The way it was supposed to work if I initiated the ejection was that my canopy would go; his canopy would go; his seat would go; then my seat would go.

But nothing happened. I used the alternate system. Nothing happened. Then I tried to jettison the canopy. Nothing happened. Then I tried to open the canopy. Nothing happened. By this time the airplane was out of control—completely out of control. I wasn't flying it any more, because there wasn't anything left to fly. It was just falling, and I saw the ground coming up rapidly.

I knew I was going to die.

I thought, "There's no use of dying all cramped up." I just kept moving handles, and then there was just one left to go. The "canopy unlock" handle was the last one we normally would use. So I unlocked the canopy, and, surprisingly, it came off.

Then, I pulled the face curtain again, and my seat left the airplane. One-and-three-quarter seconds later the parachute opens, and at that time I heard the airplane crash. So I was pretty low.

My backseater was still in the airplane, and being so low I'm sure that he just didn't get his canopy off and he was killed in the airplane.

I looked down at the ground and saw I was going to land in a rice paddy. I saw some people coming toward me. And I looked back up and then I hit the ground. So, I was in the parachute a very short period of time.

Rowan: Before we continue with this, let's pinpoint your attitude toward the war in those busy days before you got shot down.

Wilber: The biggest question in my mind before going to Viet Nam was the question of why we did not declare war. It seemed to me that we had advanced so much as a civilization, in domestic law and international law, that we had an obligation to do things according to law.

But, I went to Viet Nam as a volunteer, so to speak. I certainly didn't want to get out of it. I didn't want to have that stigma attached to my career. I felt I had an obligation to my country, and to the Navy, to serve it well. I like the Navy. And I love my country.

I rationalized the whole thing. We had a lot of troops in South Viet Nam, and what I was doing as a fighter-bomber pilot was trying to stop supplies from going from North Viet Nam to South Viet Nam which sounds very logical in a narrow scope. It sounds very logical that if we have American troops there, I should do my best to help protect American troops. And that's as far as it went with me.

Rowan: How long was it after you hit the ground before you were captured?

Wilber: Just a minute or two.

I had a chance to unhook my parachute and move about 15 feet to a little clump of grass on a teeny hill behind a small tree, and I was going to hide there and make some radio transmissions. Well, it was ridiculous to try to do it, but I did move there and made a couple of transmissions.

Then, a guy got my attention by hitting me over the shoulder with a carriage bolt. Then, they were all around me, taking off my clothes and tying me up.

Rowan: From that moment of capture, when you were down in the Panhandle, how long did it take to get to Hanoi?

Wilber: It took nine days. Moving over to Highway One took about seven days, and then I spent two days in a truck.

At first we just walked a little way every night to different houses. I was taken out of the various houses several times, and there'd be crowds of people outside, saying whatever they were saying in Vietnamese. A few people would shake their fists and make other gestures, but nobody really hurt me.

Rowan: What was your reaction to meeting the Vietnamese for the first time that way, seeing that hostility?

Wilber: At the time, it was a rather traumatic experience, the whole thing. Being shot down. Being rather close to death. Having my partner in the airplane killed. And finding myself completely controlled by ropes and by some people who didn't speak my language at all.

But, I think that they did exhibit a remarkable amount of

discipline. I think they hated me. They wanted to hurt me, but they didn't.

They'd throw little clods of dirt, or take some little sticks and try to stick them through the building to hit my feet. But anyone who has been through an initiation into a club has probably had more physical maltreatment than I experienced.

We had been told that many bad things would happen. I was kind of waiting for those things to happen because I was prepared for whatever they were—if they had taken me to an execution point, or had me dig my own grave and then put me in it. I expected the worst.

But the guards tried to keep people away from me. And when we were traveling at night, if they saw anyone else coming down the path, they would hide me and let the other people pass. That showed me that there was a possibility that officially anyway they wanted me captured safely and they wanted to make sure that I didn't escape. They were very cautious about keeping the ropes tight and keeping armed guards around me. They were also trying to make sure that I was not harmed as I was moved from place to place.

Rowan: What happened when you got to the Hilton?

Wilber: I was told that I would die there; that I would never go home. It didn't scare me because I knew that the government would never abandon the prisoners, me or anybody else. I knew that when the war was over, I would go home.

Rowan: Tell me about your physical condition the day you arrived in Hanoi. What were your reactions?

Wilber: There were two of us, an Air Force Major and myself, who came up in the truck. The day we arrived in Hanoi—it was early in the morning—I noticed that I was dizzy in the truck. To me it was a rather pleasant experience. It was like vertigo. To me it felt like I was doing maneuvers in an airplane. But, anyway, when we got there and they said to get out, I stood up and fell right back down again. I would try to get up and would fall down. Of course, I was blindfolded, which would have some bearing.

Then, they apparently carried me into the prison camp blindfolded. And, when I got into the room, I couldn't stand up in the room either. In fact, when I sat down on a little stool, a little bench, I would fall off the bench. And this started to worry me, to say the least. So, I sat in the corner to try and take stock of myself, and I found out that the left side of my face . . . all the muscles in my face . . . were paralyzed. And, the right side of my body had no feel as far as skin sensation. Pressure and temperature just didn't register on my skin on the right side of my body. All the muscles worked OK, and I seemed to be able to do everything except eat, drink, wink my eye or move any of the muscles in my face.

Rowan: Do you think it was a stroke of some kind?

Wilber: I think it was a stroke caused from a lack of water. It was the summertime and I perspire heavily anyhow. And just before I was shot down the whole air wing had had diarrhea, so we were debilitated from a lack of water. So, when I was shot down, I was probably weak from that. I think I just ran out of water.

Rowan: Did they take you immediately into interrogation that same day?

Wilber: No . . . I think it was the next day. And here again these things are a little bit hazy to me. I have not been debriefed by the Navy so I haven't had to recall them for anybody. I remember the camp commander say that he would have the doctor look at me. And the doctor did come in . . . I think it was within a few hours. He took my blood pressure with a regular standard blood pressure cup. Took my pulse. Listened to my heart and lungs . . . Then they started giving me injections each day which I think were just plain vitamin injections.

Rowan: What was your first interrogation like?

Wilber: Well, there was some discussion of what questions I would have to answer. They said I would have to answer *all* the questions they asked.

I was able to reverse some of this stuff by saying: "You don't want me to betray my country. If you ask me a military question, I will have to deny answering it." And this was bought.

In 1968, at least, I was able to get away with it. Now, maybe earlier you couldn't do it. I don't know.

Rowan: Can you give me an example of how that would work on a particular question?

Wilber: You have to decide whether a question is in the area of being classified or not.

Rowan: Suppose they asked you what type of airplane you were flying?

Wilber: Now that information *to me* is not classified. There are a lot of questions which are not name, rank, service number, date of birth which have nothing to do with military information. [For example], "What squadron are you in?" It's written right on the side of my airplane. It's ridiculous to take any lumps because they ask you what squadron you're from. But, if they ask you: "How many miles range does your radar have on it?" This is military information. You just don't answer the question. Now, if they'll accept this, that's fine. If they will not accept this, you can do what other people did, and that's lie about the answer. And, with the language barrier, you can get away with that too.

Rowan: Did they ask you the range of your F-4J radar?

Wilber: The only time they asked me was about two years later and I said I don't know what it is. The questions about military information is one of the big points we have to worry about.

Rowan: Did they ask you about targets?

Wilber: I happened to be on an intercept mission so the question didn't apply to me.

Rowan: Do you remember having any mental struggle in your initial interrogation after they had asked the four approved questions: name, rank, serial number and date of birth? What happened when they got to the fifth and sixth questions? What was the internal dialogue going on inside of you?

Wilber: I don't recall. (*Pause*)

Everybody knows that it's just a matter of time before

somebody says more than the four things.

I think we all rationalized that the answer to the fifth question was something that doesn't really matter anyway. And we'd wait for the sixth question, and if it didn't matter we'd answer it.

In most cases, there comes a time when you have to refuse to answer. And then this puts the enemy—the interrogator—in the position of deciding what he wants to do.

There *are* ways of getting information out of people. We all know this is true. They can physically torture you, or mentally torture you, or put you in positions of degradation, or duress, or withhold medical treatment. There are a lot of ways to make people decide to answer.

Rowan: Did you give them more than the four approved answers?

Wilber: You couldn't say I followed the Code of Conduct literally, but I did not reveal any national security information.

I was able to control the questions by saying, "You (the interrogator) do not want me to betray my country, do you?" This puts him on the spot. [The interrogator], being an official representative of the DRVN [Democratic Republic of (North) Viet Nam], then has to follow the official policy. It puts him in an official capacity, not as just another person, or a Gook. It gives him some kind of status. You have a status and he has a status.

It puts him in the position of making a decision. And he decides it's not worth it to ask a man to betray national security information which they probably know anyway. It worked for me in 1968.

Rowan: So you were not tortured.

Wilber: No.

Rowan: How long after that was it before you got in contact with other Americans?

Wilber: About 20 months.

Rowan: In that period of isolation, did you suffer the deep depression some of the other men have described—the result of providing more information to the enemy than they believed they should have and the result of just being out of contact with other Americans for so long.

Wilber: No. I don't think you could say that I was deeply depressed, any more than average. I tried to look at things objectively. It's quite hard living alone. I asked myself where I came from, why I was here, what do I intend to do about myself, where am I going. And I found myself very busy thinking through my whole life. And I didn't find myself being sorry for *me.*

I found myself being sorry for my fellow Americans in prison with me, and I found myself being sorry for the military men who were not yet captured because they were in a position where, if they fell into this, they were going to experience the same thing.

Then, I got back to the old question of why we were in Viet Nam. I tried to find some Constitutional basis for it. And the question I had in mind before I went to Viet Nam was a hard one to answer.

Rowan: How quickly did you come up with your negative answer to that question?

Wilber: I can't really tell you whether it was after one week or six months. The decision made represented such a change in my actions, that I've really had to evaluate it every day òf my life since then. (*Spoken slowly, with thought*)

Rowan: What was the decision?

Wilber: I told myself that I had been supporting the Viet Nam War, and I can't find any basis for it. Therefore, I'm going to support the best way for us to disengage ourselves from Viet Nam. I'm going to use my energy to do that.

I could find no legal basis for our involvement in the war. It seemed to me as a Naval officer that it was my duty to report the problem to my superiors. It was my duty as a citizen to report the problem to the country.

Rowan: Were you being subjected to propaganda?

Wilber: Oh, yes. We had little radio speakers in each room, connected to an amplifier system which could play tape recordings. We had a news broadcast every day.

We also had a limited amount of reading material. Most

all of it concerned the war in Viet Nam. A lot of it was history written by the Vietnamese. A lot of it was anti-war literature written in America. Some of it was official State Department information. If it pertained to giving the *other* side of the story, we would get it. We had almost zero amount of information which would be considered pro-U.S. policy in Viet Nam.

Rowan: Do you think your decision was influenced to some degree or another by the fact that you got only one side of the story for those many months?

Wilber: Well, that's hard to say. I'd *like* to say it was not influenced by propaganda. I would *like* to be able to say that I decided the war was illegal and wrong and I decided to do something about it, myself.

But, I'm sure I was influenced by a lot of things.

I've tried to find information back here that would balance what I learned over there, but I have yet to find enough that would tend to topple it.

The thing that *I* was asking for was a negotiated political solution and a safe military withdrawal from Viet Nam. This is what we got in 1973. This is what I was asking for, and what many people were asking for.

Rowan: Once you got in contact with other Americans, did you argue about this?

Wilber: Well, we talked about it a lot.

There are three subjects which Naval officers are told *not* to talk about in the wardroom: sex, politics and religion. And you know that the prisoners talked about everything, including those three subjects.

I did not have any arguments with anyone. Physical violence never occurred. However, we did talk with other people.

Rowan: Did you convert anyone to your views?

Wilber: I didn't try to convert anybody. I don't consider myself a convert either. I was discussing this with other prisoners to get their points of view, and if they got my point of view, that was fine. They could accept it or reject it. I didn't try to pressure anyone to accept what I had to say.

Wilber was not at all anxious to go into conversations or disputes that he had with other prisoners about the legality of the war.

Rowan: There were policies laid down by the senior ranking officers. For example, men were told they must take torture rather than give certain information. What was your reaction to that kind of direction from within the system?

Wilber: I had to look at that direction the way I'd look at any other military order. Each person has to look at it and decide whether the order is legal. A senior officer can't order me to rob a bank, for instance. I know robbing a bank is illegal. Strict authoritarianism, which goes on in the military, we just can't buy. "Forward march right over the wall" sounds great in text books. But, when it comes time to applying these things in real life, you have to listen to what you're told and try to apply it to the legal and moral situation you're in.

Because I'm a military officer doesn't reduce my citizenship rights a bit; in fact it just *emphasizes* them. Being in prison probably made me hyper-critical about anything I was told to do. But, I *do* believe the First Amendment—the right to free speech—applies wherever I am in the world.

So, if it came time for somebody to tell me not to write to my congressman, I would have to look at that differently than if someone says, "You must wear shoes," or, "You must report to me at eight o'clock in the morning."

Rowan: Were you told by the senior officers not to make statements or write letters?

Wilber: Yes . . . But I felt that the war was illegal, and if we were ever going to end the war, we were going to have to get more people to make that decision personally.

Rowan: Was there any pressure put on you after you took that position?

Wilber: No. The senior officers were very kind and very understanding, and they did not interfere. They acted very honorably toward me.

Rowan: Did the Vietnamese keep those of you who had mixed feelings about the war away from the older—in terms of POW status—guys who had strong pro-war feelings?

Wilber: I think so. I would say the people at the Zoo probably were those who at least were able to think in both directions.

Rowan: Do you feel that anything you did or said harmed anyone else?

Wilber: No American prisoner was ever harmed by what I did or said, and I'm *sure* that many of them were helped by my actions, because I spent most of my time trying to get more things for everyone.

Rowan: Do you feel *you* got any better treatment because you were doing and saying things that agreed to some extent with the North Vietnamese position?

Wilber: Yes, I'm sure that I did. Not much more. I think I got a lot more smiles than anybody else. I was able to say "Good morning" and get "Hello" back.

I know I got the same amount of food. I know I wore the same clothes. I had the same number of blankets. I had the same kind of wooden bed that everybody slept on. I wrote the same number of letters home—one a month. I got the same number of packages.

I got a total of 20 letters from my wife in five years, which is a lot less than some other people got. If I put a value on the letters, I was treated *worse* than a lot of other people.

Rowan: Some guys think you broke faith with the system.

Wilber: I don't think I did.

The system—the Navy—is a constant decision-making process. I think what I was feeding into it was just another factor. If what I said about the illegality of the war is not true, they have a perfect chance of squelching it, of telling me I'm wrong. This has not been done yet.

I feel that we were wrong in Viet Nam. That came from my own moral makeup, my own definition of justice, my own concept of the meaning of words like "loyalty" and "citizenship" and "duty" and "honor" and "responsibility."

I may be unpopular, but I didn't join the Navy to be popular.

7

Son Tay and Its SRO

Gene Wilber was in the Zoo. Hundreds of other Americans were confined in prison camps they had dubbed with names like the Briar Patch, Alcatraz, Plantation Gardens, Dogpatch, the Rockpile, Camp Faith, Skid Row and, of course, the Hanoi Hilton. But 55 men were in a camp which is far better known by its Vietnamese name, Son Tay, because of something that happened in November of 1970.

The first 20 men went to Son Tay on May 14th, 1968, and one of the first things they did was hold an election to name it. Some of them favored Mexican Village, but, Camp Hope won the support of a majority, and that's what it became to the men who lived there until July 14th, 1970. On that day, the 55 men at Camp Hope were told to gather up their personal belongings. They were moving. And, for reasons known only to their communist captors, the camp was emptied that day.

Four months later, it was Son Tay that hit the headlines, not Camp Hope. A daring raid had been staged by some of the Army's best-trained Special Forces troops—the Green Berets—who went in aboard Air Force helicopters nicknamed Jolly Green Giants, accompanied by some of the sharpest para-rescue men in the Air Force—men who wear maroon-colored berets. It was a colorful operation, designed originally to pluck the POWs out from under the noses of the North Vietnamese. But, the fact that it was carried out in

November—four months after the POWs had been moved elsewhere—triggered a controversy in this country.

Critics in the press suggested that either military intelligence was woefully inadequate or that the raid had been staged with the full knowledge that no POWs were there, simply to bolster the hopes of POW and MIA families and to rescue the falling prestige of the Nixon administration. The Pentagon argued that aerial reconnaissance photographs showed that the prison was still guarded.

Whatever happened in 1970, in April of 1973 the Son Tay POWs and the Son Tay raiders finally got together under somewhat different circumstances. The Fairmont Hotel in San Francisco was the setting for a two-day event staged by Texas multi-millionaire H. Ross Perot, who had once tried to ransom all the POWs out of North Viet Nam.

Between the cocktail parties, luncheons, dinners, sightseeing tours, shopping trips, and, most important, the get-acquainted meetings with the wives of other POWs, three of those who had lived at Son Tay shared some of their recollections with me.

In this catch-as-catch-can atmosphere, I got together first with Navy Commander Render Crayton of La Jolla, California—whose A-4 had been shot down in February of 1966—and Air Force Lieutenant Colonel Robert L. Stirm of Foster City, California—whose F-105 had been downed in October of 1967. We were joined later by Air Force Captain David E. Ford of Sacramento, California—a November '67 shoot down.

Bob Stirm is a sharp, good-looking pilot—everyone's idea of what the man in the cockpit looks like. He talks with the self-assurance of someone who knows that he knows what he is talking about. Of all the men I talked to, Bob was one of the best prepared for capture by the enemy. He had read up on the most recent survival techniques and knew exactly what the Code of Conduct meant. He understood that the operative survival theory recognized the necessity of sometimes taking a fall-back position. Consequently, he suffered less physical torture and less mental anguish during his interrogation sessions than others.

David Ford has a lean face, a lean body and a full head of dark hair which makes him look much younger than his early 40s. He is quiet and intense, but with a sense of humor that readily emerged during our discussion. Dave is an enlisted man who worked his way up through the ranks. He loves the military life and, as much as anyone I talked to, is eager to get back to it.

Render Crayton is a lean, long, balding man who reminds one of Jim Nabors except that his voice is deep. Crayton was to become the SRO [Senior Ranking Officer] at Son Tay when that camp was opened in 1968. But, at the time of his shoot-down, two years earlier, he knew very little about the way American fliers were being treated by the North Vietnamese.

Crayton: There was very little information about prison life when I was shot down. I didn't know what to expect.

I thought we'd be interrogated; military information at first, and probably political interrogations later on. I wanted to follow the Code of Conduct, and give only name, rank, serial number and date of birth. After being tortured, however, I found out this was impossible to do—that they were going to be able to get some sort of information out of you. From then on out it was just a matter of trying to give them false answers and do whatever I could to keep from giving them any useful information.

Rowan: There must have been a sense of real horror when you realized that you were with people who were going to torture you.

Crayton: Real horror, and a sense of disappointment in myself that I could not withstand more torture than I did. I would like to think that I could have done a better job.

Stirm: I was led to believe by my previous training that they would go to any ends to get military information, and I was told by one of the Air Force experts that there had only been one man he had ever seen who had been able to withold information. He was an old German sergeant during World

War II and he was too stupid—just a blockhead. So it had been my intention to plan on a second or third line of resistance all the way along.

Psychologically, I felt I was pretty much prepared for getting tortured for military information, but not for political information, or for military information that I couldn't possibly possess. But they wanted answers. They wanted answers.

It appeared to me that they felt we knew the entire plan—political, diplomatic and military—for the entire conduct of the war, and they wanted answers. And, of course, we didn't have them.

I had a great disappointment, psychologically, when protesting protection under the Geneva Convention. They had a prepared document showing why they were not adhering to it, and that was a shock to me.

It appeared to be a pretty official-looking piece of paper, saying that they were not obligated to follow this because of it being an undeclared war. And it seemed to me that it left me without any coverage.

Rowan: Were you disappointed in yourself when they started getting information out of you?

Stirm: No, I can't really say I was disappointed in myself. On the contrary, I knew that they had the capability to get information out of me. I personally felt that their interrogators were very poor, that they didn't know what kind of questions to ask to get valid information, and they dwelt too long on meaningless military or political or diplomatic questions that I couldn't possibly have the answers to. So, I personally felt pretty good about being able to withold the military information, any information that I did have.

Rowan: You didn't feel, then, that you were in fact broken?

Stirm: No. My connotation is different, possibly, than yours.

To me "breaking" is when you no longer have control of your mental faculties, and then, anything that they ask, you'll give them; you'll yield that information. If you still have control of your mental faculties, you can give them a different story, you can make up a story, you can throw confusing facts into the story to such a point that they're going to have to evaluate what's right and what's wrong. That is very difficult information to use.

So, when you say "broken," I think of a man who's been completely shattered, that he's a vegetable, that he'll do their very bidding. In my case anyway, and with most people I've talked to, I haven't heard of anyone who was completely broken in that manner. They had to fall back.

Let's take their diplomatic side. We didn't know exactly what was going on, but they wanted answers. Well, finally, they got answers. But they got a different answer from everyone they talked to. Now, what good is that information going to do them?

Let's take what I call *hard* military informtion, versus *soft* military information. Soft military information is published in the paper. Hard military information deserves a cover story, and it *can* be withheld from them, or shaded to a point. If you do plan on withholding that information, and you can make your story plausible, plan it in your mind while you still have control of your mental and psychological faculties. You can give them a story that they will buy, that will yield no information that they want. It may be yielding what I consider soft military information, but I don't consider that breaking.

Rowan: Render, in your position as the SRO, did you find that there were additional pressures put on you?

Crayton: I'm sure they knew that I was the SRO. They knew the dates of rank of everyone, and they knew the organizational structure. However, since they didn't realize the state of our communications, they would not admit to me for a long time that I was the senior officer there. Later on, when they did admit that I was the SRO, they accused me of leading the rest of the people and causing them to resist. Their way of combatting this was to try to isolate me from the rest of the group. They did not realize that when they isolated me, the next man down the line was going to take over, down to the last man. They just couldn't seem to get that through their heads.

Rowan: Were you ever tortured or pressured for information about the way you POWs organized yourselves or about the methods you used to communicate and pass along your orders?

Crayton: I was not physically tortured then. This was after what we called the "good guy" days began, in 1969. I was just isolated and put in a "hot box." They isolated me in a small room with no air and no ventilation. But, I considered information about our organization and communcations almost as sensitive as military information. You cannot give this kind of information to them. So, on my part, I tried to resist giving them any of *this* information just as hard as I did try to resist giving them any *military* information.

Rowan: Did you get any kind of pressure, Bob?

Stirm: I was in on one com purge [to determine how we were communicating]. As a matter of fact, it was while I was at Son Tay. And I was able to withhold all information on communications because they switched the questioning over to the political. Then, they wanted statements to the President on amnesty. And pretty soon that switched. So, it was just a matter of time. So that I had no problems withholding that kind of information.

Rowan: What happened when a guy *did* get to the breaking point, as you described it, and lost his ability to maintain a cover story or give false information?

Crayton: If someone reached a point where he could not withhold—where he had to give this information—we all understood. We just had to fall back and regroup.

If one com link was divulged, we'd have to start another com link. After awhile, it became some sort of a game we played.

We were never able to completely hide each com link from the Vietnamese. They would discover our com links and they would stop communications between certain buildings. We would just have to think up other ways and devise a new system. Americans are Americans. They're going to devise something.

There's a tremendous psychological advantage to being in communication—having someone else to lean on and to talk to—someone else to discuss things with.

Stirm: We made a special point whenever a person was in solitary confinement to always communicate with him and to always let him know that the rest of us were with him. And so, even though people were in solitary confinement, at the camps I was at anyway, communications still went on. There's the old saying about strength in unity. It holds true.

I think a strict solitary confinement, strict isolation, is one of the most barbarous forms of treatment you could ever imagine. No man was designed to live alone, out of communication.

Rowan: Did either of you have periods of strict isolation?

Stirm: Yes.

Crayton: Yes, I did also.

Stirm: I had a grand total of 280 odd days of isolation, but probably only 70 or 80 days of that was strict isolation.

Crayton: I had about four months of strict isolation. However, during this period, I knew all the people were behind me. I knew they were there. There was no question in my mind that there were Americans behind me, and that they were pulling for me, and that gave me a lot of help.

Rowan: Bob, you said this was one of the most barbarous forms of torture. What did your mind do when you were strictly isolated?

Stirm: I found the best way to overcome it was to program my day; to allow certain periods for certain types of thought processes. I'd go over my classmates in different grades of school; different courses; old girl friends. I went over anything that you could possibly think of as a method of trying to maintain some sort of stability.

Rowan: What was a typical day's program like?

Stirm: The first thing I think most of us did was exercise. And I think in solitary confinement we tended to exercise a little bit more, because it not only tired you out physically, but I think it gave you some sort of emotional outlet. You could sleep better, and at times sleeping was a problem, even after you get accustomed to sleeping on concrete slabs or the hardwood boards.

Then, there would be a period of time that I might think about my schooling—say Spanish. I had studied Spanish and I had studied French. So I would think about that, and I would try to reconstruct as much as I could for a certain period of time. Then, I might go on to Math. Then, I might go on to manufacturing processes. Then, I might think about what kind of a house I'd like to design or build; what are going to be the problems of raising my four children when I get back; how I'm going to accomplish that; what's going to happen when my daughter starts dating and my son starts dating and he wants a car. So I would just come up with anything that would be a normal part of my life, and try and program that in, without ever thinking of the obvious: How long were we going to be there?

Rowan: Were you aware of your own personality changing?

Stirm: Absolutely. I could see it in myself in isolation and solitary confinement. I could see the changes in my psychological and emotional makeup. And you could definitely tell it in other people, when they came out of solitary confinement.

Crayton: I think periods of isolation had a definite effect on personality traits. As Bob says, you could really tell it, not only in yourself, but in other people also. It was something I thought about a lot. While I was in solitary confinement I would see these changes and I would realize that I had to do something about them. So then I would spend part of my day trying to get myself straightened out.

Rowan: Can you think of an example of something that bothered you?

Crayton: Well, yes. I've always been an impatient sort of a person and when I was in solitary confinement, if I would get impatient and think, "I wish this day were over," I would really try to sit down and say, "Well, the day's got 24 hours in it and, let's face it, I'm going to have to fill this 24 hours today, just like I'm going to have to fill the next 24 hours, and let's do something about it."

Then I would start thinking about math, as Bob says, or taking a trip, to occupy myself and calm myself down and get rid of this impatient feeling.

Stirm: I think that one of the biggest things that most of us have had an opportunity to do is to get a good inner view of ourselves, of the mistakes we've made in our past lives, and to think about every single one of our actions and how they related to other people.

I know that I certainly have changed quite a bit. I think I understand myself much more than I ever would have been able to, had I not spent that time in prison.

Rowan: Armed with that greater understanding of yourself, do you expect to lead a different life now than you did before you went away?

Crayton: Well, I did a lot of soul-searching while I was there. I went back over the years to see the things that I'd done wrong—the way I'd treated my family, the way I'd treated other people, the thank you notes that I didn't write, the errors that I made. Since I've been back in my new life, I have tried to put into practice what I said I would put into practice. As I said, I was impatient, and I vowed while I was in prison that I would not be impatient when I got out. However, I found I have failed along those lines, to some extent. So, maybe in some of these other factors I said I was going to improve in, I may not have done too good a job on those either.

Rowan: I imagine that it will take a period of time—six months or so—to settle down and to understand what long term changes you really have made in yourselves.

Crayton: I think so. One good thing about it is that at least I realize now what changes I wanted to make in my life and in my personality and so forth, so I've got something to start with. The only problem is putting it into effect.

I think that, to some extent, this time that we spent up there was certainly not wasted time, because it does everybody some good to do some soul-searching.

Dave Ford joined us at this point and Bob Stirm departed. I asked Dave to add his observations on the way prison life changes one's personality.

Ford: There's no doubt about it. We had a bit of time to sit and think about things up there. Whether or not you were living alone, you still had the same amount of time. Under the net at night, you were left to yourself. It was very quiet and about all you had was memories.

I found that I have changed. My wife agrees. I've become much more tolerant than when I was first captured, and I don't lose my temper. I've been back in the States since the 18th of March and I've lost my temper exactly once in that period of time, which is a record for me. (*Laughter*) I find that it is much easier to try and understand someone else, and listen to what he is saying and try and find out what he means. For instance, when I was living in the big room [in the Plantation], we had over 50 men in there, and we'd set up discussion groups. We'd set aside a Sunday morning or a Sunday afternoon and just have a great big room discussion on some subject: married life versus bachelor life; buying clothes; anything like that. The subjects were so varied that they covered the whole spectrum.

Rowan: Did you lose your temper over there?

Ford: Oh yes.

Rowan: And what happened in a room of 40 or 50 guys when you lost your temper?

Ford: You'd have an argument, and it would flare up and die, just about as fast as it started. You really didn't have a vent for your emotions, so you learned to control your temper.

Crayton: I used to get very disgusted with the North Vietnamese. This was something that I really had to learn to control.

Some of the older, wiser people I had contact with when I was first captured told me one thing you never want to do is lose your temper with the Vietnamese, because this, in a way, is taking a step backwards. You don't know what you're going to do. You don't know what your next reaction will be.

So this was one of the things that I worked on. I was trying to control my temper, but I don't think I've been quite as successful as Dave has been along those lines. But, I do think that I did improve it and I realize what effect losing your temper has.

Rowan: As the SRO, did you have occasion to lose your temper with the 54 guys you had in that camp?

Crayton: No, I never did. I had 54 of the best guys in the world and I had no trouble whatsoever with any of them.

Ford: Plus he couldn't get at us either. (*Laughter*)

Crayton: There were a few walls between us, but they were a real tremendous group. I just didn't have any problems being SRO. Everything just seemed to fall in place. I didn't have to tell each man what to do. They knew what to do.

Rowan: What kind of directions did you find it necessary to pass along from time to time?

Crayton: Well, basically, it was setting up the guidelines for how much torture, how much punishment, a man would have to take before he could give certain sorts of information.

The Vietnamese would ask a man to write a statement. Then, they'd send him back to his room, to "think about it." This was one of their tactics. They'd tell you they wanted you to write on something, to write on how you felt about the anti-war movement in the States. Usually, a man would refuse to do this and they would send him back to his room after an interrogation and tell him to think about it. Well, when he would get back to his room, he would usually ask me, "Should I write this or shouldn't I write this?" I would have to make the decision to guide him and tell him how much punishment he should take before writing these things.

Rowan: That must have put you in a difficult position.

Crayton: Well, it put me in the position of an SRO. There were always those same problems. You have that back here in the States. When you write a message to higher authority in the military, some senior man in the organization has got to decide whether this is the right wording to use, whether you have the right to ask for that, or whatever it is.

Rowan: Could you remain unemotional about telling a guy that he had to withstand 15 minutes in the ropes?

Crayton: No, I could not remain unemotional about this. It's a very, very difficult thing to tell someone else he has to take torture before he does something, because, first off, you've got to look at yourself and say, "Am I willing to do the same thing?" But there again, it's just like being a commander back in the United States. You ask a man to go on a mission and the first question you've got to ask yourself is, "Am I willing to go on the same mission? Am I willing to take this risk?"

Ford: I lived with him up until December of '69 when I moved out and I'll say that Commander Crayton was very realistic. He did not put down specifics. He didn't say, "You'll have to remain in the ropes for X number of minutes, or hours." He said, "This is what you'll take torture for." He was wise enough to think: "How can I tell that man he's going to do this for so long, when he may not be able to mentally withstand that?" What he would do if things started to sag a little bit was to put out a message: "Let's stiffen up resistance a little bit. Let's not become lax."

I remember one message he put out. He said, "Remember, we are military men, even though we are prisoners of war. And, as prisoners of war, it is our job to resist propaganda attempts from the enemy."

Rowan: How did you react to it?

Ford: To me, it was just a restating of the Code of Conduct. He was my boss. I was the SRO of the room I was living in. I had five other people in there with me.

Rowan: In your room, Dave, was there any questioning what was being passed down? Was there an open discussion, or was it simply a matter of acknowledging that the Code of Conduct applies?

Ford: It was just basically as simple as that. The Code of Conduct says you won't sign any written statements, or give any propaganda to the enemy. We didn't.

Rowan: Did you ever get any feedback, Render, from elsewhere in the camp, that people were questioning the judgment you had made about how much resistance to put up on a specific item?

Crayton: No. Of course, when you get five people in a group, or any number in a group, you find that people have different opinions about these things, and when I would ask them for their opinions, they would be frank in giving me their opinions. Then, it was up to me to take these and weigh them and then I made the decision as to what was to be done. After I made the decision, no one ever questioned it. Everyone followed it. It was as simple as that. I think this probably happened in all the camps. I think as I said before, that every man knew what he should do.

The Vietnamese in a lot of cases thought if they took the senior men and put them in isolation, the organizational structure would fall apart. They couldn't have been any more wrong because they would take the top man out, and the next man would take command. We were determined to do this down to the last man. We had some enlisted men there and I'm sure that if one of the sergeants we had there was the last senior man left, he would have taken charge, just like a colonel or commander or anyone else.

Rowan: Did anyone approach you with an idea for an escape attempt?

Crayton: Of course we all talked about escapes. This is part of the Code of Conduct, that we will do everything we can to escape. So this discussion came up in a lot of cases. Of course, it was up to me to determine whether or not the escape attempt was feasible.

Rowan: Is there some rethinking that needs to be done about the Code of Conduct in regard to this specific question?

Crayton: I don't think so. I think the Code of Conduct is fairly specific along those lines, but leaves you somewhat of a broad leeway as to what is to be done. The Code of Conduct requires us to try to escape if we have the opportunity. I do not feel that it's hard and fast, or says, "You will escape when somebody is standing there with an AK-47 pointed at your head."

Ford: I agree. Like everything else, it's a judgment factor. We had people who parachuted into the middle of the jungle and yet got captured. Now, you're living right in the middle of the delta, with 14,000,000 people around you, and unless you can come up with something concrete, it's rather foolish to just go over the wall for the sake of going over the wall. You need some chance of success before you should make this attempt. People are pretty badly tortured for doing something like this and it was not only the people who were involved in it directly, but others who lived in that camp.

The prisons were all comparable to Alcatraz [the old maximum security prison on an island in San Francisco harbor], with the exception that they were not surrounded by water. A prison would have an electrified fence around the top; the top of the wall had broken wine bottles implanted in it, like the French are famous for; the walls of the rooms are two feet thick; and there are guard towers around the wall. There'd be an awful lot of work getting out of that camp. The Code of Conduct says you must make every effort to escape. Well, in a case like this, you have to weigh your chances of success.

Rowan: Some men took that chance, possibly hoping to beat the odds or at least to have it show on their records that they tried. Taking that a step further, did either of you find that your views about the war or your own careers in the military underwent any changes while you were in prison?

Ford: Yes, I was expecting to be forced to retire at the end of 20 years because I had so much enlisted time and because I was a reserve officer. Now, I had a glimmer of hope for getting a commission as a regular officer, which would allow me to extend my service.

I thoroughly enjoy the service. The service has been good to me. I have almost nineteen-and-a-half years in now. I don't want to get out of the service. I like it. It's a good job.

As far as the war is concerned, my experience in prison just reinforced my opinion that we were doing the right thing by fighting the war.

Crayton: As for me, when I was shot down I don't think I had a real understanding of what the war was all about. I think I was just like most other people. I was a career military officer, and I was told to go bomb such-and-such a place and I was willing to do this. I did not understand all the political aspects of the war. But I feel that my stay there gave me a better understanding of why we were fighting the war.

After a few years of living with the Communists, I can certainly understand why we were fighting that war.

Rowan: What conclusion did you come to?

Crayton: Well, I can see how our way of life is so much better than theirs. I can understand now why we did not want the Communists to force their way of life on other people. I think this is one of our major purposes in this war. I don't think we went into the war with the object of converting the North Vietnamese into democracy, but we did go into the war with the purpose of keeping them from forcing their will on South Viet Nam, and the other countries in Southeast Asia.

Rowan: Many of the men still refer to the North Vietnamese as "Gooks." Some of them have expressed some active hatred. Some of them have said there is no time to hate. Where do you find yourself fitting into that broad spectrum of feelings?

Crayton: Well, there were certain Vietnamese that you could not help but hate. It's going to take a long time to get over this feeling of hate for certain individuals who were responsible for a lot of the torture. However, as a whole, I think the other statement that you just made is an excellent one. There is no time for hate now. This is something that is in the background. We've got other things to think about, other than hating what they did to us. I don't see that hating them serves any useful purpose whatsoever. I hated them as individuals but I think the feeling I had more than anything else is the feeling of pity for the rest of the people. I felt sorry for them because they don't know anything other than the life they live over there. They have absolutely no concept of what life is like in the United States and the other free countries of the world.

8

The Stool

One of the most heavily-defended military targets in North Viet Nam was the bridge at Thanh Hoa, a coastal city south of Hanoi on Highway One. It became a symbol to the Communists of their resistance to the "American air pirates." The area around it was peppered with anti-aircraft guns and surface-to-air missile launching facilities to a degree hardly in keeping with the military significance of the bridge. And those weapons took their toll.

One of the first Navy men to learn about the defenses around the Thanh Hoa bridge was Lieutenant Commander William M. Tschudy. As a young Lieutenant J.G. [junior grade], he was in the right seat of an A-6 piloted by then-Commander Jeremiah Denton, now a Rear Admiral. They were shot down just after dropping their bombs on July the 18th, 1965.

A year-and-a-half later, in January of 1967, Allen C. Brady, now a Navy Captain, was sent to hit the same area, and found it even more heavily defended. His plane was shot down, and his bombardier-navigator died when his parachute failed to open.

Bill Tschudy is a tall, handsome, rawboned man who looks vaguely out of place in a Navy uniform. Had I met him in civilian clothes on the street, I would have figured him to be a cowpuncher from Texas, or perhaps a rodeo rider. He's as friendly as an Irish setter, with an "Aw, shucks" attitude about the fame he has acquired simply by being an ex-POW. But, as I tried to get a little closer to him, I found him drawing back into a protective shell of politeness, and I realized that he is truly uneasy with anyone outside his immediate family and his close Navy friends. He's the kind of man who doesn't quite believe he is talented. His buddies say he was teamed up with Commander Jeremiah Denton because he could be counted on to be level-headed in a crisis situation, and Denton needed that kind of a person in the cockpit with him.

But, you'd never hear Bill Tschudy say anything like that. His comments about Denton reflect great respect for the man who was so much his senior at the time they were shot down. He doesn't question Denton's decision to leave the airplane, even though it was still flying level when the Commander ejected, leaving Bill with no choice but to bail out, too, since the A-6 can't be flown from the right seat.

Al Brady is a short, wiry man, with a tongue-in-cheek humor that doesn't come through on paper. His humor is very much part of his charm as a person. He was reluctant to go into the story that highlights this chapter. Yet, when I asked him to share it with us he went through it exhibiting the flair of a natural storyteller, building the interest of the listener (and the reader, I expect) by understatement and good humor. Al Brady is the epitome of the professional military man of the '60s and '70s—a family man who knows his job and does it well.

Both men now live in Virginia Beach, Virginia, and that's where Al Brady started our discussion by telling me about his shoot-down.

Brady: I got hit with triple-A [anti-aircraft artillery], probably 57 or 85mm. It hit the tail of the aircraft, and blew the tail off. The other people in X squadron said they saw one good 'chute, and a streamer, and that was all they knew. They did not hear from me on the radio.

That was the word that they sent back to the States. My wife got that word, that there was one good 'chute and one streamer, and that's all she had to go on for about 15 months, a 50-50 chance, at best, that I had survived. Fifteen months later she was shown a picture of me crossing a bridge with a little Vietnamese girl carrying a rifle. The intelligence people had picked this out of an eastern European newspaper.

Of course, I recall when this happened. The day after I was shot down, they photographed this thing. It was a typical *staged* deal by the Vietnamese. You've been captured by one guy, but the next day they break out the "duty" little girl with the gun about as big as she is. And there she is in the picture, pushing you with a bayonet.

But I was glad to have my picture taken. That is how my wife found out that I was alive, and a POW.

Rowan: Bill, you went down in '65.

Tschudy: We were numbers 13 and 14 up into Hanoi. I don't know how many were shot down earlier, but we were the 13th and 14th to come into Heartbreak Hotel.

I landed in this little hamlet. The funniest thing about it was I landed not only in a hamlet, but in a hole in the hamlet. I think everybody would have been a little shocked if they had seen the snicker on my face, because the hole was about three feet wide and about six-and-a-half feet long and about two feet deep. It looked like a grave, and I thought, "They really knew I was coming."

I landed in that thing, and there were a whole bunch of little men around. They came charging out, and they grabbed me and went through all my gear. They were trying to get me out of my parachute, which I didn't even have time to unhook because they were right there, and they were going to chop me out with their machetes. I managed to pop the snaps and get the parachute off. Well, they got me out of the hole and, when I stood up on the ground, I was so much taller [about six feet tall] than they were, they put me back in the hole.

They took away my wrist watch. I wasn't wearing any rings or anything else. They took my wrist watch, my identification cards, and my box of flip-top Marlboro cigarettes. They distributed a few cigarettes among themselves, and then the leader apparenty pocketed the box.

They took all my clothes away from me. Then, after they got me out of the hole, they tied my hands behind me with a long rope, and put me in another hole. It turned out to be an air raid shelter. There was a lot of water in it, and the rope got sopping wet, and I did, too. Then, they pulled me out of that within a short time, and led me away.

There was one little man who apparently took it upon himself to guard my modesty. Every time I moved around, the fly in my skivvies [underwear] would open up, and he would reach over and close it. Then, they finally allowed that my fly wasn't going to stay closed, so they let me wear my trousers.

Rowan: Was there any thought of how long you would be there?

Brady: I thought about it when I was first captured. North Viet Nam had always required that we have a complete troop withdrawal and all these other things in order to talk with them. Just before we came over, in November of 1966, we read in the paper that they had dropped the requirement for a total troop withdrawal in order to have talks. For some reason, this caught on, and people felt that there were going to be talks, and that the Communists probably were ready to negotiate. So there was some concern among "first cruisers" that they were going to miss their combat tour. It probably seems callous; many people would say, "What a bunch of callous people, they didn't want the war over." But, when you go all through this training, and you're just up to a peak, and you're ready to go, and then you come racing over there, and they stop the war, well . . . Of course anyone would be happy to have the war stopped, but people wanted to get in there and get their licks in before the war ended. Anyway, there was that kind of aura at this time.

So, when I was shot down, in the first hours when I was standing around thinking about it, I didn't really believe it would go on a long time. I thought it would be less than a year, so I was not too upset. I figured I was going to be reasonably well treated, and that I'd probably be out within a year.

Rowan: When did you first awaken to the fact that you were not going to be reasonably well treated?

Brady: The treatment all the way up to Hanoi, which took me a couple of days, was at times rough, but never really horribly bad. I did get one interrogation session, a very short one, where the guy did put me in the ropes the first time.

But I was expecting rough stuff. We'd been to survival schoot. We *knew* we were going to get it. We didn't know quite the severity of it. The rope treatment was more severe than I had expected. But, I still had in the back of my mind the way we'd been trained: In some short time period, you're going to get through this military interrogation business, and when that's through, then you will be in a compound situation, and join the rest of the guys.

I got to Hanoi a couple of days later, and again I got the rough stuff for a couple of days. It was really bad. The place was pretty spooky. Heartbreak Hotel, when you first get there, that's a real dungeon. That's a little shock right there. I mean it's a real dungeon, the kind that you find along the eastern coast of the United States, historical monuments now, Civil War-type things. You just walk into a dark black dungeon, and there you are, and that was a little bit depressing.

During the two weeks that I went through this initial phase, where they're still looking for military information, it really slacked off to almost nothing for about the last week or so. They hardly even bothered me. I just stayed in that little cell. But I had the feeling that I was going to move, and then, one night, after about two weeks, they came in and opened the cell door and told me to roll up my gear, and, boy, my heart just leaped. I thought, "I'm going to be with the gang in a few minutes."

I came out in the courtyard, and they spun me around a few times, blindfolded, and then took me over to the other section of the camp, which came to be known as Las Vegas, or Little Vegas. They led me around blindfolded, and they opened up the door, and they shoved me in and slammed the door, and they all walked away. There I was, alone again. I thought, "Well, what the heck." That was the first time I got a little bit queasy about the thing.

The next morning when I went to dump my bucket, I walked into the Thunderbird [an area of Little Vegas in the Hanoi Hilton]. That's a grim place, with all those little cells that are just like tanks, and stick out with separations in between them. I didn't know how many people were in each one. I assumed there was only one in each one. It was just grim. There was dead silence. You never saw anybody. It was the most depressing thing I ever saw. And as the days started to go by, I suddenly realized, "This is *not* the old compound. The gang is *not* together." And I began realizing then it was going to be a grim deal.

Then, Harry Jenkins moved in next to me. He moved in with Barry Bridger, whom I'd made contact with. I was kind of teed off and he said he was shot down in November of '65. This was February of '67. And then I weakly asked, "You've had another roommate, haven't you?" He said "No, this is my first." I thought, "My God, that's about 15 months, and if it took him that long to get a roommate, it *was* going to be a grim deal."

He told me then that he thought it would probably take me a year or so before I would get a roommate, if I was lucky.

Rowan: How long had it been before you were in communication with Bridger?

Brady: There was a set of three cells there, separate from others. They had a bamboo screen, and then a regular roof on top of that. But, the way the thing had been crudely constructed, you could actually talk over the wall. If you stood up on the bunk, you could do a pretty good job. Well, we did, but we got caught, within 24 hours. We got nailed. And the V, for punishment—it was pretty light at that time—they handcuffed you for a week. They would come and let you out of the handcuffs to eat, and to go dump your bucket, but the rest of the time, 24 hours a day, you stayed in the handcuffs with your hands behind you.

So that put a little damper on our spirits over leaping up

on the bunk and hollering across. The V told us that the next time we got caught, it would be worse. They would put us in irons, as well as cuffs. So I was a little bit gun-shy for awhile. But we still talked. We were a little bit more cautious, and checked, and tried to do a little clearing.

Then, Harry Jenkins moved in, and he was an old hand. He knew all the systems, and was able to teach us things. I was in fairly regular communications from then on.

Tschudy: We [he and Denton] came in [to Heartbreak] on the 18th of July, 1965, and I was foolishly optimistic enough to believe that I would only be there about two years. Even at that, I would not allow myself to really think it was going to be that long.

I remembered some of the problems that the British had over in Burma, and in some places, where it took nine years to clean the Communists out. And I thought, "It'll never last that long, I hope."

When I got there, I had pretty much the same thing as Allen did later, except they didn't twist us for anything, right away. It only took me overnight to get to Hanoi. They put me in cell seven in Heartbreak, and my contact with Americans was instantaneous. As a matter of fact, as the jeep pulled into the Heartbreak courtyard, I heard someone whistling "God Bless America," and "It's a Grand Old Flag," and so I knew there were Americans around.

But I also had had the same training. I expected a compound. The day they captured me, as they walked me down these paddies, they took me to a place that, when I saw it, I said, "Well, this looks just like the movies; this must be the compound." Way down, maybe 25-30 feet from the gate, there was a gathering of people around a motorcycle with a sidecar, and in that sidecar was Commander Denton. He was sitting with his leg draped over the thing. And, when I looked at him, he looked just like Alec Guiness in "Bridge on the River Kwai."

So as I walked into the gate, I said, "Hey, hi, how are you?" He told me how he was, and he asked me, and before I had a real chance to answer, they swept me away and jammed me in a little room, and that was the last I ever saw of him until the fifth of February, 1973. So my dreams of a compound were shot.

When they took me away I sort of had an inkling, right then and there, that it wasn't going to be this compound situation that I expected. That night an official came in. He took out a box of Marlboros, would you believe, and made a big show of lighting one. It was obviously the pack that had been taken from me when I was captured. He came up to me, and he asked me my name, rank, serial number, and how old I was. Then he said, "This means you can tell me what your date of birth was." So this is just what the book said: name, rank, serial number and date of birth. What more can you ask? And he didn't ask any more questions.

Anyway, they put me in this cell, and as soon as they closed the door and walked out of the cell block, I heard people talking. At that particular time, the guards didn't seem to pay any attention to us. We didn't really have guards around the area. They just sort of guarded the whole prison. There were so few of us, I received the impression that they didn't really know what to do with us. The fellows could whistle. They couldn't really talk out loud, but whenever the guards weren't around, they talked. So they started talking to me right away. They gave me a briefing on what the set-up was, and what to expect, and how everything was going to go, and where the other people were, and they passed their names to me, and everything else.

Well, within about three minutes the Vietnamese picked me up and hauled me out to interrogation. It was just a talk-talk interrogation. I didn't tell them anything. They *told me* a lot of things. They thought I was flying an F-4. All they knew was that two of us came out of an airplane. The only thing they knew that had two people in it was an F-4. So they told me I was in an F-4, and I wasn't going to deny it.

We were the first A-6 down there. The A-6 was brand new and, if I had any apprehension about being captured, that didn't lend anything but misery to it. I felt I had to protect this airplane in some way.

But we just chit-chatted around, that's what it amounted to. They'd ask questions. I'd refuse to answer. Generally you could wait them out and then they'd change their question and ask something else.

So, I wasn't subjected to any abuse, during those first years. The first time I was abused was when they asked me to write something, and that was in May of 1966, and I wasn't going to write anything for them.

But, in 1965, there I was in a cell seven by seven by fourteen feet high, with a window that was about six feet up on the wall. I think the biggest shock was not that I was a prisoner—that I was out of the war, that I probably wasn't going to see my wife for a long time or my family, or even fly again for awhile—but it was the idea that, "Holy cow, not only am I a prisoner, but I'm a prisoner of the *Communists.*" My mind was filled with all the same things as everybody else's about the Communists. And believe me, they weren't half the truth, as I found out later.

Rowan: Is it difficult to fill up the hours when you're first there?

Brady: It was for me that first two weeks I spent at Heartbreak. The last week, when I was not being interrogated, just sitting there, each day was interminable. I thought they would never end. The sun would finally go down, and I would wait and wait and wait and I would think it must be about 10 o'clock at night, and I would go to bed. I could hear a series of bells, which I didn't understand. They have a strange bell system, with some chimes over in town. Some months later, I found out what these bells meant, and I think I was going to bed about 7 o'clock. But I could have sworn I was going to bed at 10 o'clock at night. It was getting dark fairly early in January.

Then, when I moved over to the Golden Nugget, in Little Vegas, the days were long. It was cold in February. I would sit around all day, wrapped in a blanket and shivering. Twice a day we got to eat, and that was it. The hours were long. I dreaded the nights, because they were even colder. I was just miserable.

Perhaps the most miserable thing that really upset me the first two weeks was the thought of my family. I felt that under the circumstances there was a very good chance that they would not know whether I was alive or dead. This caused me a lot of concern. I knew there was nothing I could do about it.

But my spirits picked up when we had a little change of weather about the first week in March. It began to get a little warmer. I was so cold during January and February, all I wanted was to get warm. That was the most important thing in my life. Then, the weather changed. I felt much better. I remember I went out and got to bathe one day and the sun actually came out. I could feel that warm sun up there for the first time.

Then, in the middle of March, they moved me into the Thunderbird, into a small solo cell. I sat in there that morning and then we had lunch. Then the dishes were taken out. Then the siesta period came. I was sitting on my bunk and I heard a few coughs here and there. Then I heard some whispering. We had these little windows in the door that were covered. I came up to the window, and I could see through the crack. And somebody was saying, "Prisoner in room 5, what's your name?" So I gave him my name. They asked me a few more questions, and I whispered it out there. After a little while he said, "Commander, would you mind coming down and talking under the door, like the rest of us?" So I dropped down and I looked through the crack, and I could see all these eyes. Everybody was down there, lying on the deck. It was really weird.

But, at this time, the V were being very careless, and during the siesta period, when the whole camp was asleep, including the Vietnamese, they had one guard who circulated around through the entire building. We had one room in the Thunderbird from which we could track this guy. That was Ron Storz' room, and someone would get up on top of the upper bunk, high enough to see over the bamboo screen that was covering the outside of the window. They could keep the guard in sight. And he would go back in the galley lots of times and screw off, and as long as we had him in sight we would give the clear signal, and we would talk. If the guard headed back towards us, you'd hear some guy give the warning. At that time, we were using a throat clearing and everybody would shut up. You'd lie there, watching the guard come in. You'd see his sneakers go by and back the other way. And finally somebody would give a "clear." So we were able to talk pretty much over a two hour period.

Rowan: Were there ever low periods—periods of depression—when you thought: "It's never gonna end; God, I'm never gonna get out of here"?

Tschudy: The worst time, I found, was at night. For some reason or other, I'd be very tired, and I'd fall asleep, and I'd think it was 10 o'clock. I'd have dreams about leaving the prison. I'd dream that people came to get me, and then, just as I was about to walk out the door, they'd tell me, "You have to stay a while longer." And I couldn't understand that because these were my friends who were telling me this. Weird dreams.

And then, I'd wake up and I would really go into a super depression because I would realize I was still in the same place, and the radio was still on, which meant it was before 10 o'clock. And since I'd already slept, I was kind of rejuvenated, and now I was going to lie there awake and just think.

Or I'd simply dream that I was at home, and I'd feel a tremendous feeling of exhilaration, and then I would wake up and see that I was in this rat hole, and that was really depressing.

There were times when things got very low. I imagine it's self-pity or frustration, but there's nothing you can do about it.

Rowan: Did you think about your careers?

Tschudy: I didn't think about that particularly, because I didn't think I was going to be in long enough. I figured that the two years I had anticipated being in was no big thing.

Brady: I was a little concerned, but not over the time I might spend in prison. After they'd squeezed me, and got me to talk, I guess I had a tremendous feeling of guilt. At first, I had felt that I was going to be hanging in there tough, because at survival school you can pretty well do it. They can beat on you, but you know they're not going to kill you. This, of course, was much more violent, and they do squeeze you. I felt very guilty, as if I had failed. I thought everybody else had hung tough, and I just wasn't tough. I had this remorse, until Harry Jenkins moved in, which was a month or so after I arrived in Hanoi. He asked me what I'd done, and I told him. I apologized, and he said, "Don't worry. We don't know of anyone yet who has not broken. They have broken everyone. Just try to hang in as tough as you can and tell them as little as possible. Don't feel bad about it. Just hang in there." That was a great lift to me.

In 1967, we had a tremendous system going. New POWs were coming in. We were getting to them. We had a good communication systen. We were giving them information. And then, we had a purge in August of '67, and out went Jim Stockdale and Jerry Denton and some others.

This was when they opened up the Alcatraz camp. They went around and picked the senior guys and their roommates right out of each building. I had been right next door to Jim Stockdale, and I was right in there with them, passing information and so forth, when he got jerked out and worked over real bad, with Sam Johnson, his roommate.

A couple of years later, when Commander Stockdale got back into our camp and I made contact with him, the first thing he did was apologize to me, and I said, "For what?" He said, "Back there in '67, during that purge, when they worked me over, I had to give them your name." They'd really beaten the crap out of the poor guy, and I told him: "Gee, don't feel sorry, I know what you went through. And besides, they didn't do anything to us."

Fred Crow and I were living together, and when they grabbed Stockdale out and worked him over, they pulled Fred and me out and just moved us to another building. They never said anything to us.

Rowan: You said earlier Al, that there wasn't much to do at first but sit around and shiver.

Brady: Life was spartan to say the least. The food was bad; it was cold as hell; we were underdressed. We continued to stay isolated, although I had a roommate. There was no outside time. The first time I got outside to get a little sunshine and exercise was in the late spring of '69.

Rowan: That puts the lie to those films we saw about then of all the exercise you guys were getting, throwing a basketball around.

Brady: In '69, which was a bad year, I got caught throwing a piece of candy from my first package to the guy who lived next door to me. This was on the 24th of January.

His room was open. I knew it was going to be open, so I took a piece of candy with me out to the bath area, and on the way back, I threw it in his room. The guard heard it, and went in there and found it. I went in my room, and I realized I had been caught. Shortly thereafter, they opened the door and told me to put on my long clothes, we were going to a quiz. And I knew right then what it was for. I figured, what the hell, I threw the piece of candy in, and that's no big deal.

The Paris talks were going to start on that very day, the 24th of January, and I thought things were looking up, and I didn't think they'd do anything to me.

I went in there and the guy confronted me: "What did you do wrong?" He expected me to deny everything, of course. I said: "I threw a piece of candy in the other prisoner's room. I'll admit it. It was wrong. I should not have done it. I broke the regulations, but I admit it."

He was really caught back. He then threw the piece of candy out on the table and said: "What is that?" That's what he had planned to do when I denied it, and he went ahead even though I'd confessed. So I said, "Yes, that's the piece of candy." He said, "What did you do with it?" So I had to go through the whole thing and explain to him what I had done, which he knew.

He said: "This is very serious," and I said: "It was just a piece of candy." He said: "The next time it could be a note to this other prisoner." I said, "Perhaps it could be, but it wasn't." He wanted me to confess that I had done it other times, and I said: "Well, I haven't."

I never could understand what he really wanted. So he said: "You must be punished." And he stood me in the corner. This was in the morning, and he came back a couple of times and wanted me to write a confession, which I wouldn't do, and then, that night, about 11 o'clock, I thought they were going to take me back to my room. They came in and said: "Come with me," and we walked right past the building I lived in, and they put me on a wooden stool, and I spent the night on the stool.

The next day, the regular interrogator, who handled our building, came in to see me. He had not been in camp the day this happened. He came and told me, "I go away one day and you get into trouble." I said, "Well, that's it, all I did was throw a piece of candy." "Well," he said, "I'll talk to the camp commander, and you must stay on the stool until Monday morning."

This was Friday morning. I was going to stay on the stool from Friday morning until Monday morning. Of course this is a no-sleep deal. You sit on that stool all the way, 24 hours a day. I remember that Leroy Stutz had told me he'd been on the stool one time for 30 hours. So I kept in mind, "Gee, I'm going to have to stay until Monday morning. I've got Leroy beat."

So Monday, the interrogator came in for a quiz, and so I assumed I was going to get off. I was really fagged, because if you know the end is near, you really get tired. And, boy, he was *really* hard. He didn't look too friendly.

He had two objects in his hands. He put one over to the right and one to the left. "There's two ways to go. Over here, you completely surrender, and over here you resist. Now which do you want?" I said: "Well, how about in the middle?" "No, *complete* surrender." I said: "I don't understand what you mean." "Surrender. You do anything we ask, everything we ask; or you resist." I said: "Of course I have no choice. I'll have to resist." He said, "Ah ha, you resist, you oppose the camp, you oppose us on everything."

This is the way the Communists are. You're one of two

ways. You either do everything they say, or you are in complete opposition to them. There can be no in-between, and it's really frustrating. They know you're not going to say you submit. So they say, "You must submit."

Rowan: You told him you would have to resist. What happened then?

Brady: Well, he started working me over, started the business of hitting me, putting me on my knees, holding my arms over my head, tying my thumbs together, putting me up against the wall, on my toes with my arms behind me. He did this for hours, during the day, just to make me miserable and hurt, and to degrade me.

It was all bad, but it wasn't killing me. You can only stand there so long, and then you fall down.

This went on for about two days. He took my stool away from me on Monday, incidentally, and replaced it with a small saw horse. It was very hard to sit on, it kind of cut into my fanny, but I recall I fell asleep a couple of times.

It's funny, when you fall asleep sitting on the stool, you wake up. You can never hit the ground first. You wake up while you're falling every time. You're sitting there, looking straight ahead, and the next thing you know, you're at about 45 degrees, going through the air, and you just have time to flex, not too successfully, and you kneel over, and there's a big crash and the guard comes. They have a little window up so they keep watching.

I found out later that Paul Galanti was on the stool, also, for the same offense, which I didn't know he had done, two cells down from me, out at the Riviera. Paul and I went through the week not knowing the other man was there. And I'm convinced, from talking to doctors, that we were both drugged, because we had fantastic hallucinations. It turned out that Paul had many of the same symptoms.

Rowan: What were some of the things you hallucinated?

Brady: The first cues that I had were visual cues. For example, I recall sitting there about the third night, and looking down at the deck. The deck was bricks, with mortar in between, just regular old dusty bricks, but they looked very glossy. They looked as if they were made out of glass. And the mortar seemed to be raised up quite high, and looked sort of like rime ice, or ice that you have on your ice cube tray. Now, Paul Galanti had the same hallucination. And I recall reaching down and touching it, to feel if it was as smooth as it looked. And I could see into the bricks, too, some depth into them. And yet, I felt completely rational at this time. I wasn't out of my head or anything.

Then, I began to see faces in these things.

Then, I looked around the room, and the room seemed a little bit different. It seemed a little larger. The walls did not seem to be quite as true, straight up and down, they seemed to kind of go out. I recall there was a jug over there, and, right at the top where it was white, it seemed to look very yellow, as if it had a yellow stain on it. Everything white seemed to have a yellow stain on it. There was this definite yellow cast. Again Paul Galanti experienced seeing this yellow cast.

Things out of my peripheral vision would bother me. I would sit there and it would just seem like something was coming at me, and I would really jump, startled, and there was nothing there. It might be just a black spot on the wall.

Rowan: What made you think you had been drugged?

Brady: I had talked to Jim Hughes in the bath area the previous summer, and he told me some of the things that had happened to him, and he said he had been drugged. Well, I remember coming back and talking to my roommate, Fred, about that. We decided not to tell the rest of the guys in our cell block. We just flat didn't believe it. But, when these things started happening to me in there, all of a sudden, I remembered, Hughes told me that he'had been drugged. I said, "By God, they're drugging me. I know I'm being drugged." So I just stopped eating.

I would eat bread but I wouldn't eat the side dish, because I didn't think they could possibly put it in the bread.

Then, I began hearing things. I began hearing voices. And then this progressed right down to where I could understand all the Vietnamese.

The building was right next to the galley. The Vietnamese girls and guys were back there, just jibber-jabbing all day long. Well, I could understand everything they said. To me, it seemed they were speaking English, not Vietnamese. I could hear the Vietnamese radio, and I could understand it.

And then pretty soon, I had people in my room. I would have a person sitting right there, as close as you are. I could just see them as clearly as anything. They were old classmates, and they came in, and we talked. We discussed all kinds of things.

And finally, I forgot that I was being drugged, and I tell you, I wasn't here any more. And, right up until the eighth day, I was absolutely not tired at all. I lost all my fatigue. I was completely alert, and ready to go.

On the eighth day, I imagined I heard voices; people were talking and somebody told me that we were going to go on a fast in the camp. Then, the instructions came: "Do not bow anymore. You will not bow." Those were the instructions from the SRO, although everybody was still doing it at this time. And so I wouldn't bow.

Well, the next thing you knew, they got The Bug, who was the "bad news" type. He came in. There I had it, a direct confrontation with the feared Bug. He said, "Bow," and I said, "No, I'm not going to bow."

Rowan: You had hallucinated these instructions?

Brady: Yes. They had never come from anybody. In fact, I even thought I was sending messages out and getting messages in, but nobody even knew where I was. So, anyway, he said, "You must be punished." That was a joke. Here I'd been eight days on the stool and he'd been beating me, and now he was going to punish me.

They took me that night back over to Heartbreak. They took me to Room 5, off the courtyard there, and the old head man, Pig Eye, came in. I saw him, and I knew that was bad. They threw me into leg irons on the ground. I thought they were going to use ropes, but they did not bring them in. He just got on my back and started twisting my arms.

He would twist my hand and arm and raise it. This was excrutiating pain. I couldn't understand why my arm wasn't breaking. It seemed as if it should break. He was sweating. He'd pull as hard as he could, until his fingers started slipping. Each time he pulled, I really let out a scream. The interrogator was over there, and he came and hit me in the face a few times, and told me not to scream. They were afraid a loud scream would be heard throughout the camp.

This went on for about 10 minutes or so and I had "had the stroke." So I finally said, "Okay, I'll do what you want."

They dragged me over to a table and they took a couple of pieces of paper and a pen, and they dictated two statements to me, one of them saying I had come and bombed their country; that I was a criminal of war. He said, very specifically, "You are not a *war criminal.* You are a *criminal of war.*" And then the second one was a letter to the camp commander, thanking him for the "lenient and humane treatment" of the DRV, and saying that I wanted to cooperate and would do anything he wanted.

I remember one statement that he dictated to me—The Kid was the guy doing this—I had to write to the camp commander, *"I want to make for you happy."*

I said, "What was that again?"

"I want to make for you happy."

I thought, "Why that's beautiful. I'm sure glad he came through with that. That's going to really look good."

Rowan: Anyone who saw that would have known you were forced to write it. But did they ever use that material?

Brady: They never really wanted to use it. It's blackmail. By writing it, you are breaking the Code of Conduct and they now have this. They threatened me with it many times. "We will release this. We will read it to all the camps on the radio."

And also they would bring this paper out to me and say, "You have a commitment. You said you'd cooperate. Now you must do these things." And whenever they did that, I'd say: "That's no commitment. You forced me to write that, so it's not a commitment."

Rowan: Bill, you say you wrote similar things.

Tschudy: Oh, yeah. I went through the whole gamut.

But, 1969 seemed to be the year for hallucinations. I had sat on the stool for years and years and no problems, but in '69 they had me on a stool, out at the camp in Son Tay, and they had the Vietnamese radio on, over the wall. It was just far enough away that, if you could understand Vietnamese, you might be able to understand it. Well, one night, on the stool, I sat there and listened to a lecture on Las Vegas. They described the city and the beauties of it, and each one of the casinos, and just went through hour after hour, it seemed like. And this was just sort of an hallucination I had after sitting on a stool.

Then, I found out after that that it took fewer and fewer days of sitting on a stool before I'd go into this thing where I could start understanding the Vietnamese talking. Of course I didn't understand what they were saying, but it *sounded* all English to me.

I didn't feel that I was drugged.

Yes, I went through all the other purges, communications purges, biographies, "Which way do you choose?" "Who do you support?" crime confessions, letters to GIs in the South.

My favorite letter was one that was written to "U.S. Naval Aviators Flying Off of Ships of the Seventh Fleet in the South China Sea Who Have Not Yet Been Shot Down."

Rowan: What did you have to tell them?

Tschudy: Oh, it was just one of those letters where you say "I'm a criminal of war. I came to Viet Nam to sew destruction and hate among the people. I am a victim of my government." That's the introduction-type paragraph.

Then, the next one is, "Soon it will be Christmas time. I have spent ...... (however many Christmases it had been) in a camp of detention in the Democratic Republic of Viet Nam. I know I will have to spend more Christmases here. Where will you spend your Christmas? Will it be home with your family, or will you perhaps be at the bottom of the ocean where you are dead, or will you be a prisoner like I am."

This is the type of thing.

Letters to aviators, letters to Senators, Representatives,

letters to President Johnson, letters to peace advocates, letters to hawks, letters to doves, letters to anybody.

Rowan: Did they send these letters?

Tschudy: As far as I know they never did. I never expected them to.

Brady: I've a feeling they never sent anything unless you wrote the thing without being pressured. They liked to have it and make you worry about it.

Rowan: Did you bounce back pretty quickly from that?

Brady: Yeah, I think I did. It didn't take long to come back.

Tschudy: It didn't take long to come back, and all you knew is that you just had to sit around and wait 'til the next one came.

This was one of the worst things up there, the anticipation. Whenever a purge would hit, it would start someplace, not always the same place. One time I was the very first one. Usually, I was the last one. And this sort of thing was really nerve-racking because you knew you were on the list, because everybody was, and you just sat around and waited, day after day, until finally you heard that jingle of keys, coming in the middle of the night, or whenever, and they'd open the door and out you'd go, and it was your turn. But, it was the waiting that was half the problem.

Communications did help us, because we knew immediately what they were looking for, and we knew how everyone else was resisting.

Rowan: Did you get instructions from your senior officers as to what you could and couldn't give them in those circumstances?

Tschudy: During the early days when we were very spread around and communications was not nearly as good, it was on pretty much of an individual basis. Later on, the rules became harder and faster.

Rowan: Did the North Vietnamese ever just give up after you'd been on the stool for a few days?

Tschudy: Not for me. I know of one fellow they gave up on. He did a fantastic job. He sat on the stool for 21 days.

Now he was not sitting there completely without sleep. He was in a position where he was able to catch a few winks. But, it was a matter of catching a few winks, here and there. That doesn't count very much. He sat on the stool for 21 days and they finally just sent him on his way. I don't know whether they decided they didn't need what they wanted from him or what it was, but that's one time I know that they did give up.

There were a couple of other times when the person who was down at the end of the purge was never touched.

Other times they stopped in the middle of it, because they lost interest in their program, or they finally decided after they had 125 copies of the same thing that maybe this wasn't such a good idea, after all.

Rowan: Was there a point at any time in those years when you thought that you were losing your minds?

Brady: No, never.

Tschudy: We used to kid each other, though, occasionally. We'd say: If we are going crazy, we're all going crazy at the same rate of speed, and we're not noticing a thing.

Brady: When the new guys came in in '72, Larry Guarino was out with them, then he moved back in with us. He got plucked out during the B-52 bombing late in '72. He came back in, and he was a real funny guy, anyhow. He said, "Boy, you don't know how crazy you are until you talk to those new guys."

Tschudy: After we got the news that the new fellows brought in, about what was going on back in the States, we figured we were the only sane ones.

Brady: That's right. We thought everybody back home was going crazy.

Rowan: Give me a couple of examples of things you heard, and how you reacted to them.

Brady: Well, when the new guys came in in '72, I was over with all the seniors. We were isolated. Our communications were all by what we called "chit." We had fancy ways of getting it, different ways. The new guys—they were '72 shoot-downs; they were really a great bunch of guys—came into the camp, and they caught on to the communications stuff real well, and they gave us the most complete, comprehensive bunch of stuff. We were getting chits that concerned morality, economics, the Common Market, NATO, fashions, automobiles, just about anything you can think of . . . haircuts, regulations in the services, changes, and just on and on and on. They just seemed to be a real goldmine.

We discussed a lot of things. Of course, the economic problems in the United States—the cost-of-living increase was a little bit of a setback to us. We had recieved some word about pay raises, and the pay sounded real good, but then the prices took most of it away. That was one thing we were a little bit conerned about.

The crime rate was big. We knew it had always been big. It didn't sound overly alarming.

This business about drugs seemed to be a real problem, it was greater than even we had suspected. Of course, we were concerned about our own children, and the widespread use of marijuana and all that. I think most of us there were probably pretty square, compared to society today.

One of the most interesting chits I got was a complete rundown on the play *Hair*, and that was pretty interesting. They told us about these X-rated movies, and all that sort of thing. I was definitely against that trend.

Rowan: Was there concern in those later years about what was happening to your wives, what your place in their lives was going to be?

Brady: You've heard about divorces that've come up, and there probably will be more. In my own case, I felt I had a strong marriage when I was shot down. I received letters from my wife, the last couple of years, and I got enough of them to convince me that everything was four-square back home. And, when I called Louise from Clark, everything sounded great. And when I got home everything was four-square. We readjusted, and we're cruising right along. She's back chipping at me (*Brady started to grin*), just like before. We got back to normal so quick, I kind of expected better treatment for a little longer. We're back to normal too quick. (*Laughter*).

Tschudy: It was the same way with me. I was raised in a small town. The cosmopolitan world has sort of passed me by. You read about movie star divorces, but that happens to other people. Perhaps all my life I've missed that type thing. But, I didn't feel any different the day I came out than the day I went in. I just knew everything at home was just fine.

We talked about how the long period of time was going to affect marriages, and just from the comments made by people and from what I knew about them—and you know people pretty intimately there, probably more intimately than you ever will anywhere else—I detected that perhaps their marriages were not as stable as mine was.

Since I came out I've been amazed at the number of divorces of peole I knew back here at home. Now, out of a group of 500 POWs you're going to have some of this sort of thing, too. A lot of these people would have had divorces if they hadn't been prisoner types.

Brady: It would be interesting, and I'm sure someone will attempt to do it, to study POW divorces. There have been a number of them while people were in prison, and I think there are quite a number coming up here, now that they're back. But I feel as Bill does. I really think if you look closely at every one of these divorces, there was always something wrong before. It might be something small, but I think there was a weakness in the marriage somewhere, and boy, if you started off a six or eight-year stint in jail with a weak marriage it would have to be an absolute miracle to come through with flying colors.

Tschudy: One of the things I noticed when we were talking about this marriage situation was everybody sort of was holding his breath. They didn't know what to expect. And unfortunately, in about '71 or '72 we started getting word that a few of the wives had divorced their husbands, and I think this concerned some people whose marriages might have been a little shaky. Everybody was reassuring everyone else that divorce was not possible, under the Soldiers-Sailors

Act, while you're a prisoner of war, or while you're overseas. Yet, all of a sudden, we found out that they'd been going down to Mexico and getting divorces. And I think some people were wondering about that, hoping if their marriage was unstable that they'd have a chance to get back and work on it.

A lot of people did a lot of self-reviewing while they were up there. I can't remember how many guys told me: "Oh gee, now that I think about it, I used to treat my wife terribly." They'd feel remorseful, and they'd make all those great vows about how they're going to do things differently. Well, a lot of fellows hoped that they could get out and do those things to prove themselves, and to improve their marriages. But, for some of them, it just isn't going to work out that way.

9

. . . and Never the Twain Shall Meet

More than most of the millions of Americans who went to Viet Nam, the POWs discovered the truth in that old maxim about East being East and West being West. They didn't understand what made their Vietnamese captors tick, and it was obvious that the Vietnamese didn't understand their prisoners either.

For example: torture is an accepted part of Vietnamese prison philosophy. Virtually all the prison cells—north and south—contain leg shackles, or stocks, in which inmates are locked for lengthy periods of time.

The prisoner in Viet Nam has no rights. This is quite a contrast to prison philosophy in the Unied States, where inmates have staged insurrections to support their demands for more variety in the meals they are served, or to establish the right of quasi-religious organizations, like the Black Panthers, to hold regular meetings. In this country, a guard accused of physically torturing an inmate would be suspended, pending an investigation.

But, the differences between American and Vietnamese are far greater than that. We just can't comprehend their form of nationalistic Communism, and they have no comprehension of democracy as we know it. Their backwardness offends most Americans, just as our technological advances baffle most Vietnamese. To them, dog is a gustatory delight, while the thought of eating "man's best friend" makes us ill.

This clash of different backgrounds, tastes and ideologies was never more jarring than in the prison camps of North Viet Nam. There were a couple of added factors: the Americans had to learn to play the game by the other guy's rules—something few Americans do very well. But, the ultimate outcome of the POW War was never in doubt to the Americans. They knew that most of them would be going home to the familiar comforts of the United States, while their captors would be remaining behind in the poverty of their war-ravaged homeland.

In San Antonio, Texas, I talked with three of the POWs about their difficulties in dealing with the North Vietnamese.

The discussion took place in the hospital room of Army Master Sergeant John Anderson of Niagara Falls, New York. He was the first of the POWs I had met in March, just after Hanoi started releasing the men. John Anderson was not a fighting man. He was a broadcaster helping to run a television station for the American armed forces in the northernmost provinces of South Viet Nam. At the time of his capture, during the Tet offensive of 1968, he was stationed in one of the country's lovelier places, the ancient imperial capital of Hue.

Air Force Major Glenn H. Wilson, who lives in the San Antonio suburb of Universal City, Texas, also had been stationed in a beauty spot in South Viet Nam. He was flying F-4s out of Cam Ranh Bay, an area which boasts one of the best stretches of beach in the world, and which was largely untouched by the war. Glenn and his back-seater were captured in August of 1967, after their plane was shot down on a mission in the Dong Hoi area of North Viet Nam. He joined me at Brooke Army Hosptial, where Andy Anderson and another Army man, Sergeant First Class Cordine McMurray of Fayetteville, North Carolina, were undergoing some follow-up medical treatment.

Mac, a Detroit-born black, also had been stationed in one of the fabled areas of South Viet Nam—the lush central highlands, where wealthy Frenchmen used to ride native elephants as they went out to hunt mountain lions. But, on the day he was captured, Mac was hunting an even more elusive game—North Vietnamese Army troops—and they found him first.

Mac was a "grunt"—an infantry soldier—out on a search and destroy mission with his platoon from the 4th Infantry Divison. He and four other grunts ran into some "Charlies" who had been setting up an ambush. (Charlie was the grunts' name for enemy troops—a derivative of Victor Charlie, the military radio code for VC or Viet Cong.) Mac told me what it was like to be captured in the dense jungle, out near the Laotian border.

McMurray: I figured that they weren't going to kill us, not then, unless they figured that we had information that was vital to them. I calmed one of the other guys down, trying to make him believe that they weren't going to kill us. Then, everything was all right.

Rowan: Were you allowed to maintain contact with the other fellows from your platoon?

McMurray: No, I was separated from them. I was wounded in my right leg, but we walked three—maybe four —thousand meters [two or three miles] before I actually realized I had been wounded, and the only reason I knew it then was that my leg started burning when we crossed a stream. I saw then that I was wounded, so they bandaged me up. We got to another creek. They wanted me to cross it. I told them, no, I wasn't going to cross it. And I thought that I was going to die right there. But, the Charlies realized that I wasn't going to do it, and they didn't try to hurt me or anything like that. They ran off and about a half-an-hour later they came back with a hammock and they carried me the rest of the way.

Rowan: Was there any American artillery coming in your direction as this was going on?

McMurray: At this point, the choppers and artillery were a great distance away. We could hear it. In fact, even all that night when they were sleeping, I could hear it. I estimated it to be maybe 10-11,000 meters [about six or seven miles] away.

Rowan: You weren't worried about being killed by one of your own shells?

McMurray: No. I was in a foxhole. I slept in a foxhole. It was pretty well fortified.

Rowan: Were the North Vietnamese pretty well prepared? Did they know the territory pretty well?

McMurray: This area had trails—small, but high speed trails. They were well worn down, and had no jagged branches sticking out in them. And there were foxholes all along the trail, behind bamboo thickets. They moved with confidence. They knew where they were going.

Rowan: What were your feelings that first night? Did they tie you up?

McMurray: Right, they tied me up inside the foxhole, and gave me some milk, and then, they all just went to bed. I untied myself and got up to the top of the hole, to look around, to see if there were any guards. But I did not have the energy to get up and try to get away. I couldn't walk any farther.

Rowan: What was your mind doing?

McMurray: At first, it was wondering what was going to happen to me, how long I would stay a prisoner. And I was wondering if my unit had sent out patrols looking for us. The second night, I began to have bad dreams or hallucinations— I thought my unit was right out there, and I would raise up out of my hammock and say, "Hey, I'm over here." But nobody was there. This went on for about two nights. Then, that's when I got the idea that it was really going to be a long war. There was no chance of me getting away.

Rowan: How long did you think it might be?

McMurray: Well, one of the doctors who spoke fairly good English explained to me that the longest they might keep me would be maybe nine to twelve months, and this depended on my behavior.

Rowan: Then, what would happen to you?

McMurray: Then, I would be released. Now this was what I had on my mind at this particular time.

Rowan: You figured you could make 12 months, standing on your head?

McMurray: Right. No problem.

Rowan: Andy, the circumstances of your capture were extremely different. You were captured in the sudden onslaught against Hue in the Tet offensive of '68.

Anderson: Yeah, they hit the city three days before they actually came in to our building. They cut off all water, electricity and telephone lines, and we lost communications with the MAC-V compound [Military Assistance Command—Viet Nam]. We had a portable radio, and we were listening to AFVN [Armed Forces—Viet Nam] broadcasts, and according to what we heard on AFVN, our section of the city had no problems whatsoever. Everything was to the north and east of the city. The southern area was pretty much under control. They had mortared the city the night of January 30th—when Tet began. We shut down the TV station and the generators completely, because anything that was sounding off in the city at all was mortared, immediately. And we set up a perimeter defense around our quarters.

Well, the night of the fourth, our guard spotted a combination of Viet Cong and NVA [North Vietnamese Army] troops, moving down the street. So we pulled back into the house, and set up our defenses. They blew off the front of the house with a satchel charge, and we fought them off all that night.

The next day, they started blowing the building down around our ears with B-40s [anti-tank rockets]. The roof caught fire and started falling in. We decided to make a break for it, to try to get out, and not burn up in it. I think they let us get out.

We caught some machine gun fire. Lieutenant [James V.] Dibernardo was wounded. We started up the main street, to try to make it back to the MAC-V compound. They pinned us down again, in back of another house. I was hit in the chest and the hand.

We lost one boy up there, and each of the men there was wounded to varying degrees. When I came to, they were yelling for me to surrender, and a man was standing there pointing an AK-47 [automatic rifle] at me.

They had an interpreter there who had obviously been educated by the French, because he had a French accent. He was asking our names, and we got the impression from talking to him that they were actually looking for us. When I gave him my name, the Lieutenant who was there just looked at me and nodded his head and smiled, and wrote the name down in his book.

A medic gave me some field treatment. He bandaged up my chest and my hands, and they tied our arms behind our backs and started running us out. They took us up to an old pagoda on the outskirts of the city, and kept us there overnight.

Rowan: What was your initial reaction to the realization that you were a prisoner?

Anderson: I was hit pretty hard in the chest, and I think there was a lot of shock involved there. I don't know why I got the impression that they were looking for us, but I got that impression, and it kind of worried me. I didn't know exactly what they had in mind.

The Vietnamese television station had been in the same compound we were in, and I think the NVA thought we were running the Vietnamese station, as well as our own.

In fact, they asked me where my CO was. I told them I didn't know. They didn't get him until about 15 minutes after they got me. And when they brought him in, they *told* him his name, they didn't ask him.

Rowan: That was Lieutenant Dibernardo?

Anderson: Right. So it looked pretty obvious that they knew who they were looking for in the city—those people they wanted. There was no question about being killed. They told us immediately they were going to take us to Hanoi.

Rowan: Did you get the feeling there was a price on your head?

Anderson: We heard this rumor several times before, that all of the AFVN people, particularly in the news media, had had a price put on their heads. But I heard the same malarkey in Korea, back in the 50's.

I do know that, later, when I was in my first camp west of Hanoi, some of the North Vietnamese civilians claimed there was an offer by the U.S. government of $10,000 per man if they would turn Americans back in to the American government. It didn't seem to affect these people at all, as much as they were in need of money.

Rowan: What about that trip to Hanoi?

Anderson: Well, after about 25 or 26 days on the trail, we ran into another group of prisoners, and the troops who had been bringing them in took us all into the north.

Rowan: So you were really never out of contact with Americans from the very beginning?

Anderson: No, I went north with three other people, and then we met up with a group of eight.

Rowan: Glenn, for you it was 34 days before you got to Hanoi. Were you alone?

Wilson: No, within an hour after we were shot down I saw Denny [Captain Carl Dennis Chambers], my back seater. We marched together that night. And the next day we marched together up to this staging area right north of the airfield at Dong Hoi, where we stayed for 18 days. He was in one bunker and I was in another one, about 15 feet away. We were kept separated, but we got to talk to each other a couple of times during those three weeks.

And then we made an escape from there. We made it to the coast, and got two boats out, both of which sank. It was right after a big storm, and the water was real rough. They sank and we were captured the next morning. The next day after that we started up to Hanoi. We picked up two more fellows that night who had been shot down on the ninth of August, two reccy troops [reconnaissance pilots] and the four of us then made the trip to Hanoi. It took us 11 days by truck, with a four-day stopover just outside Vinh, at a kind of an interrogation camp. That's where we were first interrogated. A place called "The Half-Way House." A lot of guys who were shot down in the southern part of North Viet Nam made that stop.

Anderson: They held *us* there from April to August, and then moved us north. So that must have been a big general staging area.

Rowan: Glenn, had you and Denny worked out any kind of a cover story?

Wilson: No, I didn't see where we really needed a cover story. I figured it was common knowledge to anybody who had any brains at all that we were just up there bombing and got banged. So that's exactly what we told them. We were bombing up there and got shot down.

By the way, the interrogation had absolutely no military significance at all. By the time we got to Vinh, we'd been down three weeks, and by the time we got to Hanoi, we'd been down over a month. I got very little military interrogation. Most if it was predictable stuff like: "Who was your squadron commander? What kind of airplane were you flying?" and stuff like that. You could lie to them if you wanted to and they'd buy it. It didn't make any difference. You could tell one guy you were flying an F-4. You could tell another guy that you were flying a 105. It didn't make any difference, just as long as you gave them answers. The big thing impressed on me real early in the interrogation game was: "You aren't going to say 'no.' You aren't going to say: 'I'm going to stick to name, rank, and serial number!' " They impressed on us very early that they weren't going to let us do that.

Rowan: How did they impress that on you?

Wilson: With ropes, straps, beatings, things like that.

Rowan: What was the first question that you refused to answer?

Wilson: Well, the first question that I refused to answer was what kind of airplane I was flying, and where I was flying out of. They made it very plain after a while that they weren't going to accept name, rank, serial number, date of birth.

Rowan: But you felt at that point that you could have told them anything?

Wilson: I did tell them I was flying out of Cam Ranh; I told them Danang; I told them Ubon, And as far as I know, there was very little coordination between their interrogators. They just didn't seem to check with the other fellows as to what you were telling them.

Anderson: I can go along with this. I probably had as many as nine different people come down during a period of two years that I was there. I'd tell the same man different things at different times. Now he'd make notes, very complete notes, of everything I'd say. He'd come back maybe two days later with the same list of questions, and in many cases they were going back to my military history, like: "When did you make PFC?" Well, hell, I didn't remember when I made PFC and so I gave him *another* date. And it might be six months later before they came in and said, "Well, you told us one day the 15th of March, and you told us later the 30th of March." I told them, "I don't remember." They'd say: "When was it?" So I said, "Well maybe it was the first of April." And now they had all three dates down.

These people they sent in to interrogate us, if you went above the sixth grade level as far as words were concerned, you were talking over their heads. They didn't know what you were talking about.

Rowan: Did that help you or hurt you?

Anderson: It hurt in some respects, because you couldn't get through to them. They'd ask you a question and ask for an answer. For example, people who don't comprehend electricity don't have the foggiest ideea what small cooking utensils are. I made the mistake of mentioning that my mother had an electric frying pan.

He said: "Describe it for me."

Of course you can't talk with your hands, that's supposed to be an insult. So try to describe an electric frying pan to a man who doesn't know anything about electricity. And you could be punished if you didn't come up wth a decent answer.

Rowan: Mac, you were out in the field. Did they interrogate you? Did they try to get military information out of you?

McMurray: It was some days after we had reached our first camp, I'd say about the early part of August. They asked me a lot of questions concerning my unit. How many machine guns we had in our platoon. How many officers there were. How many men were in the company. What was our mission. What was our CO's name. I just told them, "Well, our company commander's name was John Paul Jones. Our first sergeant's name was Nathan Hale."

This one particular guy we had knew American history, and he said, "Well, John Paul Jones was a great naval captain." I'd say, "Yeah, yeah, yeah. Maybe he had a son or somebody else who is named John Paul Jones." I told him, "there's more than one person named Jones in the United States." And he wrote it down. That was it.

Wilson: We'd always been told in our survival schools that once you start answering questions, it's a good snowball type thing, and that you *never* try to duke it out with a good interrogator, because he'll get to you. I found that it was definitely not true in this war. The interrogators that I ran into, without an exception, were very, very poor at what they were doing, and you could get them off on a subject that had very little to do with their original questions. And you could B.S. with them almost indefinitely.

A lot of guys went through an awful lot of punishment because they were afraid that once they started talking, a sophisticated interrogator would get to them. As it turned out, they just didn't have any sophisticated interrogators.

Anderson: If the interrogators had been a little sharper, I think they would have capitalized on the feeling of depression that hit you when you first broke down and gave them something more than name, rank, serial number. You're tremendously depressed. "My God, what have I done?" If they'd been sharp enough to stay on top of you, if they'd hit you at that time, and kept working, they'd have got more.

Wilson: The thing that got me was that when they did break me, they were breaking me on something that really wasn't that important. They finally got me to say, "OK, I'm flying an F-4 out of Cam Ranh Bay." Then, I thought, "OK, they're going to come up with some good questions here pretty soon. I've been in the service a long time. I've been involved with nuclear weapons all my career. Boy, they're going to get some good interrogators in here now that I've started to talk, and they're really going to put some questions to me." But, surprisingly enough, they never came.

Aside from those military matters, I was scared I would be forced to do propaganda things—like war crimes statements, amnesty statements, germ warfare statements—things these people are so famous for getting out of people, even though they're complete lies. I thought, "Boy, now that they've got me broke they're really going to put it to me." It never came.

Now, they did get the anti-war statements out of some guys, while they were down. And they signed amnesty statements, and things like this. But, in my case, I kept waiting for the hammer to fall and it never fell.

Rowan: Was there ever a time when you just didn't think you were going to be able to hack it?

Anderson: The only time it hit me was on the trail, about 20 days out. I had had dysentery for several days, and there was one particularly rough mountain we were going over, and I just got to the point where I said, "The hell with it. If they're going to shoot me, let them shoot me." Surprisingly enough, the man in charge said, "All right, we will stop. We will stay one night and give you a chance to rest."

They were afraid of us dying on the trail because they had to sign for us when they brought us north, and they had sent a message north telling what people they were bringing up, and I think they were afraid of the repercussions if they lost any prisoners.

I don't know whether this was true in everybody's case, but I think the more they kept on me physically, the madder it made me. And I think this is what kept me going. I got to the point where I said: "I'll be damned if you people are going to kill me," especially after I'd gone that far. I wanted to go home.

That survival instinct is awfully strong, *awfully* strong.

When I was down in D-1 [a holding area for prisoners moving north], when they had me in solitary for a while, I was living on boiled water and some bread about the size of a couple of hard rolls. I was down to about 165 pounds [from over 200]. And a couple of times, when they were working me over, I hoped that I'd die.

But the survival instinct was always there. I'd wake up in the morning after a couple of hours sleep, ready to go again . . . well, not ready, but it was there again.

Rowan: Did you ever think about taking your own life?

Anderson: It crossed my mind a couple of times. They got to us one time on a com thing, and I was afraid I was going to blow the whole works, and I thought about it then.

But, then I started playing the question and answer game with them. I'd say: "I don't know what you're talking about. What do you mean?" They'd let a little bit drop. Then, they'd let a little more drop. And it got to where I could feed them back enough of what they were telling me to satisfy them.

McMurray: Most of the interrogators would tell you more or less what they wanted you to tell them. Or you could just come right out and ask them.

Anderson: You couldn't get to all of them that way, but the one I had then, Winnie the Pooh, I could get to him with, "I don't know what you're talking about."

Of course, this was the third time they'd had me in a bind, and I'd play the old game: "Now you people did this before and I didn't have anything to tell you. What the hell do you want from me now?"

Wilson: One thing that we used quite a bit was: "Okay, we know that you can break us and make us talk and we will give you answers to your questions, but we honestly don't know the answers. We'll give you answers, but they will not be true answers," This always kind of baffled them, They'd say: "What's the sense of pressing on with this guy, because he'll break, but then he'll give us lies."

Anderson: The sad thing about it was that what they wanted out of us was so ridiculous. They went through all of this business of working a guy over physically and psychologically, in one case that I know of, for almost three solid months, and then, the end result was that they had the guy sit down and write a letter to one of the peace groups telling them that he protested the war.

Rowan: Did they ever send those letters?

Anderson: I have no idea.

Wilson: I know that a couple of guys wrote letters to the President and to Senator McGovern and Senator Mansfield, and they really felt badly about it. They had gone through a lot, and when they came back to the room, they were really broken up, saying things like, "My career is ruined" "I'm a traitor." All this kind of stuff. But I haven't heard anywhere that any of those letters ever made it back. Or, if they did, those people just completely disregarded them.

McMurray: I liked to tell them about things that I own. They'd call me over to ask me how I could afford to own an automobile and five rooms of furniture, and have two televisions when I was a black in the service. It was their belief that blacks didn't own anything.

One interrogator told me that no blacks in the United States owned anything. I told him that was wrong, because I did. He said: "When were you captured?" I said, "July 12th, 1967." And he said: "Well, on July 13th, 1967, things changed." (*Laughter*)

Wilson: They weren't very sophisticated with their interrogation.

Anderson: We had an interrogator who came in one time and he said to me: "Do you have a water-making machine in your house?" And I said: "What do you mean?" And he said, "You know, where you turn it and the water comes out." I said: "Yes, I have a water faucet. Most everyone has them in their houses."

He was baffled by the idea.

Many of these people had been pulled off the farm. I won't deny that they had the intelligence level, but they just didn't have any familiarity with what goes on in the United States.

They would tell us about the havoc in the stock market— that the economy was falling apart. At the same time, they'd give us the ball scores, and we'd notice that there were four or five new teams in the baseball leagues and the football leagues. And they couldn't understand why we didn't believe them about the economy. But, we knew that there had to be a lot of money coming from somewhere to start new teams, and that the people had to be getting enough money to go to the games.

McMurray: They'd ask me whether I was going to get a job or stay in the service once I got home. And I'd say I was going to stay in the service. They'd ask me why. And I'd tell them, "There's money to be made." Then, we'd go back to the business of being a paid killer. They thought the only reason a man would be in the service is to kill. They never thought a man would be trying to better himself, and learn a skill, so he could get out and work on the outside, eventually.

Anderson: After each one of these sessions we'd have to do a taped apology to the camp commander for breaking the regulations, and so forth.

Wilson: I only had to do that once, but I've written probably half-a-dozen apologies to the camp commander, and they were ridiculous. I told them what I was apologizing for, like not answering a question about why I was flying over North Viet Nam and bombing it. And I'd say, "I was punished by being put on my knees for three days, and I won't do it again."

If they ever made that thing public, it would make them look ridiculous.

Anderson: Like the letter that Bruce Archer wrote home to his mother one time. He said: "My weight is not losing." *(Laughter)*

Rowan: I heard that they would dictate things.

Anderson: Right. They would dictate the letters to you.

Wilson: During my first week in Hanoi—after I'd been broken—they had me write things on close air support for coastal landings. I was supposed to describe how the Air Force would support an invasion from the sea.

They gave me some paper and a pencil, and I started writing it.

I wrote for five days, I wrote about fuel. I wrote about tires. I wrote about four pages on how to change a tire on an F-4. How to refuel an F-4. They already had all this information. They've got technical orders [manuals] for every airplane in the American inventory.

But, this guy would come in and he'd see that I was really stacking up the paperwork, and that really impressed him. He didn't bother to read it. He just asked me if I was through, and I said: "No, I'm not through."

I figured as long as I can keep writing, they're going to leave me alone.

When I had a stack of papers an inch high, they finally got sick and tired of me saying I wasn't through, and they wanted to read what I'd written. And they started reading it and immediately blew up and said I'd been wasting their time.

And sure enough, I had.

And another thing. I normally print everything I write. But on this, I wrote longhand. And my longhand is something that you can't believe. It takes me about an hour to do a page, and I only get about three words to a line.

But, if they had ever turned that loose, I figured someone would know all I ever do is print. And a lot of guys did that— change their handwriting to indicate that this was not done voluntarily.

Rowan: What was it that gave you the strength to hold yourself together through all those years in prison?

Wilson: We had a desire to make it through because we knew that one day we'd come back to the United States.

McMurray: Land of plenty!

Wilson: That's one thing we used to tell those guys: "We feel sorry for you because when this war's over we're going back to the United States, and that's the most beautiful country in the world. You bastards have to stay here, and live here the rest of your lives. And you're probably going to have it worse, because, when you don't have us, you can't sit around on your duff all day pretending you're working. You'll probaly have to go back to the rice paddies, and start working for a living. We're going back to the United States, and drive a car again, and watch movies, and television, and play sports and stuff."

McMurray: And eat real food.

Rowan: Did you argue with them about the way they treated you?

Wilson: While I was going through my six months of solitary, we were living in these little cells, and they had just come out a few days before and said: "The punishment's over. You guys are through being punished. We're going back to normal living again." But nothing changed. We were still in the same room. We still weren't allowed to talk to anybody. We were still in solitary.

I got into a pissing contest with the guard and went out to a quiz, and I was talking to the officer, a guy we called "Spot."

I said, "Well, when are you going to start treating us like human beings? You're treating us like animals. We treat animals in the zoo back in the United States better than you treat us, in these cages." And he said, "Do you know that we're treating you better than the American government is treating the American people?"

I said, "Send me back to my room. There's no sense in me even talking to you anymore. I don't want to discuss it with you."

When he said it to me I could tell that he was sincere; he believed it. He'd been getting information on how badly the people were starving to death on the streets back in the United States, with many millions of people on welfare.

Anderson: They took us out to the pagoda out there at Redemption Lake one time, and we were going down through Hanoi and they were talking about the great advantages of socialism. We saw this old woman down there, with one of these big straw brooms, sweeping the street. Her clothes were totally patched. She looked like she was probably 65 years old. Her arms would have made a good broom handle, back in the States. When we got back in, and I was again talking to Winnie the Pooh, I said, "How can you talk about poverty? Did you see that woman who was out there sweeping the streets?" And he said, "Well this is part of what the government gives her to make her feel that she is earning her own keep."

Wilson: Yeah, I think that's very important. They didn't have anything to relate to, as far as anything better, but we did. And there was no way they could sell communism to anybody that I was associated with over there, not only from the way they tried to sell it, but just from what was so obvious to everybody. It's a sick form of government. The whole philosophy is sick, as far as I'm concerned.

We'd get the news that Saigon had just closed down 34 newspapers because they were pro-Communist, or something like that. I'd ask them, "Well how many newspapers do you have in Hanoi? All we've ever seen is one, and that's obviously run by the government." They'd say, "Well, we don't have any other newspapers. Our government wouldn't lie to us."

We couldn't get it across to them. If we want to read five different newspapers, and get five different opinions on something, we can. We never take just one person's word for it.

Rowan: Out of this all, I take it that your views about communism are perhaps even stronger. How about your views as to war as a way of settling matters?

Wilson: I don't think war is a way to settle anything. There's never been any doubt in my mind about that and this didn't change it at all. But, I definitely got the opinion up there that you're going to have to put the hammer on them to get them to shape up. You're not going to negotiate with Marxist-Leninist hard-line militant Communists. If they're going to use force, the only way you're going to stop them is put the hammer on them.

I think the last ten days in 1972, when the B-52s showed up, there was no doubt in my mind or anybody's that I was living with that this thing was coming to an end. The United States had finally decided, "We're going to hammer you beggars, and we're going to continue to hammer you until you come around." I just think they could have done that five years earlier.

10

Hogan's Heroes

One hundred and thirty-one Americans were captured and put in prison camps during the final years of the war in Viet Nam—most of them pilots.

For those shot down in 1972, prison life was a much different experience than it had been for the more than 400 other POWs captured earlier. For them, there were threats, but there was no torture. There was adequate food and there was medical treatment. There were times of the day when they could get together in the fresh air and talk or play games.

At the time of Alan J. Kroboth's graduation from high school in Burke, Virginia, in 1965, there already were a couple of dozen men in the Hanoi Hilton. Four years later, he joined the Marine Corps. By July of 1972, he was a First Lieutenant and a bombardier-navigator in the right seat of an A-6. On a bombing run over South Viet Nam, near Khe Sanh, his plane was hit. He blacked out, and within minutes was a POW.

Navy Lieutenant J.G. Joseph E. Kernan was yet another pilot who ran into the defenses around Thanh Hoa, in North Viet Nam's southern panhandle. In May of 1972, Joe was flying an aerial reconnaissance mission over the Thanh Hoa area when his RA-5 was hit and he parachuted.

When I talked with these two men at the Bethesda Naval Hospital outside of Washington, D.C.—where they were undergoing medical examinations prior to being sent home to their families—I found them to be considerably different than the other POWs I had met. They were younger, of course, but that was only a minor factor. They had escaped the torture experienced by earlier shoot-downs, but even that doesn't explain everything. I suspect the major difference is that they never suffered that feeling of terrible guilt which has been so vividly described by others—that period of days or weeks or months after having been broken when each man thought he was the only one who had ever sold out, and when many wished for death rather than have to face family and friends. The earlier prisoners carried a terrible burden of shame.

For most of the '72 shoot downs, the only real horror was the uncertainty about what would happen after they drifted to earth on their parachutes. Al Kroboth and Joe Kernan didn't even suffer that, since they blacked out when their planes were hit. But Joe does have one fleeting memory of that moment.

Kernan: I remember a sensation of light flooding the cockpit. I think it was the canopy jettisoning. From that point, I don't remember anything until I woke up on the ground. I started to get up and, for about five seconds, I was removed from the situation and was *watching* myself get up. It was the weirdest thing I'd ever experienced in my life.

I was talking to the doctor yesterday, and he said it's what they call "depersonalization." They can't explain it, it happens. I think I just didn't want to be there so badly that I tried to get away.

I think I regained consciousness within a minute after I hit the ground, and, by that time, the Vietnamese people were already arriving. I landed about 15 feet away from a house and they were coming from everywhere. This is the fuzziest part of my whole experience, but I remember glimpses of faces, and people screaming.

Rowan: Did they actually attack you?

Kernan: Yes, Most of the people who were on me were

boys, from the age of about 13 to 15, and some women and some little kids. It was the boys who were the most violent, and yet, looking back, that's certainly a natural reaction for them, me having dropped in the way I did. I received a few small cuts and bruises, and I remember hoping that somebody in uniform would show up. About five minutes after I landed, three or four militiamen came running up. As they waded through the people, one of them grabbed me and tied my arms behind me, and they started talking with the people. I had the feeling they were trying to decide what to do with me, and the militiamen were saying, "Well, we're going to take him, because that's the way it ought to be." I was pulling for the militia.

At that point, I remember thinking, "Maybe this is a dream." That lasted for about five seconds, and I said, "No, it's not. You're really here."

Rowan: Alan, what happened to you when you woke up on the ground, and what were your first thoughts?

Kroboth: My first words were, "Oh, hell! God damn! What have I done?" I lay there. I couldn't move my arms. My head was up on a log. And, about 10 feet away was an NVA army man with an AK-47, to make sure I wasn't going to go anywhere.

They put me in a stretcher and then they carried me westward for about 20 or 30 minutes. I was in and out of consciousness at that time. There was never really any apprehension on my part. They couldn't speak English at all, and of course I couldn't speak Vietnamese. They tried to talk to me a few times, but nothing was ever conveyed. They did ask me about the aircraft, indicating that it had been diving and then it exploded. I just shrugged this off. I didn't believe it.

I really didn't have any problem until I started getting into North Viet Nam, going up the trail. The villagers, the people themselves, they don't like us at all. If you weren't a B-52 pilot, you were lucky. They wouldn't string you up right there. But there were times when I actually thought we weren't going to leave certain villages alive.

I had been shot down on July 7th, and I arrived at Hanoi on September 20th, after a two-and-a-half month trip.

Rowan: By the time you both were shot down, an awful lot of men were being held in North Viet Nam, and a much greater number were missing in action. What did you expect to have happen to you?

Kernan: On the truck, on the way up to Hanoi, I had a feeling that I had been challenged, and that now I was going to find out quite a bit about what I was made up of. I don't think that I was really worried about torture. The possibility existed, certainly, that I would be, but I felt that I wouldn't.

Rowan: Alan, you were en route to Hanoi for a much longer period. What happened to you during that trip?

Kroboth: I tried to escape, at one point, while I was being held in a camp. I had it all laid out. How I was going, where I was going. I had it all planned. I was ready to go during their siesta time, about 12 o'clock during the day. I wanted to get about three or four miles through the mountains, and out towards the coast.

But, the escape didn't last long. Just after I slipped out of camp, I thought someone was shooting at me, and I went right back to the hootch [thatched hut] my 6'5" running about three feet off the ground.

I sat down and gathered my thoughts,·and then I walked out and looked up to the top of the hill, and there were two kids, pointing up to the top of a tree. One of them had an AK, and they apparently had been shooting at a bird. But, the sound of that gun had scared me, and I didn't try to leave again. That was the only chance I had to get away.

Rowan: Did any of the North Vietnamese find out about it?

Kroboth: No. But the next day, by coincidence, I was interrogated by an officer. He pulled out a pistol, and said, "I can shoot you for all the crimes you've committed against the Vietnamese people."

I didn't say anything, just nodded my head, and he commenced his questioning. He did ask some military questions and a lot of personal questions. I wasn't about to give him

any information that would give them any type of help whatsoever. In general, if you're going to say anything, lie like
hell, but remember your lies.

Rowan: Did you reach a sticking point with him?

Kroboth: No. But, this [interrogation] was almost a
month-and-a-half after I was captured, so I knew they
weren't after military information. As for what I told them,
there was nothing of value, if not lies. When I got to Plantation Gardens, I was isolated for about five days for intensive
interrogation. Then, I was let out with the other Americans.
Those first five days didn't bother me that much. The
hardest thing was remembering some of the false statements
I made. I thank God that the guy I talked to down south
never correlated those statements with the ones I made up
north, because if he did, I wouldn't be here right now. That
was the roughest thing that first week. Other than that, I
really wasn't afraid.

I really never thought of being tortured. They had different
ways of doing torture: lack of medical treatment, a cut down
in food, this type of thing. By the time I got there, this is the
way they were getting people to do things. There was no
physical torture. In that first five days, they were convinced
that all first lieutenants were very stupid. That was their
comment to me.

Rowan: What did you tell them to convince them of that?

Kroboth: I told them where I lived back in the States. My
family has lived in a cemetery for the last 25 or 30 years. I
told them they live in a cemetery. Trying to explain that to
the Vietnamese took almost a half a day, and they didn't
believe it. I think they just kind of gave up at the end.

They told me, "If you do not tell us what we want to know,
we will not treat your wounds." All I said was, "Okay."

Altogether I had two major interrogations, and what we
called "attitude checks." The attitude checks happened
once a month. I'd be sitting at a table. The interrogator
would be on the other side, and he'd start talking. I'd spend
the time counting how many times he said, "You see" and
"You know," And then, at the end he'd say, "Well, what do

you think?" I'd say, "Can I have a cigarette?" He'd say, "You have a very bad attitude." That was the end of it.

They wanted me to know what all the [POW] camp regulations were of course. They asked me about a few of the regulations, and I told them I had never seen them. Every time I said that, they'd hand me another set. I had stacks of them.

Rowan: Joe, what happened when you were first questioned?

Kernan: My interrogation lasted about three days. The fact that I was only a J.G. [lieutenant junior grade] and it was my first cruise, early in the cruise, helped me a great deal. Not only was I able to say that I didn't know the answers to many of their questions, but in fact I *didn't know* the answers.

There were subtle hints and threats that I had not answered the questions seriously or correctly, with the proper attitude, and that I must try to do better. I was asked once if I thought I would be tortured, and I said, "Well, I don't know, but I don't think so," and they just smiled and left. Like Al, I didn't think too much about being tortured.

Most of my time, initially, was spent resigning myself to the fact that I probably was going to be alone for about a half a year. So, after the first three days, I'd exercise, and make up games; like running through the states and state capitals; arranging them alphabetically, both forward and backward. I would do that once a day with the state capitals, because I didn't want to get to where it was rote for me. I would save that as long as I could into the day.

I'd also multiply three and four digit numbers in my head. Generally, I tried to work up a program that I felt would keep me going for however long I was going to be alone. That ended up being just 25 days.

After that, I was moved to the Zoo. There were three other rooms in my building, and there was an American in each one. I'd wait at the door for 20 minutes, trying to get a glimpse of somebody through the crack, and see if it really was an American, and possibly one I would recognize. It was probably a week before we got to talking.

Rowan: Do you have any special memories from that period in the Zoo?

Kernan: One of the prettiest things I've ever heard came during that period. I was in the room one day, and one of the other guys was out sweeping the leaves in the courtyard. I was looking through the crack in the door and I had a pretty good view of him. He was scooping the leaves into a wicker basket, and the holes in the basket were bigger than the leaves. He kept putting them in, and he'd pick up the basket, and there'd still be eight or ten leaves on the ground. This went on about three times and I was watching him get more and more frustrated. And he said the first words I had heard from an American in a long time. He said: "Goddamn fucking basket." And it was great. I was in heaven.

Rowan: Alan, you said you were isolated for just five days. How did you feel during that period?

Kroboth: I just wanted to *see* an American, that's all. I began looking out the cracks and the holes to try to find somebody. I thought I heard some American voices, but later I found out it was the Vietnamese. The Vietnamese had tried a few taps on the wall a couple of times, to see if I would answer any kind of code. I didn't respond to this.

After five days, they finally let me out, and I stood in the doorway and there was a group of Americans, 14 of them, and they said: "Welcome to Plantation Gardens." That was the greatest day.

Major Floyd Kushner, who was a doctor, was in the camp, and he immediatley diagnosed all my injuries. I had many boils, all over my back. He said, "What you need is a good bath." It had been a month and a half since I had taken a bath. I got some soap, and, because my shoulder was broken, they all helped to clean me up.

I was in a state of depression when I first got there, because I was still running through my mind what had happened, and wondering what was going to happen. But then, I just woke up one morning and said, "I'm more of a problem to them alive and active than if I just sit around and do nothing."

So I thought I'd make a little trouble here and there. I really didn't think they were ever going to torture me. Threaten me, yes, but not torture me. So we'd do things. We started singing at night. We made up a Christmas song. We wrote new words to "The Twelve Days of Christmas." Of course, the guards would get mad, so we'd sing for the guards now and then, and laugh at them.

I'd compare a lot of it to Hogan's Heroes on TV. Very close to it. The morale and the spirit of everybody was like that.

11

Heartbreak Hotel

Within the walls of the Hanoi Hilton was a cellblock where almost every American shot down in North Viet Nam—and kept alive after being captured—spent the first few days or weeks of his confinement. It was nicknamed Heartbreak Hotel, and hard by it were the interrogation rooms in which North Vietnamese men nicknamed The Cat, The Rabbit, Pig Eye, The Bug and so forth conducted their activities.

Dick Stratton described it this way:

"I was there in January of '67. The temperature was down to 40 degreees Fahrenheit and I was in my skivvy shorts for seven days until they determined whether I was going to live or die. I was sleeping on cement, so I was cold, and there was one little 40-watt light bulb covered with dust in a ceiling that was 14 feet over my head. It was dim.

"When I think of that period I think of cold, I think of dimness, I think of hordes of mosquitoes cascading through the windows, even in that temperature, like waves coming in. It was a high window. Even if you stood on your bunk and tried to look over the boarded-up portion, you could barely see any portion of the outside courtyard, where some Vietnamese prisoners were being held.

"Heartbreak Hotel was a holding place for those who were undergoing intensive interrogation and torture. Most of the torture was done in what we called Room 18—the Star Chamber—the Violent Room—near the main gate. It had been soundproofed for purposes of muffling the sound, because there were Vietnamese living in that area, too. They also took one of Bob Shumaker's old cells and put concrete all over the walls and ceiling to muffle the sound. That became known as Shu's Room, and Shu's Room was an alternate torture room.

"Room 18 was probably about 20 feet long and maybe 12 to 14 feet wide. It had a stucco soundproofing material on the walls, and it was painted what we in the Navy call wardroom green. If you've been on a ship, you know it's kind of a sickening color, and I don't know why the Navy sticks with it. It was sort of hilarious in some ways to be sitting there looking at wardroom green in that room. There were marks —rust colored marks—on the wall, which I discovered through my own experience were blood stains.

"In the center of the room was a piece of angle iron which was broken off in the red tile floor. They utilized that in their interrogations, and also a hook in the ceiling, which apparently had been intended for a fan or a chandelier. Over in the right hand corner, as you came in the door, there was a hook in the wall, which they also used. And when I was there, there also was a hook underneath the table that they used. They would handcuff a guy with his hands behind his back and then hook him under the table and just leave him for hours while they were rephrasing their questions or something.

"The doors were glass.

"The country is falling apart and they don't have any idea of preventive maintenance. For example, the light switch wasn't working, so they simply bypassed the switch and hooked two wires together to turn the light on. It was a more powerful light—I'd say a 100-watt bulb. In place of a fuse they just put in a piece of tinfoil from a cigarette wrapper. It's a wonder the whole country didn't burn down around them.

"In that room you could hear a ping pong game going upstairs and I had the illusion, even as I was going through my ordeal there, that tomorrow or the next day I'd be up there playing ping pong with my friends. I wasn't prepared for the isolation that followed."

Two of the Navy pilots who went to Heartbreak Hotel and to Room 18 later in that year of 1967 were Commander Claude Douglas Clower—a native of Belzoni, Mississippi, and Commander William R. Stark—a native of Michigan City, Indiana.

Doug Clower was just 11 days short of being 37 years old when his F-4 was shot down south of Haiphong in November. At home he had left his wife and his nine-year-old daughter. He also had left a nine-year-old automobile, promising his wife that he'd replace it when he got back from his cruise to Viet Nam. She still had it when he got back in 1973.

Doug is a former college football lineman who speaks with an animated Mississippi accent. Laughter readily creeps into his speech and he has a way of making you interested in everything that he has to say—important and not. He reflects the inner peace of a man who is not dissatisfied with the overall direction that his life has taken.

Bill Stark had celebrated his 37th birthday just nine days before his F-4 was shot down in May of 1967. In contrast to Doug Clower, he speaks in soft, measured tones. I had the feeling, listening to him, that he was reliving his experiences as he spoke to me. When *he* got to Room 18, that makeshift light switch wasn't working, or the tinfoil fuse had burned out or something.

As we met in San Diego, where both men now live, Bill started the discussion by telling me about his visit to Room 18.

Stark: It was dark in there.

After a few minutes an interrogator came in, alone, and he had a lantern in one hand and a pistol in the other. The room was empty except for a little table and a wooden chair. He walked behind the table and, in the best Grade B movie tradition, he dropped the pistol eight or nine inches to the table, as if to indicate to me, "Boy, are you in deep serious."

I looked down at my condition. I couldn't walk; my arm

was broken and really sore; and I was just crap and corruption all over. And the thought that this guy had to have a pistol sort of struck me as funny. As a matter of fact, I laughed.

I wasn't too smart, from start to finish. When I laughed, he came around from behind the table and gave me a shot in the head with his foot; and that got us off.

His opening remarks were, and I'll paraphrase them: 'For you, the war is over and you're going to tell us everything that we wish to know.' I said nothing. And then we got on with it.

He said, "What's your name?" I gave him that. "Your rank? Your serial number? Your date of birth?"

We got through the first four questions just outstandingly. And then he said, "What ship are you from?" I didn't say anything.

He repeated the question several times and I said, "Well, you know and I know that I'm not required to answer that." He said, "Well, you're going to answer that," and he repeated the question.

This went on for a period of, oh I don't know, half an hour. He was threatening me; telling me that I *must* answer the question. I told him, "I'm not going to answer the question."

Then, he stepped outside for just an instant and came back with his helpers, and they had the straps [the ropes] with them. And they put me in the straps.

Initially, they did not put the broken arm in the straps. They just put the right one up behind me, wired me around the throat, and down. And they worked on that for awhile, and it hurt.

After a time, I don't know how long, they took the broken arm and doubled it up behind me, wired it in. I can remember looking down—there's no other direction to look when you're in the straps. I could see the fingers of my left hand coming over my left shoulder, and I was wondering, "How in the hell can they do that?" It hurt quite a bit.

This went on for a couple or three hours and after a time they undid the straps and I fell back down on the floor. I thought, "Maybe I've toughed it out. Maybe they're going to let me alone."

Well, I was wrong again.

The two guys apparently got some more help. I'm not sure how many were in there now. They still had the ankle shackles on me, and the bar that ran through them, and there was a meathook overhead. They got on their stools and they put the bar up over across the meathook. Now I'm hanging, inverted, and my head doesn't quite touch the ground.

It's getting on toward dawn now, of the 20th [of May, 1967] and that hurts, that hurts quite a bit. They beat me and they hammered on me and they kicked me. I don't know how long that went on, although I do remember that about twilight, on the 20th, the shadows in the room were beginning to get a little long and I realize it's late afternoon—I've just about come to the end of my rope. I just can't handle it anymore. And along about dark, on the 20th, I said, "Okay, I'll tell you what ship I'm from." And at that, immediately, they took me down off the hook and put me back on the floor.

I said, "Okay. I'm from the Kittyhawk." Another mistake.

As soon as I said Kittyhawk, the interrogator reached into the little drawer in the desk, and pulled out a book about the size of a Coronado, California, phone directory, and opened it up. I couldn't see what it was, but I assume now that it was a directory of people, and he went down the page and said, "Who's the Commanding Officer of the Kittyhawk?"

Well, hell, I'd heard the name, but I couldn't remember it.

He said, "You lie." Well, I didn't agree, but I didn't have any comeback. They knew I had lied. He said, "For this now we will punish you."

The thought occurred to me, "Well, what the hell do you call what's been going on for 24 hours, now?"

As punishment, they hoisted me back up on the hook and he left. The helpers took a few parting shots and they left, as if to convey to me the idea that I was going to be there awhile.

I don't know how much longer I was there. I'm guessing it was about four hours because when I realized the "error of my ways" sufficiently to understand that I've got to tell them, it was after dark. He came back and he said, "Are you ready to tell us what ship you're from?" I said, "Okay, I'm from the Enterprise."

He left me up there a little longer, as he's fumbling around checking in his book—picking his nose—and I was just hurting like hell up there. Finally, he took me down.

Back on the floor, he said, "Now, who's the Commanding Officer of your squadron?" Well, I'd already seen the book displayed and I'd already seen the futility and I didn't want to go back on that hook. I just couldn't.

I was hoping all during this period of 24 hours that they'd kill me, that I could die. But, unfortunately, that was not one of the alternatives. It would have been a whole lot easier for me right then to do that.

So I said, "Commander Lefty Schwartz." He said, "What's the name of the Commanding Officer of the Enterprise?" I said, "Captain Holloway." He said, "What's the name of the CAG [Air Wing Comander]?" I said, "Captain Shipman."

And then he said, "You must tell us something about your ship or the people. You were a senior officer, you know these things." I said, "Lefty Schwartz is a damn fine airplane driver." And he quit. He left it at that.

Rowan: Why do you think he left you alone at that point?

Stark: I think part of the explanation for the fact that he left it there was that there were a lot of other guys down on the 19th of May and they were probably spread pretty thinly around Heartbreak at that time. But, that was the last question that I had.

I think, also, a good part of the explanation lies in the fact that the purpose of that quiz was not to get information from me, but to demonstrate to me that they were *able* to get information from me.

Rowan: Most of the men have indicated that this is the toughest moment—after they've broken you, and before you've had a chance to find out that *everyone* has given *something*. How did you feel during this period?

Stark: I don't mind saying I felt very badly. I was *heart-broken*. I never thought of myself as the "toughest mother in the valley," but I thought that I might be able to tough 'em out. And then, I thought I had failed myself and everything else.

After 20 or 30 minutes of lying there in the dark by myself, and I don't mind admitting that I cried, a Vietnamese came to get me and he indicated that I was to follow him.

I finally made it up on my one good leg and I hobbled along. He gave me a crutch, which was pretty useless in my case, because the left knee was broken and the left arm was broken, and I couldn't hang on to the crutch. But, I sort of got it underneath my arm and then kept it there with my armpit and picked it up from one step to the other. My right arm was also numb because of the straps.

He was very patient. He offered no help, but he was patient, and I hobbled along after him. He took me to a shower area, a little spigot in a room, and pushed me in there. He took my clothes. All I had left at this point was a flight suit and he took that off and took it away, and turned on the water, and I just stood underneath the water for five or six mintues. Pretty soon he came back and he had some prison stripes, the long pants, long shirt. He helped me put those on. From there, I hobbled out into another area and he wired my hands behind me and put a blindfold on me and pushed me into a truck.

The truck got underway, and traveled for five or six minutes to a hospital that was in downtown Hanoi. I thought, "Well, okay. Now I'm going to get some help."

He took me out of the truck, and took me in an x-ray room. I figured it was an x-ray room because I saw an x-ray machine in there that was twice as old as I was. I had to take my shoes off and walk barefoot on the dirt floor because they didn't want contamination in the x-ray room.

I was pushed onto a bench and after a time a technician came in and a guard dragged me, pushed me, helped me over to the x-ray machine. And the technician, in a not very gentle way, put the arm under the x-ray machine and he took two pictures of it. We left, and the guard pushed me back over to the bench and I thought, "Well, I'm going to sit here and wait for the prints to dry, and be read, and pretty soon the doctor will come and set this arm." Well, I was wrong there.

After a period of waiting, two soldiers came in and they were not medical personnel. One had a pistol. The other had an AK-47 automatic weapon. They had with them a little wire splint that had been made out of a coat hanger and then wrapped with gauze. The two of them put the splint on the arm and they tied it in three places. And they really tied it tightly.

I thought, "Well, this is a temporary measure until the doctor gets here."

Wrong again.

After a few minutes, the guard who had taken me in there came and got me, wired my arms behind me, splint and all, blindfolded me, put me back in the truck, and I went back over to the prison.

I was taken out of the truck and taken to another area of the prison; the building I later was to learn was the Stardust. I was put into a room. There were four beds, with stocks on the end, and I was by myself. They just sort of pushed me into the room. It was then about 10 or 11 o'clock at night. I sat down on the edge of the bed to consider what my next move was going to be. And, as I looked down, I noticed this hand [the left one] was getting black, and very discolored because of the lost circulation. And that bothered me. I figured I had to get that splint off. I couldn't use my right arm, so I chewed it off. And, as soon as I did that, then the color came back.

Well, they fed me the next day. I ate like a dog, out of a bowl because I couldn't use the spoon.

Rowan: Were you still feeling as if you had let down the entire world?

Stark: Yes. I thought they had gotten to me, and perhaps someone else they would not have been able to get to. I felt very badly about that. It wasn't until I got to living with peo-

ple later on—the first time I got a roommate was in August—
and it wasn't until that point that I came to realize that they
got to everybody. I don't know personally of anybody, short
of giving up their mentality or their life—which I just
couldn't figure a way to do—who was able to successfully
stick to name, rank, serial number, and date of birth.

Clower: I was a little luckier. By the time I got there in
November [of '67], they were getting crowded, and as soon as
they were through with my initial interrogation, they put me
in a room with three other people. So, within four to five days
of being in Heartbreak, I was to realize that at least some
other people had talked.

One of the first questions that one of the other people
asked me was had I talked, and had I given them more than
my name, rank and serial number. And I said, "Yes."

He said, "Well, we all have, too."

Since we were all within a month of shoot down, and there
were four of us together who had talked, we felt then that we
were the "soft crowd"—we were the ones who couldn't hack
it. We were to spend nine months before we were to have a
roommate who had had communications, and who told us
that this had happened to everyone.

Rowan: Gosh, what did that feel like?

Clower: When you feel like you're with a bunch of losers?
Well, it's a pretty bad feeling. I always tried to be a pretty
good fighter all of my life. It's really a "down" feeling.

Now, in this nine-month period we *did* know we had to
come back. We ended up with a policy of living that we were
never to change. We reached the same conclusions under this
setup that others were to reach. So, once we got roommates,
there was no change in our procedures.

But, it was a feeling of defeat, one which I don't think
anyone likes.

I don't even like losing a ball game. I don't play cards unless it's to win. And this was, as Bill says, a real losing feeling.

Stark: Particularly when you go there with the idea I had,
based on some reading that I had done on the subject, that if

you can tough it out, if you can take your licks, they may be inclined to let you alone after a period of time and go on to greener pastures, and you can beat them that way. And I took my best shot. I just couldn't handle it anymore.

Rowan: Did you get the idea: "If only I could have lasted another hour," and, "Why didn't I?"

Stark: That's right. And I think this applied to every torture session we experienced later on. If you can just get a few minutes to yourself, to get your guts back, then you can go back.

I feel that a couple of times they failed to trade in on that fact. Had they pursued it more at the time when they had broken you, they could have gotten a lot more than ship, commanding officer and so forth. But they didn't. They let me up. They let me get my breath. And this was pretty much the way we all had to work from that point on. Just get the feeling back in your knees.

Clower: A good deal of the time I found that they would give you the information they wanted. They would actually tell you what they wanted you to say.

I'll give one instance. They finally were on me about targets in Hanoi. I did not know any targets in Hanoi. But, they kept torturing me for targets in Hanoi. And finally they put a map of Hanoi in front of me and I just reached up on the map and pointed: "That one right there," not knowing where I was pointing. It happened I was pointing within three blocks of where we were. Then, they asked me what it was. I said, "A small army boot factory." All they had to do was run out the door and check it, but they just dropped it right there.

They knew they had reached the point where you're going to lie. You're going to answer every question.

What was so funny about this was that then he said, "What is the most important target in Hanoi?" I said, "I don't know." Then, he went to hinting about lights and all that, and I said, "The power plant." He told me what he wanted me to say.

Then, he said, "Well, who hit it last—the Air Force or the

Navy?" "Well," I thought. "I've got a 50-50 chance on that. I ought to be pretty good on that." He told me if I don't answer this question he will punish me again. Well, I thought I was keeping up pretty good with the Navy, so I figure it's got to be the Air Force, so I said, "The Air Force." He said, "You lie. It was the Navy." And they put me back in the ropes again.

I would have said the Navy if I had known. I think he knew that then. And that was about all they gave me. They put me back in just one more time, to show me.

Stark: They were very much hung up on the idea that we knew what future targets were to be.

Clower: When I first got to Hanoi, they had an organization chart of my air wing, and sitting across the table from the interrogator I was able to read the chart. I looked over there and read my own name. Later, when I was going through a bunch of torture sessions, they said: "We know who you are. You are the Operations Officer of VF-151." They knew it. Now they said: "You must tell us that you are the Operations Officer."

Later on, while he was still looking at his list, he said: "Who is your Commanding Officer?" I could read the list, and they still had the name of the old skipper, even though he had been shot down the month before. So I gave him the name of the old skipper.

I got all the way down to the name of one squadron skipper in the air wing and I couldn't read it. I told him that was a new man and I didn't remember his name. He said, "If I give you the name, do you think you'll recognize it?" I said, "Well, maybe." And he gave me the name and I said, "Yes, that's right."

There was other information they could have gotten and they never seemed to try for it.

Rowan: What might they have gotten on the day you were shot down?

Clower: They were interested in Hanoi, but we weren't going to hit Hanoi the next day. I knew what we were going to hit the next day, but they never asked me that.

I got the impression that they were extremely worried about Hanoi. The did not want to talk to me about anything but Hanoi. I had been into Haiphong time after time after time. In September and October and November [of '67], I had been hitting Haiphong as much as twice a day. There were no questions about it. They were worried about Hanoi.

Rowan: Why was that, do you suppose?

Clower: I think for the same reason that brought the end of the war.

They knew they had lost everything else.

I'm convinced that they were hurting; they were really hurting in '67. The only thing left that wasn't hurting was downtown Hanoi. That's my opinion.

Stark: I have the impression that Hanoi was very much in the same order of importance as that bridge down at Thanh Hoa. It was a symbol.

With Hanoi, the fact that they might lose a lot of productive capacity was not the primary reason. That was the capital. Just like the bridge at Thanh Hoa was symbolic of the resistance effort.

Clower: That bridge is an interesting thing. While I was hitting Haiphong practically every day in September, October, and November, I went down to that bridge just one time. Compared to the defenses they had for the whole port of Haiphong, there was just no excuse to have the guns, antiaircraft, the support trying to cover that bridge.

Haiphong meant something to them. They needed that for supplies. But yet, you could go into Haiphong and not have half the trouble that you did at Thanh Hoa. All it was was a bridge. A pontoon bridge.

> The Thanh Hoa bridge finally was knocked out on May 13th, 1972.

Rowan: What did you have in the way of a symbol of *your* resistance to the North Vietnamese?

Clower: I think the thing that gave me strength was God.

I don't know how it was with others, but boy, I never even went into interrogation or anything before I said a little prayer. I had a little one that went with me, and I've stopped and said it in the middle of an interrogation. If nothing else, it gives you that time to calm down.

Rowan: Will you share it with us, Doug?

Clower: "Lord, give me the strength to do those things which are right in your eyes, the eyes of my country, and the eyes of my fellow men."

It gave me the time to calm down.

I've sat behind a table and I knew I was shaking, and I did not want to let the interrogator see me shaking. I'd say that prayer and then perhaps act like I was doing exercises because it was cold.

We worked hard on our church services, too, and they became a symbol to us, too. We *were* going to have that choir, and it didn't make any difference what the V said, or how much torture they handed out. We *were* going to have that church service. That was the one thing we were going to stand on.

They pulled people out of the rooms because of it. They put guards in the rooms. They told us we couldn't go over five minutes. They told us we couldn't sing. But we did.

I think they knew good and well we were going down to the last man.

Stark: They would impose phoney and artificial constraints on the conduct of the service. For example, "You're singing too loudly. Now, instead of having 11 people in the choir, you must have only eight." And they'd come around and count. Eight people can make more noise than 11 if they put their minds to it, and this was the phoniness of it. In the room in which I lived, we used it as one more means of resistance. We're going to have 11. We didn't need 11. We could get along with eight. We could get along with two. When it's all said and done, you could get along perfectly well without the damn choir. But, you've got to fight them. You've got to fight them at every turn. And it doesn't stop, notwithstanding what The Cat told me on the 19th of May. It does not stop when you're shot down.

Clower: When I was the SRO of one group, the V told me we couldn't have any choir at all.

I can't sing. I'm tone deaf, but I've got eight in my choir and the leader makes nine. I've been told, if they don't quit, that they will be "punished," which is the way the V had for saying, "We're going to torture you." So I walked back in and I got them together and I told them what he had said. They stood there and waited for me to say something. I said, "I do not want to tell you to continue, but I think it is best, although each and every one of you may be tortured." I said, "Now, if any of you wants to stop, I don't want you to be influenced. I will not feel badly about it one way or the other." And, to a man, each one of them said: "If I am pulled about this, and then tortured about this, I would feel it an honor."

As it was, the V didn't do that.

Dick Stratton described another battle with the North Vietnamese over church services which *did* result in a form of torture for many of the senior ranking officers. It occurred in February of 1971, when Stratton was in a cell on the back side of the Hanoi Hilton—in an area called Camp Unity—with many of the seniors, including Jim Stockdale, Jerry Denton, Robbie Risner, and George Coker.

"Any type of group gathering within the cell was considered by the Vietnamese to be a potential hazard to them. No man could stand up and speak in front of a group. There could be no play-acting, no church services, nothing where one man got up in front of the others.

"You see, they used plays and songs to drum up hate for the Americans among their own people, and they presumed we did the same.

"But, church was a good issue for us to resist them on, because they were on bad grounds in prohibiting church services. So, we did indeed have a choir, and Robbie Risner, George Coker, CAG Stockdale, all these people stood up in front of the group and we had church services.

"We told them ahead of time it was going to be done; invited them to come in and watch, or *participate* if they cared to. We said: 'In America, we do this, and we're going to do it here. And *your're* not going to stop us.'

"What happened was they immediately skimmed off the leaders. First, they took George Coker and Robbie Risner and we rebelled by singing. There was a camp order out against singing: 'You will make no noise that can be heard outside your cell.' So, we were violating the camp regulations. So, they hauled off the other leaders, CAG Stockdale, Jerry Denton, Jim Mulligan, all those guys. And we went on a hunger strike. And they continued to scrape all the leaders off. The humorous part of all that was that we had just finished organizing [the 4th Combined POW Wing] and they ended up scraping off 28 of the leaders."

Clower: I found out that my men only got angry when I did not put harder restrictions on them. They wanted leadership, strong leadership.

After we moved from Son Tay to Hoa Lo, I had sort of a basic policy. I put a restriction on my men. They cannot speak to the V. Now this builds up pressure among Americans when I tell them they cannot talk. Americans don't like this.

Rowan: What are some of the circumstances in which a man would want to speak to the V? Wanting to ask for a bar of soap or something?

Clower: That's right. You must go through the senior man. You just can't go out and say, "I want a bar of soap." If you need medical, you go through me and I'll say, "This man, this man and this man need medical." You just can't go out and shoot the bull with him, you just can't talk to him. If he asks you, "Is there enough water inside?" You will say, "You will have to ask the senior man."

Well, the other rooms are having these flare-ups. This one was having a flap so they're going on a sit-down strike, and this one over here's having some other flap, and *we're* not having them. Some men felt, "We should be having more flaps. We're not doing our share."

Well, there's no reason to have them unless you have a reason to have them. We don't have any reason to have them. But the tension is growing among the men.

To back up a bit: It seemed to me that the older a man was, the better he was able to adapt to the diet, the better he was able to resist a lack of medical treatment, and the better he recovered from normal everyday ailments. The only thing we could ever attribute this to was that those of us around the late thirties and early forties had grown up during World War II and the years prior to the antibiotics. Our systems had immunities without the antibiotics. So we had a little more stamina.

Rowan: But, it was the younger men who felt that you should be doing more to resist?

Clower: Yes. Well, I get my flight leaders together, and we're sitting there talking and finally one of the senior flight leaders says, "I recommend that the next time *anything* goes wrong, we go on a hunger strike, regardless of how little it is." I said, "Why?" He said, "Well, as soon as we go on a hunger strike, you know they can't handle it. The younger men can't handle a hunger strike. We can't either, but they'll fall before we do. They want to do something, so the next time something comes up, let's just do it for them, and just wait around a couple of days, and they'll be the ones hollering, 'Let's get off it!' "

So my senior officers and myself decided this is what we'll do. I don't know what the flap was, it was immaterial, but we went on a hunger strike.

As soon as we go on a hunger strike, the V take our water away from us, so now we don't have food *or* water. Well, by noon that day, two or three of the younger guys came by yelling, "This is what we should be doing." That was the first day; that was even through the first night. We went to bed saying, "Boy this is great. We really should keep this up and just show them who's boss." Well, by the next morning I had about eight or nine who couldn't even get out of bed. That day those who had had ailments say they can't go in on it. So I waver in my cause, and the two or three sick now also have permission to ask the V for food. They ask for food, and the V take them outside and feed them, and they came back in. Now the sick had been fed.

By evening, I've got about 20 who can't even get out of bed, begging me to please break this thing. All that afternoon they were begging me for food. This is just the second day. And I look around at my old and senior men and they're just smiling, and they say, "We think we have shown them our point."

So , I went out and talked to the V and they gave us food. We did not have any more problems. The psychology of the thing worked. We had *resisted*, and that was important. The young guys felt that now they were a part of the camp-wide resistance. Up to this point, they had felt that they had not done their share.

Rowan: But, you can't even remember what you were resisting?

Clower: I can't remember what it was.

But the men wanted leadership. They wanted a hard core leadership. So although at times it bothered me to tell a man to be tortured, I found out later that that was the degree of leadership they wanted. They would rather go that line than go the other. They were willing to take hardships. They were willing to take less. And, in some cases, we got things later than others did.

Rowan: What kind of things?

Clower: Educational material. A few of the luxuries. The Bible.

I cannot over-emphasize how important these things are. Next to food, clothing and shelter, the most important thing is something to occupy the mind. They became nearly a necessity.

I am a big note-taker, and have been all my life. I have a little book in my pocket right now and it's just full of things, telephone numbers, what I will do tomorrow. I've been this way most of my life. And now, not to be able to write anything down, well, it was probably good for me in the period of solo because now I would try to memorize things.

For one period of time, I was memorizing the square of all numbers through a hundred, while I was solo. I don't know what you're going to do with the square of all numbers through a hundred, and I doubt if I could remember any of them right now.

But, I did learn a pretty good amount of poetry. I learned it line by line.

With the help of Jim Ray, I wrote two sonnets for my wife:

The puffy clouds that dot the summer sky,
Their fleeting somber shadows signify
The mood of wives and mothers of the men
They possibly may never see again.
This cruise is different from the ones before,
For duty calls us to some hostile shore.
I hear your words of comfort now to one:
"This duty calls my husband and your son."
Let's hope that duty alone will suffice,
Your cheerful smile, your poise, your stylish dress,
Assurance of your strength to meet this test.
With our most precious memories with me,
The winds of freedom blow us out to sea.

The years of war required much sacrifice,
And now I too have had to pay this price.
Shot down and captured in a hostile land,
Deprived of all the hopes we once had planned.
Our Ginny has now grown to womanhood,
But I am confident she understood
Just why for freedom's cause I wasn't free,
And why both Mom and Dad you had to be.
All those whose men were missing felt this pain,
But none so much as those who hoped in vain.
Sweetheart, you took it well, I'm proud of you,
Our life and love and dreams we'll now renew.
And, though my love for you will strong remain,
You know, when duty calls, I'll go again.

I was afraid to give these to my wife because it says in here
I'm going back. But, when I got to Clark [Air Base], there
was a letter, and in that letter she said, "I don't know what
your plans are, but, whatever you want, it is alright with
me." Knowing her as I do, after being married to her for over
20 years, I knew that she was saying, "If you want to go back
and fight again, or whatever you want to do, I'll be here to
support you."

Epilogue

On a morning in March of 1973, one of the POWs looked out into the courtyard of a prison in Hanoi and spotted a familiar face out of the past. "My God," he said to the men who shared his cell, *"Walter Cronkite is out there!"* But it would have taken more than the presence of even a Cronkite to dispel all the doubts and fears built up over the years. Peace had seemed so close so many times, only to fade away into the distance again, that the men had learned not to allow their hopes to get raised.

On the buses going to Hanoi airport, many of the POWs continued to resist the notion that they were actually going home at last. Perhaps this was just another trick being played by the "V." Perhaps they were being moved to another prison camp. Worse still, perhaps they were to be taken out en masse and executed, as a final gesture of the defiance of the North Vietnamese. The fear clutched again.

At the airport, their fears at first seemed to be justified. No American planes were in sight. Some groups were kept waiting for what seemed like interminable periods. Then the buses started up again and moved to an open area on the other side of the airfield.

But, finally, the big C-141s arrived, and the POWs were handed over to Americans in crisp military uniforms. Even then there was a nagging doubt in the minds of many of the prisoners. Something might still go wrong. In fact, most of those to whom I spoke said they didn't allow themselves to really believe they were going home until "the wheels were in the well"—until the big transport planes had lifted off the runway and the landing gear could be heard retracting and clunking into place in the wheel wells.

Even before they arrived at their first American outpost—Clark Air Base in the Philippines—the men were confronted with evidence of how much "home" had changed. Copies of *Playboy* and other men's magazines had been brought along by some of the crew members of the 141s, and they contained hints of the relaxed moral climate that had developed in America—the pubic hair of the models, there for all the world to see. There was even a suggestion in some of the photographs that the models were masturbating. More than a few of the POWs looked around nervously as they flipped through the pages of the magazines, embarrassed at the thought of being caught with such pictures in their possession.

At Clark, higher prices in the base exchange bore out the truth of what they had been hearing from the '72 shootdowns—inflation was eating away at the pay raises given to military men over the years. And there were letters from home, and strained, artifically bright-sounding voices on the telephone to remind some of the men that even more serious problems awaited in the United States.

They expected no hero's welcome. When all was said and done, they had survived in pretty good shape. More than 40,000 men had been killed. Hundreds of thousands had been crippled for life, and *they* were the men, most POWs thought, who should have been given preferential treatment, free trips, cut-rate automobiles and all the other "goodies" which were to be lavished on these few former prisoners.

More than anything else, they found themselves out of step with the rest of the nation on the issue of the war, itself. They still saw it as a contest between communism and democracy, a contest in which Viet Nam, as Ed Flora put it, "just happened to be the country where we had to put our foot down." Ned Shuman remembered that Harry Truman once had said: "The only way to talk to a Communist is with one foot on his throat." And Rob Doremus said that many of the POWs were so eager for a victory over the Communists that they would gladly have died in a nuclear explosion in Hanoi.

They had seen all the propaganda pictures, and as human beings had been sickened by the twisted and torn bodies of little children. But their sense of values puts "country" ahead of life. And, in any case, they weren't *trying* to kill little children; they were trying to destroy military targets in an enemy country. This was their work and they had done it as well and as sincerely as they knew how.

They had come to know that there was a growing dissatisfaction with the war among the people of the United States, but they understood that. They too were dissatisfied with the way their civilian bosses in the Johnson and Nixon administrations had sent them in to fight—with one hand tied behind their back. They were disappointed that their country had not seen fit to support them in the same way it supported its fighting men against Japan and Germany. But they were realistic enough to know that "that's the way the cookie crumbles." And they took what strength they could from reality. As Red McDaniel reasoned, "I think the division of our country prolonged the war, but at the same time it gave the Army in South Viet Nam time to strengthen itself."

And there was another strength to be gained from such division in the country, for that is the stuff of which America is made. As Dick Stratton put it, talking about his sister, Ellen Cooper of Buffalo, N.Y., who strongly opposed the war: "As long as she sticks within the legal methods of protest in bringing out her position, I'll fight a war tomorrow for her to say what she wants to say. That's what democracy is all about."